SECONDARY EDUCATION

SECONDARY EDUCATION

Editors
Monica Tomar
D.S. Srivastava

ISHA BOOKS
DELHI-110 033

Secondary Education

Rs. 750

ISBN: 81-8205-162-2

Published in 2005 in India by
Isha Books, D-43, Prithviraj Road,
Adarsh Nagar, Delhi-110 033

Laser Typesetting at: Shree Vaishnavi Creations, Delhi
Printed at: Mehra Offset Press, Delhi

PREFACE

Secondary education is the connecting link between primary education and higher education and it is often considered as the most important segment of an individual's learning. In India, secondary education starts with classes 9-10 leading to higher secondary classes 11 and 12 and is expected to prepare young persons between the age group 14-18 in the world of work and entry into higher education.

The objectives of secondary education are formulated on the basis of the guidelines prepared by the National Policy of Education. The major aim of secondary education is to enable the learners to acquire new knowledge, skills, use modern science and technology, develop positive outlook and scientific attitude, to acquire skills for self-employment and to inspire them with patriotism, and religious, moral, cultural and social values.

The system of secondary education is supported by the organisations such as National Council of Educational Research and Training (NCERT), Central Board of Secondary Education (CBSE), National Institute of Open Schooling (NIOS), Kendriya Vidyalaya Sangathan (KVS), Navodaya Vidyalaya Samiti (NVS), Central Tibetan Schools Administration (CTSA), Central Institute of Education Technology and State Institute of Education Technology, under the administrative control of the Union Department of Education. The development of secondary education sector is also supported by the specific centrally sponsored schemes like Vocationalisation of Secondary

Education, Integrated Education for Disabled Children, Computer Literacy and Studies in Schools (CLASS), Education Technology, Improvement of Science Education in Schools, Promotion of Yoga in Schools, Strengthening Culture and Values in Schools, Strengthening Boarding and Hostel Facilities for Girls, Environmental orientation to School Education, etc.

The present volume describes the history, status, role and development of secondary education in India in an elegant style. The role of government policies, centrally sponsored schemes and supporting organisations in the development of secondary education are elaborately discussed. The book will be highly useful for education students, education planners, teachers, principals and others related with secondary education.

Editor

CONTENTS

1

VOCATIONALISATION OF SECONDARY EDUCATION

CENTRALLY SPONSORED SCHEME OF VOCATIONALISATION OF SECONDARY EDUCATION

In accordance with the priority accorded to Vocational Education in the National Policy on Education, a Centrally Sponsored Scheme of Vocationalisation of Secondary Education was launched in February, 1988. The main objectives of the Scheme of Vocationalisation of Secondary education, as spelt out in the NPE are to provide diversification of educational opportunities so as to enhance individual employability, reduce the mismatch between demand and supply of skilled manpower and to provide an alternative for those pursuing higher education.

Components

— Creation of separate administrative structure at the State, District, school level to manage vocational education programmes.

— Strengthening of SCERTs to provide technical support for research, development, training and evaluation.

— Conducting district vocational surveys in all the districts for assessment of labour market demand.

— Development of curriculum, instructional material, text books and guide material.

— Provision of two full time teachers per section, honorarium for part time experts, training of teachers.

— Provision for one workshed per section and basic equipment for the course.

Pattern of Funding

One hundred percent Central assistance is given for district Vocational surveys, workshops for development of curriculum, instructional material, a text book, training of teachers, equipment, construction of whorksheds, monitoring, evaluation and field visits. The Central Government bears 75% of expenditure on salary of management staff at the State Directorates, SCERTs and district levels and for raw material. The State Government have to bear 100% expenditure on contingencies, examination, certification and vocational guidance.

Management Structure

A Joint Council of Vocational Education has been set up at the National level under the Chairmanship of the Minister for Human Resource Development for co-ordination, policy planning and review. State Governments were also requested to set up State Council of Vocational Education as the overall co-ordinating and implementing body at the State level.

EDUCATIONAL TECHNOLOGY PROGRAMME

An Educational Technology Programme was started in the Central sector in the year 1972 during the Fourth Plan period for widening access to and bringing about qualitative improvement in education. Under the scheme, a Centre for Educational Technology was set up in the NCERT and 100 per cent assistance was provided to twenty- one States for setting up Educational Technology (ET).

Cells.

In view of expansion of broadcasting facilities with the advent of INSAT and concomitant demand for educational software, the Ministry of Education decided to take on the responsibility of production of educational television programmes for relay through satellites. Accordingly, a scheme was prepared by the Ministry for creating Educational Television (ETV) programme production facilities within the education sector on a decentralised basis by setting up a Central Institute of Educational Technology (CIET) in the NCERT and State Institutes of Educational Technology (SIETs) in six States, viz., Andhra Pradesh, Bihar, Gujarat, Maharashtra, Orissa and Uttar Pradesh and strengthening of ET Cells in other States.

To meet the objectives of NPE, the Educational Technology Scheme was revised in 1987 with the broad objectives of strengthening of both ETV and audio programme production capabilities and providing wider access to the same by supplying one lakh Colour Television (CTV) sets and five lakh Radio-Cum-Cassette Players (RCCPs) to primary schools during the Seventh Plan.

A group with Dr. Kiran Karnik as convener was set up in August, 1987 to study and make recommendations on the use of satellite services on education and the media time requirement of various sectors of education. The recommendations of the group are under consideration of the Government.

Programme production has commenced in CIET and all the six SIETs. In fact, from the academic year 1988-89, responsibility for programme production, which was until then being shared between CIET and Doordarshan on 50:50 basis, has been taken over by CIET and SIETs. The satellite based ETV service presently provides telecast of educational programmes for the children and their teachers at the primary level in the morning for 45 minutes duration in each of the five regional languages, namely, Gujarati, Hindi, Marathi, Oriya and Telugu on time sharing basis. The programmes for children are telecast from Monday to Friday and for primary level teachers on every Saturday. There are separate programmes for the children in the age groups of 5-8 and 9-11 years on each day.

The ETV programmes are relayed by all high and low power transmitters in the six INSAT States. The programmes in Hindi are relayed by the other five Hindi speaking states also, namely, Haryana, Himachal Pradesh, Madhya Pradesh, Punjab and Rajasthan and the Union Territory of Chandigarh.

With the availability of uplinking facilities from Bombay and Hyderabad, the telecast timings have been rescheduled from November, 1991. The CIET has produced 646 ETV programmes upto October, 1991 and 914 language versions. It has also produced 450 capsules for the programme of MOST during the summers of 1986, 1987, 1988 and 1989.

The SIETs have been a bit slow in achieving adequate production capability of the required standard because, of management and technical manpower problems faced by them. The Working Group set up to suggest ways and means of improving the functioning of SIETs, among other things, suggested conversion of SIETs into autonomous organisations in the form of registered societies under the aegis of the State Governments. SIETs in Orissa, Andhra Pradesh, U.P. and Maharashtra have already become autonomus. SIETs in Bihar, is likely to be registered as societies shortly, while the matter is being pursued with the Government of Gujarat.

Efforts are also on to involve private producers in production of ETV Programmes. The NCERT has set up a committee to evolve modalities for involving outside producers to produce videofilms for CIET. As many as nine ETV video programmes commissioned to outside producers have been completed and another eight programmes are nearing completion.

An ambitious programme of distribution of CTV sets and RCCPs was undertaken under the ET Scheme. Funds are also being sanctioned for audio programme production by State Governments and non-Government organisations. The CIET has also produced more than 1100 audio programmes on various educational themes at various levels of school education. SIETs have also geared efforts towards production of audio programmes either by themselves and/or through outside agencies. A list of about 40 video and audio programmes produced by the CIET have been identified for providing meaningful media support to the DIETs in their teacher training activities.

EDUCATION AND TRAINING

Education and training also improve individuals' productivity and income earning opportunities at work, their mobility in the labour market, and widen their choice of career opportunities. An American study found that private returns of two year Associate degrees were as high as 20 to 30 per cent, particularly in the business and technical fields of men, and health fields of women. In France, during the 1970-93 period, possession of vocational post-secondary qualifications conferred substantial benefits to the individual, in terms of access to employment, reduced likelihood of unemployment, and significant increases in life-cycle earnings.

Education and training help individuals escape poverty, by providing them with skills and knowledge that raise their output as farmers and workers. According to the World Bank, primary education is the single largest contributor to growth and development in developing countries. A farmer with four years' schooling is much more productive than one who has no education. As poverty is increasingly concentrated among women, increasing girls' and women's access to education will reduce poverty significantly.

Enterprises also reap rewards from education and training. By investing in their human resources, enterprises can improve productivity, and compete successfully in increasingly integrated world markets. The economic performance of 62 world-wide car assembly plants around 1990, measured in terms of labour productivity and product quality (assembly-related defects per vehicle), proved to be closely associated with the presence of three dimensions of business strategy: lean production, team working and innovative human resources management (HRM) practices. Training provision, for both new recruits and ongoing employees, constituted two out of five practices in the HRM dimension. The benefits of training in terms of improved productivity was found to depend strongly on the choice of a compatible organization of production, work, recruitment and remuneration (pay) structures.

In Denmark, enterprises that introduced process and product innovations, combined with targeted training, were more likely to report output growth (11 per cent versus 4 per cent, job growth (3 versus 2 per cent), and labour productivity growth (10 per cent versus 4 per cent) than those who had not introduced these innovations. In the U.S., on-the-job training was found to have a positive effect on productivity and wage growth.

Economic growth and social development of countries are invariably associated with large and sustained investments in education and training. Countries with the highest incomes are also those where workers are most educated. Witness enrollments of high income countries in primary education, which is universal, secondary education, which is almost universal, and tertiary education, which is approaching 50 per cent of the relevant age group. Some 98 per cent of the adult population in these countries are considered literate. By contrast, in the poorest countries, primary education enrollments were in 1997 around 71.5 per cent, secondary education enrollments 16.4 per cent, and tertiary education enrollments a mere 3.2 per cent of the respective age groups.

Basic literacy, essential for learning and "trainability", and for employability and access to decent work in today's world, eludes a significant share of adults in Sub-Saharan Africa and Southern Asia. Advanced countries invest at least 30 times more per student in education and training than the least developed countries. Human resources development and training contribute to improved productivity in the economy, reduce skills mis-matches in the labour market, and promote a country's international competitiveness. A comparative study of Germany and the UK found that the greater willingness of German employers to offer apprenticeship training, as opposed to the regular youth employment and informal training which came to dominate in the UK, contributed to Germany's higher productivity and better trade performance.

Finally, and beyond any economic considerations, education and training bring benefits to society. Human resources development and training underpin the fundamental values of society - equity, justice, gender equality, non-discrimination, social responsibility and participation of all in economic and social life.

Knowledge and Skills-based Society

Every individual has a right to education and training, as do many national constitutions, for example, in Argentina, Bolivia, Brazil, Chile, Germany, Guatemala, Italy, Mexico, Spain and other countries. This right is also acknowledged at the international level, for example in the Universal Declaration of Human Rights (1948) and the American Declaration of Human Rights and Obligations (1948). Similarly, at the regional level, MERCOSUR's Social and Labour Declaration (Declaracion Sociolaboral del MERCOSUR) (1998), and the European Union's Charter of Fundamental Rights (2000) recognize these rights.

More than ever before, individuals want to master their own lives and expect to contribute to the economy and society.

The development of individuals as active citizens of society is increasingly given a central place in statements of learning, education and training objectives. According to the EU Memorandum on lifelong learning, active citizenship is about how "people participate in all spheres of economic and social life, the chances and risks they face in trying to do so, and the extent to which they feel that they belong to, and have a fair say in, the society in which they live". Decent work underpins individuals' independence, self-respect and well-being, and, therefore, is a key to their overall quality of life. Many countries, both industrialized and developing, are putting the individual in the center of the education and training process, buttressed by financial means that help him/her access learning.

Denmark is pioneering a learner-centred approach to vocational education and training. Others, for example Tunisia, Egypt, Singapore, Argentina and many other Latin American countries, are introducing fundamental basic education reform that emphasize "essential", "basic", "key" etc. skills that are intended to promote the independence and initiative of the individual. In Sweden, the Adult Education Initiative (AEI), the largest adult education investment initiative ever undertaken in the country, explicitly puts the focus on the individual. All AEI programmes are governed by his/her needs, wishes and capacity.

Education should help to improve the individual's opportunities in the labour market and provide for further study opportunities; it must be demand-led, be it in terms of organization, planning or actual courses provided. Every individual is given ample scope to make a personal choice of the study he/she wants to undertake, its timing and location8.

The individual is becoming the architect and builder responsible for developing his/her own skills, supported by public and enterprise investment in life-long learning. Democracy is about empowering the individual. Several factors - economic, social and technological - account for the growing emphasis on the individual.

Firstly, in any modern economy today, the production of goods and services increasingly relies on human, rather than physical, capital, i.e. on its workers' individual and collective endowment of knowledge and skills. For example, Germany's endowment of human capital is today more than twice the value of its physical capital. The difference is increasing. In the 1920s, however, physical capital outstripped by far the importance of human capital9.

Secondly, from a passive, and teacher oriented, approach to gaining knowledge and skills, there is a shift towards learning for life and work, centred around the individual. The process of formal education and training is becoming less one of passing on information - as there is too much of it in today's world - and more one of individuals learning to learn so that they can find out for themselves. The relevance of knowledge about facts is diminishing, while the need to learn how to access, analyze and exploit information and transform it into new knowledge is increasing. It is only by giving the individual the desire, and tools, including financial means, to take charge of her/his own learning that he or she will be able to live and work in the knowledge and information society.

Thirdly, modern communication and information technologies (ICT), in particular the Internet- based technologies, offer great opportunities. ICTs are used by increasing number of people as learning tools, since access to them is expanding rapidly in the advanced, as well as in many middle income, countries and free courses are becoming available on the Internet. A recent survey of ICT workers in Vietnam, found that 70 per cent of those trained in computer skills had learned them via CD-ROM or on the Internet.

These learning opportunities are not restricted to computer and ICT skills but cover now a vast, and rapidly expanding, range of learning opportunities for life and work in the knowledge economy and society. However, the "digital divide", i.e. unequal access to ICT and the Internet - between countries and within countries - runs the risk of growing even wider unless serious efforts are undertaken nationally and internationally to reverse the trend.

Objectives and strategies of training

Objectives and strategies of training can be formulated at various levels, e.g. national, enterprise, training institution, individual level, etc., and also at the international (e.g. OECD) and regional (e.g. European) level. Below are given a few examples.

National human resources development and training objectives have often been (re)formulated in the context of countries' efforts to undertake major education and training reforms in order to make their training policies and systems better meet their contemporary economic and social needs, e.g. in Australia, Chile, Ireland, Malawi, Portugal and Zambia.

The reforms have invariably been undertaken in the context of extensive social dialogue and engagement of various stakeholders in education and training. In many less developed countries, particularly in Africa, economic stagnation and mushrooming growth of the informal economy has made a redefinition of human resources development and training objectives imperative.

Lifelong learning objectives

Many countries increasingly formulate their human resources development objectives in terms of lifelong learning. At the individual country level, Finland is a country that has formulated a clear vision and objectives of lifelong learning. The Government's development plan for the 1999-2004 period calls for, among other things, helping more young people to apply for upper secondary general or vocational education and complete their studies; develop student's learning skills in all sectors of the education system; increase the provision of non-university higher education; expand the opportunities for adults to study for upper secondary and post-secondary vocational qualifications and to pursue other studies that improve their employability and capacity for further learning; and develop methods for recognizing non-formal and informal learning.

The 'learning chain' has been identified to include the following: early childhood developmental education accessible to all children; universal free and compulsory basic education; increased access for all to secondary education; training and learning opportunities in schools and enterprises; widespread opportunities to obtain further and higher education and training; accessible continuing education and training for adults; gender balance in access to education and training; access to education opportunities of minorities and other disadvantaged groups.

Primary and secondary school enrollments increase, in Sub-Saharan Africa primary school enrolments declined from 59 per cent in 1980 to 51 per cent in 1992. With declining output per worker, economic stagnation and no employment growth, incomes and living conditions plummeted. Recently, however, investments in education and training have been maintained and even increased in many African countries.

In South Africa, private training is expected to play an important role in expanding access to further education and training, in particular by responding to labour market opportunities and learner demand. The key challenge is "to create an environment that neither suffocates educationally sound and sustainable institutions with state over-regulation, nor allows a plethora of poor quality, unsustainable "fly-by-night" operators into the training market". Therefore, the country's Further Education and Training Act, 1998, endeavours to ensure that only private institutions with the necessary infrastructure and resources to provide and sustain quality training will be registered and accredited.

According to the World Bank however, experiences in Chile, the Czech Republic and Russia suggest that national accreditation systems - intended to inform people about the quality of training - may neither be necessary nor sufficient for a balanced system of privately provided training. In fact, they may rule out innovative and non-conforming training providers and discourage a vigorous training market.

Decentralization of Decision-making

Social dialogue and partnership in training typically involve significant elements of decentralization, in both policy formulation and implementation. The rationale for decentralizing decisions on training is that these are best done at the regional, local and sectoral levels, close to economic demand and social needs. For example, decisions on training in say a booming area of economic growth, will differ greatly from those where de-industrialization and job loss are prevalent. Such differences can be accommodated by devolving training decisions closer to local realities. Institutions and local organizations are given local autonomy, and, most importantly, accountability, within a framework of national policy, priorities and targets.

Greater innovation is likely to follow when local initiatives can be harnessed effectively. However, devolution can impair the attainment of national objectives by allowing local actors to pursue their own (parochial) agendas. Devolution is not an easy process. Vested interests among those with central decision-making power may need to be overcome. Local bodies will need the necessary resources, both human and financial, to be able to execute adequately their newly acquired functions and responsibilities. Notwithstanding these possible drawbacks, devolution of decision-making on training is a common trend in most countries.

The United States offer perhaps the best example of a decentralized, loosely coordinated, locally administered and strongly market-driven approach that is responsive to local training needs. Local training networks, based on a complex set of relationships between training providers and enterprises, are able to secure training services and funds, and also influence policy decisions. Nevertheless, the role of the Federal Government remains important as it provides fiscal incentives for initiating such local capacity building.

In the Philippines, the national Technical Education and Skills Development Authority's (TESDA) centralized functions - e.g. planning, setting of standards, monitoring and evaluation - are balanced by decentralization of decision-making and training functions. TESDA is expected to formulate, implement and finance specific plans to develop the capability of local government to assume the responsibility for promoting community-based technical education and skills development. Similarly in Indonesia, planning and implementing skills training programmes, previously a function of the Ministry of Manpower and Transmigration, have been devolved to provincial and district levels.

Recently, the Governor of East Java identified key training issues that demand action at the provincial level, including development of skills for income generation activities and retraining of laid-off workers. These issues are being addressed, with support from the ILO, jointly by the provincial government, the province's Chamber of Commerce and Industry and other provincial and local partners.

Integrating Lifelong Learning

Ensuring "lifelong learning for all" remains a goal that no country so far has achieved. Integrating lifelong learning into the institutional framework for human resources development demands a resolution of the following major issues:

— ensuring the foundations for lifelong learning by, in particular, emphasizing learning-to-learn skills. With the massive increase in information available today, people must learn to access, discriminate and exploit information that is relevant to their needs and transform it into knowledge;

— developing policies and institutions for ensuring equity and access, particularly of disadvantaged groups, to lifelong learning opportunities. A multi-pronged strategy, e.g. by means of offering financial incentives and more opportunities that are better tailored to individuals' needs, is necessary in order to encourage wider, and more equitable, participation in lifelong learning;

— mobilizing the necessary resources for making lifelong learning opportunities more widely available. All the parties concerned, including the state, the enterprise and private sectors, and also the individual, will have to contribute to increased investment in institutions and programmes of lifelong learning;

— ensuring collaboration among a wide range of partners and stakeholders. Partnerships have important advantages. They are likely to increase the resource base available for investment in human resources development. They will also promote programmes that are relevant to economic and social needs;

— developing policies and institutions for the recognition of all forms of learning, even informal learning. Recognition of an individual's skills and knowledge acts as a powerful incentive for him /her to learn, and improves his job and income prospects. Also, it promotes labour market mobility and transparency and guides employers in their recruitment of employees;

— designing guidance and counselling for lifelong learning. People need assistance in "navigating" and choosing between alternatives in a vast array of learning and training opportunities that can enhance their careers.

Corporate online learning

Siemens Information Networks Inc. (United States) needed to train at short notice 600 high-level engineers on data/voice convergence technology. Traditional classroom training would have taken three years to reach all 600 engineers and would have cost some US$ 4 million in lost travel and production time, in addition to the direct training costs. At a cost of only US$ 75,000 for hardware and learning software - and an additional charge of US$ 1,500 for 100 classroom seats - the company was able to create interactive online classes via the company's Intranet. Over time the course evolved from being merely cost-effective to improving productivity, raising the company's market share and generating high rates of return. At present, Siemens' voice data course is one of 64 online classes offered to 7,500 employees.

ICT-BASED LEARNING WITH TRADITIONAL METHODS

In addition to their penetration in the workplace, ICT and e-learning are also making in-roads in schools, colleges, community centres, training institutions and universities. As ICT and Internet applications in education and training proliferate, they are increasingly used in combination, or "blended" with other more traditional learning and training methods, like classroom teaching. Blending can overcome the often observed sense of isolation and lack of human contact that pure ICT-based learning imposes.

Distance learning programmes that exploit ICT are expanding at a rapid pace. As the costs of new technologies plummet, traditional distance learning tools (e.g. correspondence, radio) are being supplemented or even replaced by ICT-based technologies. Eleven mega learning institutions (in China, France, India, Indonesia, Iran, Republic of Korea, South Africa, Spain, Thailand, Turkey and U.K.) enroll altogether 2.8 million students and provide distance learning programmes at an average yearly cost of $350.

Distance learning may increase access of disadvantaged groups to learning opportunities. Physically disabled people who cannot attend training programmes in an institution for lack of mobility and transport or because costs are prohibitive can, with the help of a computer, access Internet-based learning programmes at home. In Portugal, the THINK project illustrates an innovative use of telework for creating new opportunities for disabled people. A training package has been developed that prepares teleworkers for providing consultancy services, including computer programming, translations, direct marketing, web design, among other services. The project has enabled people with disabilities to become active contributors to society, providing a quality service to customers. Based on its success, the approach will be applied in four other European countries.

The potential of harnessing ICT in education and training is therefore huge. So are the challenges. A shift from instruction and passing on information to learning and knowledge creation will demand a huge effort of teacher and trainer (re-)training. Ingrained professional and cultural habits and attitudes will have to be overcome; resources need to be invested in new learner-based techniques of education and training; and the ICT infrastructure, including in schools and training institutions, will need strengthening. These are challenges even in the richest countries. They are even more formidable in large parts of the developing world, where communication infrastructure is weak, incomes are low, education systems are resource poor, and teachers lack materials and equipment that could support a shift to learner- and ICT-based education and training. But perhaps the greatest challenge of all is providing basic education to all people, as a prerequisite for accessing the information and knowledge society.

As contemporary societies become more complex, many countries are broadening the scope of basic education to incorporate new knowledge and portable skills for the world of work and for living in the knowledge and information society. Secondary education at lower level is increasingly part of compulsory basic education and its objective is more than just preparing students for higher education. Basic education "ensures to each individual the full development of the human personality and citizenship, and lays the foundation for employability". Initial training helps to develop "further his or her employability by providing general core work skills, and the underpinning knowledge, and industry-based and professional competencies which are portable and facilitate the transition into the world of work".

Vocational education and initial training should instil knowledge of science and technology within a broad occupational area and develop the requisite technical and professional competencies and specific occupational skills. A critical issue for vocational education and training is the emphasis placed upon general academic education and development of portable skills on one hand, and on occupationally-oriented training on the other, in order to facilitate the smooth transition from school to work and enhance individuals' basic employability.

In most countries, at some intermediate age between 11 and 15, students tend to be channeled into streams of the education system that emphasize either academic or vocational skills. The academic stream usually prepares for tertiary education and entry to university and has relatively little job-related content, given the pressure to meet the competitive entry requirements of higher education. Increasingly however, academic education in schools also develops portable core work skills, like teamwork, problem solving, ICT skills, understanding of entrepreneurship, communication and language skills, and learning to learn skills. These are skills needed to build-up individuals' employability, which will subsequently help them to adapt to rapid changes in the workplace and society.

The vocational stream includes a wide range of programmes with various levels of work-based content, but entry into these tends to occur later as the duration of compulsory basic education is extended. Like academic education, vocational education and training also emphasize more and more portable core work skills and employability. At one end of the spectrum is school-based learning, which includes work familiarization and practical exercises designed primarily to prepare students for work or for post-secondary vocational training. At the other end, alternating periods of accredited learning are rigorously organized at school and in an enterprise, often in the form of modern apprenticeship. The aim is to produce skilled workers who can gain access to jobs smoothly. These streaming decisions, which generally involve some form of individual assessment, have traditionally been immutable, but they are becoming increasingly permeable.

Education systems increasingly facilitate new pathways and progress between various types of education and training. Changing the content of education and initial training demands a new relationship between education and the world of work and a shift in responsibilities between the public and private sectors. Training programmes outside the formal education system are also common. These are often supervised by Ministries of Labour, and run by independent bodies and financed by governments or employers, or by both. Entry requirements and the duration of training vary considerably. They often target school leavers, with or without school-leaving certificates, unemployed youth and employed workers who need to improve their skills.

Vocational training courses of short duration are more work-oriented and flexible compared with vocational education. In some countries, e.g. in Latin America, these programmes have grown into major institutions (INACAP, SENAI, SENAC, SENAR, SENA and others), often having many more students than school-based vocational education. Many training programmes have also, like in vocational education, expanded their apprenticeship type programmes by integrating school-based education with workplace-based learning in enterprises. Hence, many countries have witnessed a progressive convergence of their education and training systems and a standardization of education and training supply and occupational profiles in response to broad skill requirements.

Proprietary training, provided by private training firms and institutions, has traditionally been a large supplier of skills in the industrialized world, and has recently grown rapidly in many developing countries. Growth in proprietary training has mostly been in the area of non-industrial skills such as service occupations, computing and information technology, management, and accounting; it has largely avoided training for technical and industrial occupations, which tends to require more costly investments.

Proprietary training have grown in response to employer and individual demand for increased opportunities for initial and continuous training. Responding often to short term demand, proprietary institutions tend to focus on specific work related skills. Private training institutions finance their operations primarily by charging fees, sometimes complemented by government subsidies. A large share of the tuition and other fees charged by these institutions may also be underwritten in the form of state grants and low-cost individual student loans.

Informal apprenticeship is a form of proprietary training common in countries that have a large informal sector, both rural and urban. Informal apprenticeship often absorbs a large number of young people, and is now also being examined for wider use in other countries as a means of augmenting the supply of skilled trainees for informal employment. By giving artisans economic support, and training and learning materials, governments and NGOs hope to overcome some of the shortcomings of informal apprenticeship, in particular its little education and portable content.

Private education and training supply have been spurred less by pure market forces than by public policies that offered private agents incentives and subsidies to engage them in executing programmes. However, profit making private institutions are unlikely to become the principal purveyors of education and initial training in most developing countries. In the present context of often severe income and social inequalities there, the participation of disadvantaged population groups in education and training cannot be assured by privately run education and training.

Also, education and training are often long time endeavours that are less conducive to be met by private profit making institutions, frequently operating in a short term perspective. Nevertheless private institutions, and also NGOs, community organizations and other actors have been instrumental in adapting education and training to local economic and social needs and constitute a valuable source of learning opportunities supplementary to public provision.

Education and Initial Training Reforms

Inequalities of access to education and training in and between countries remain formidable. In 1998, the net enrolment rates in primary education was 60 per cent in sub-Saharan Africa, 74 per cent in South and West Asia, 76 per cent in the Arab States and North Africa, 92 per cent in Central Asia, 94 per cent in Latin America and the Caribbean, 97 per cent in East Asia and the Pacific and 98 per cent in more developed regions. The enrolment rate in primary education in sub-Saharan Africa fell between 1980 and 1997. Basic literacy eludes over 40 per cent of adults in Sub-Saharan Africa and South and West Asia. The funding impact of structural adjustment programmes in many African countries has often negatively affected educational enrolment and quality.

In the advanced industrialized countries, which have extended basic education to most of their populations, the emphasis is on improving educational quality and access to education and initial training opportunities of disadvantaged population groups, and addressing the still considerable gap in access between the sexes. In many transition economies in Europe and Asia, the main task is to address the mismatch between available skills and existing education and training programmes on one hand, and, on the other, the demand for new skills that their economies need as they embrace the market economy.

Countries in Latin America, North Africa, and East Asia have high education participation rates, but inequality in access, and quality shortcomings are considerable. Issues of equity, financing, and definition of the roles between the public and private sectors need to be resolved as they make the transition from elitist to modern systems that embrace their entire population in lifelong learning. The least developed countries, especially in Sub-Saharan Africa and parts of South Asia face the huge challenge of providing all school-age children with the core skills identified in national curricula. Many girls and children, in rural areas in particular, are unable to attend school, while others drop out of school before mastering essential basic skills. Illiteracy rates among women and girls are sometimes double those of men and boys.

National and international public investment should ensure a minimum level of quality and universal access to basic education, particularly in rural areas and for women and other disadvantaged groups. Many countries must undertake the often politically difficult task of changing investment priorities in favour of basic education. In 1990, the Jomtien Education for All Conference in Thailand developed a plan to increase learning and educational quality in schools, and to attain universal primary education before the year 2000.

In Dakar, the World Education Forum (2000) pushed back the date to 2015, with the commitment that "all children, particularly girls, children in difficult circumstances and those belonging to ethnic minorities, have access to and complete free and compulsory primary education of good quality". Most recently (July 2001), the High Level Panel of the Youth Employment Network formulated a set of recommendations that the heads of the United Nations, the World Bank and the ILO invite all heads of state and government to mobilize national and local actors to, inter alia, make basic education and initial training more accessible to young men and women.

EXPANDING COMPULSORY EDUCATION AND INTEGRATING GENERAL AND VOCATIONAL EDUCATION AND TRAINING

Several countries have integrated vocational and general education by merging various types of educational institutions, by increasing the general studies content of vocational streams, or by integrating vocational subjects into general upper-secondary education. The duration of compulsory education has been extended. Initial training is provided in schools and in specialized institutions, and it also increasingly includes workplace-based learning.

In Norway, in 1994, a major reform of the entire upper secondary school system gave all 16-19 year olds the right to receive three years of upper secondary education that makes them eligible for further studies or an occupation. The reforms increased the general, portable content of vocational education, raised the number of those awarded vocational certificates and qualifications for entrance into higher education, while it endevoured to reduce, or even eliminate, the number of dropouts from upper secondary, education, both academic and vocational.

Vocational education, including apprenticeship training, is today an integral part of upper secondary education. The basic vocational education model offers the student a three-year education, with different vocational streams. Schools often give both general courses and vocational courses. The number of foundation courses during the first year of study was reduced from more than hundred to thirteen, while a broader vocational education curriculum also put stress on the development of general, portable skills such as Norwegian and English language skills, mathematics, natural science, and sports and physical education.

In Norway, the first two years of upper secondary education are given at school. The student must choose different, more specialized courses during the second year. These are provided in schools while others are workplace-based. The academic track entails three-year courses. Under the vocational track the third study year has been transformed into two years of apprenticeship training. Apprenticeship schemes were extended to economic sectors that had no previous experience of them, and many vocational courses, previously entirely school based, were transformed into the new model of two years of school based education followed by two years of apprenticeship training (2+2).

In Spain, the 1990 Law on the General Organization of the Education System (Ley de Ordenacion General del Sistema Educativo-LOGSE) extends free compulsory education to the age of 16. All students follow some general technical training and are given the opportunity to take optional subjects that allow for some pre-employment experience or activity. After completing compulsory secondary education, the students can continue to upper secondary education, either general education or intermediate vocational training. On top of these strearns there will also be higher vocational training. (Spain Education System).

In Brazil, the Ministry of Education is modernizing vocational education, adopting a competency-based approach and developing systems of certification in order to facilitate continuous education and labor market insertion. New legal instruments provide for the development of vocational education curricula. Vocational education is complementary to basic education, and can be acquired in schools, specialized institutions or in the workplace.

In order to encourage further study, the law provides for pathways between various levels of education and access to certification through the recognition of knowledge and skills gained at work. Vocational education has become more generic, and definition of trades has been discontinued. Local education authorities are free to develop curricula according to local needs and circumstances, on the basis of occupational areas defined in the directives.

Chile has undertaken successive education reforms. Mirroring international and domestic workplace trends, the most recent reforms of mid-level technical-professional education in Chile expanded the general education content of the first two years, and redefined the role of vocational education, which is now part of general secondary education, and intended to prepare students for labour market entry and promote their social inclusion. The Ministry has used the competency approach to develop educational trajectories that facilitate life-long learning. The reforms emphasize linkages with industry. In 1999, a "dual" programme of vocational education was introduced, in collaboration with the Government of Germany.

Denmark, Hungary, and Sweden have also increased the general education content of upper-secondary vocational education, giving students the conceptual knowledge and skills they need in working life. They also have better access to tertiary study. In Sweden today, students who go on to further studies represent nearly all vocational areas. However, weaker students often face difficulties meeting the higher demands of general education subjects, while teachers sometimes find it difficult to relate some general education content to the world of work. Also, vocational students tend to gain access to further study only if they have done well in general subjects.

Australian state governments have recently integrated vocational education and training into upper secondary education in an effort to equip young people with the skills that employers need. Senior secondary studies will provide expanded and better quality opportunities for nationally recognized vocational education and training qualifications.

The new VET in Schools initiative allows secondary students to take vocational education courses at school, or with public and private training providers, and combine work with general and vocational education, on a part or full time basis. Students will graduate with full or partial VET qualifications and a senior secondary certificate that will boost their prospects of finding jobs. They will also be able to use the credits so gained towards VET qualification at higher levels.

Modernizing apprenticeship

Workplace change and technological innovation and their upward skill bias generate demand for higher technical and specialist skills, combined with an understanding of the broader economic and social context of occupations, work and industry. Efforts to reform apprenticeship, for example in Germany, attempt to broaden the content of apprenticeship learning and training, often expanding the educational, contextual part of the learning programme.

In South Africa, the new learnerships are a flexible form of apprenticeship. They have, in common with apprenticeship, the addition of workplace learning to the learning programme and a practical assessment of competence. The "new apprenticeships" in Australia, introduced in 1998, have expanded rapidly, a testimony to their appeal among individuals and employers. New apprenticeships aim to broaden the industrial and occupational base for apprenticeship learning. Individuals can today take up apprenticeships in virtually all sectors and industries, groups of companies, and occupations. Considerable success has been achieved in making the new apprenticeships better reflect the country's employment structure.

In 2001, 32 per cent of jobs were in the clerical, sales and service occupations; in that year these same occupations had 30 per cent of new apprenticeships. However, the share of managerial and administrative occupations among jobs (7 per cent of total) has not been matched by an equivalent increase in apprenticeships, presently at 1 per cent. A few countries, e.g. India and Pakistan, apply compulsory apprenticeship training schemes.

Employers' training responsibilities are recognized legally. In India, the apprenticeship training scheme (The Apprenticeship Act, 1961) is an important source of skilled workers in the country. Employers are obliged to engage a certain number of trade apprentices based on the number of their employees and the type of industry they represent. Industry is required to impart on-the-job training while theoretical instruction is offered in government's training centres. In 2000, some 17,800 establishments engaged some165,500 apprentices (150,000 in 1996) covering some 254 industries (218 in 1996) and 138 designated trades (130 in 1996). On completion of training, trade apprentices have to pass the All India Trade Tests conducted by the National Council for Vocational Training (NCVT).

Apprentices receive stipends, paid by the employer, which increase with each year of training. There is also apprenticeships for graduates and diploma holders in engineering and technology and for students graduating from the vocational stream of general education schools ("technician (vocational) apprentices"). In addition, the Apprenticeship Act encourages employers to offer places to people representing disadvantaged groups. In 2000, scheduled castes accounted for 7 per cent of places, scheduled tribes 1 per cent, minorities 7 per cent, physically handicapped 0.14 per cent, and women twenty per cent[6].

New Institutional Arrangements for Providing Education and Initial Training

Reforms of education and training content and curricula have been undertaken in a rapidly evolving institutional context. The growth of private provision has been significant. Regional, local and community organizations, including NGOs, increasingly provide education and initial training services.

Local management of vocational training

In Brazil, the regional bodies of SENAI (National Industrial Training Service), SENAC (The National Commercial Training Service) and most recently SENAR (The National Rural Training

Serice), enjoy a high degree of autonomy vis-a-vis their National Directorates. Rather than an outcome of a central decision to delegate policy, administrative and organisational decisions to the regions, their autonomy rests on local Chambers of Industry and Commerce which are responsible for managing, maintaining infrastructure and allocating resources of the Regional departments. By engaging local entrepreneurs in the Departments' management, a range of co-operation and business initiatives with local authorities, trade unions and civil society organisation have become supportive of the State's social, economic and cultural objectives.

Non-formal initial education and training

A wide range of non-formal initiatives have been developed to provide various groups, including young people, poorly educated workers, rural workers, women, migrants and disadvantaged groups, basic education and skills to improve their employability and facilitate their labour market and social integration. These programmes are generally provided outside formal systems and are not formally recognized. However, countries like Australia, Singapore and South Africa are integrating also such non-formal training supply into national systems of recognized qualifications.

In Singapore, the Skills Development Fund has actively encouraged employers to enrol their employees in non-formal, recognized basic education programmes that are administered by the Institute of Technical Education. These include Basic Education for Skills Training (BEST) Programme which provides basic literacy and numeracy training, and Worker Improvement through Secondary Education (WISE) programme for adults to improve their competency in English and maths.

In Thailand, 3 months to 1 year long non-formal education programmes are run by many governments departments, state and private enterprises, NGOs and schools. These target students who have completed primary education, but have no secondary education. Pre-employment courses include basic skills training in electrical, automotive and construction technology and include an industry-training component. In 1995, the two Government departments responsible for major non-formal education programmes enrolled some 375,000 students. However, these programmes do not allow for progression in the formal education system.

In Barcelona, Spain, Workshop Schools help marginalised young people, who have never worked, have no vocational qualifications, and are looking for a manual job. Training develops their basic vocational skills, helps them gain self-confidence and self-esteem and assume responsibility for their own lives. It combines theory and practice in a socially relevant context. Students learn trade and job-search skills, and also basic management skills to help them become self-employed. Trainers work part-time which enables them to maintain another job and keep in touch with labour market and technical developments.

Students' insertion into employment is being assisted and monitored by a special agency Barcelona Activa. In the Netherlands, regional training centres (ROCs) assist young people who risk dropping out of school or who have left school without a certificate but want to complete their education. These Centres integrate and consolidate various programmes of vocational training and adult education, providing educational assistance, basic vocational training and training for self-employment, intermediate management training and specialist training.

Students can move from one type of study to another if they are experiencing difficulties in the one chosen. The Centre guides students, mediates between teachers and students and advises on training and employment problems. In Brazil, rather than running physical training centres, SENAR (The National Rural Training Service) has opted for a "virtual" network of services that are outsourced to private providers. These provide education and training services to rural populations, e.g. literacy programmes, training for young people and social promotion activities.

The Somaliland Education Initiative for Girls and Young Men (SEIGYM), supported by the Africa Educational Trust (AET), uses vouchers to encourage disadvantaged youth gain essential reading and work skills. Technical and vocational training institutions invariably demand that entrants have school qualifications. The vouchers allow disadvantaged youth to locate and pay for literacy and numeracy training before they go on to skills training for employment. More than 5,000 disadvantaged girls, young women and young ex-militia men have been given literacy, numeracy and vocational training. SEIGYM uses a variety of providers of non-formal education and training: carpenters, driving instructors, painters, tailors, nurses, etc. Vouchers are redeemable through AET only if it has inspected the provider and certified its standard of training.

EVALUATION FOR VOCATIONAL EDUCATION AND TRAINING

Individually sponsored training

Private sponsorship of training starting with that individuals sponsor for themselves, ie VET conducted largely or wholly apart from employment. Self-sponsored training all vocational courses taken in post-secondary education, such as secretarial vocational courses at American community colleges, technical institutes and proprietary schools, *Brevet de technicien* courses at French colleges, teacher training courses in British universities, and upgrading courses for *Meister* qualifications in German *Fachschulen*.

The importance of self-sponsored training varies greatly across countries. In the United States it accounts for nearly three-quarters of the private sector training experiences reported by young adults, dominating training for the 'mid-skilled' labour market in particular. In the United Kingdom, by contrast, only one-fifth of privately sponsored training episodes are sponsored by individuals; the rest are sponsored by employers. Second, sponsorship of one's own training is a predominantly youth affair in many countries, its incidence declining sharply with age- though in the United States there has been a steady increase in numbers of older students, particularly in community colleges.

The evaluation of self-sponsored training has relied heavily on quasi-experimental methods and single outcome criteria. The standard human capital earnings function applies more directly to self-sponsorship than to other categories of training. Individual pay and employment rates are related statistically to the various types of post-secondary VET, using regression analysis to remove the effects of other individual attributes such as race and sex. Although the selection biases potentially associated with unobserved attributes - notably ability and motivation - have occasionally been addressed, the effectiveness of such 'controls' remains dubious and, in any case, most studies simply ignore selection issues.

American research suggests private returns to two-year Associate degrees of the order of 20 to 30 per cent- somewhat lower than to a four-year first degree - and returns to one-year certificates of 10 to 20 per cent. The benefits are higher in particular areas, notably business and technical fields for men and the health field for women. When students complete occupational subjects in community colleges, the private returns tend to be higher than for the equivalent general subjects if they find employment related to their area of training, and lower (even zero, particularly for women) if their employment is unrelated.

A smattering of evidence indicates that the returns to the highly vocational courses offered by proprietary schools and technical institutes are lower than those in comprehensive community colleges. Finally, people who take but fail to complete post-secondary programmes, taking only a few courses, receive small net returns, generally less than 10 per cent. Such findings are probably affected by selection bias. For example, lower returns to vocational than to general subjects in community colleges may reflect lower student ability in the vocational category.

One study found that correction for selection bias removed the earnings effect of vocational Associate degrees for American men, though not for women. Another found that the marked effects of self-sponsored training on the pay of young American adults survived both the two step and the fixed effects corrections for selection bias.

The parallel French literature on the links between qualifications and employment suggests similarly that the possession of vocational post-secondary qualifications, notably the *Brevet de technicien* and the *Diplome d'ecole d'ingenieur*, confers substantial private benefits, in terms of access to employment, relative to the less vocationally qualified at the same level of attainment. During 1970-93 such training reduced the incidence of unemployment, and of employment on fixed-term contracts, during the first year of labour market experience, as well as increasing life-cycle earnings powerfully. The findings survived attempts to, for unobserved selection processes. They are not, however, capable of indicating whether such training is a success on wider efficiency criteria.

Finally, evidence has begun to emerge on the private returns to formal upgrade training in Germany, which we treat as sponsored by individuals rather than by employers. Skilled German workers who wish to upgrade their qualifications from *Facharbeiter* to *Meister* or *Techniker* level do so typically by taking part-time courses outside working hours, relying on local public technical colleges. The training might be expected to pay substantial dividends, given large pay differentials between these qualifications, together with strong employer demand for higher vocational qualifications.

Quasi-experimental evaluations of adult training in Germany unfortunately tend not to distinguish between upgrade and further training (*Fortbildung*, *Weiterbildung*), on the one hand, and retraining (*Umschulung*), on the other. Moreover, those who make the distinction have studied effects on employment rather than pay. In any event, positive effects on employment have been inferred by two studies. The first used a comparison group to analyse adult training in Hamburg, finding even stronger effects for upgrade training than for retraining. The second dealt with eastern Germany, finding that part-time adult courses are associated with lower exposure to unemployment, and full-time ones with the opposite. To the extent that upgrade training is conducted part time, and retraining full time, the implication is that upgrade training reduces the probability of entering unemployment.

In sum, in its highly varied national forms, individually sponsored training appears to improve markedly participants subsequent labour market fortunes, even allowing for unobserved positive selection into such training. That is perhaps no surprise - and it is just as well that it is the case - given that the individuals who take the training have to invest their own time and money while doing so. It is not easy to establish the merits of such training from the efficiency standpoint, as most studies use only partial outcome measures and ignore costs. Its merits from an equity standpoint are intrinsically limited, in so far as individuals must typically already possess resources in order to undertake such training. Public subsidies do, however, reduce the costs to individuals of some forms of VET, notably community college courses in the United States, helping less advantaged individuals to undertake training.

A NEW POLICY FOR EDUCATION

Education was given high priority after India gained independence in 1947. The new Constitution called on the State to provide free and compulsory primary education and gave the federal government the responsibility for maintaining standards in higher and technical education. By a subsequent amendment to the Constitution education was also declared to be a concern of the provincial governments. India opted for a planned economy, and each five-year plan indicates the directions for educational development.

Dramatic expansion of education has taken place since independence. The number of primary (including upper primary) schools has tripled and enrolment has increased from about 30 per cent to 80 percent. The increase in the enrolment of girls at primary level has been particularly impressive, from 17.7 per cent in 1950-1951 to 64.6 per cent in 1986-1987.

Increase in enrollments has been even more spectacular in secondary education, and the number of schoolteachers has risen from 750,000 to 3.7 million. In higher and professional education, the number of institutions and enrolments has increased eightfold and in technical education about tenfold.

In 1964, the government of India appointed a commission to advise on the national pattern of education and on the general principles and policies for educational development. Four years later, an education policy formulated on the basis of the commission's recommendations called for a transformation of the education system which would relate it more closely to the life of the people; a continuous effort to expand educational opportunity; a sustained and intensive effort to raise the quality of education at all stages; an emphasis on the development of science and technology; and the cultivation of moral and social values.

The most remarkable change which took place after the adoption of the 1968 Education Policy was the establishment of a common structure of education. This consisted of ten years of common schooling for all children, followed by two years of higher secondary education and a three-year degree course.

In 1985, the Central Government again reviewed the educational situation and decided to initiate a new National Policy on Education, which was debated extensively by students, teachers and people in all walks of life before it was passed by the two Houses of Parliament in February 1986. A detailed

Programme of Action was completed a few months later to ensure that the policy would be implemented without delay.

The1986 education policy envisages a national system which will take determined action to bring about universal primary education an promote the spread of adult literacy, thereby helping to reduce inequalities. The education system will be based on a national curricular framework which contains a common core as well as components specific to each region. The core will cut across subject areas and will be designed to promote such values as India's common cultural heritage, egalitarianism, democracy and secularism, equality of the sexes, protection of the environment, observance of the small family norm, and the scientific approach.

Pace-setting schools called Navodaya Vidyalayas will provide quality education to particularly gifted chil&en, irrespective of their families' means, and will promote excellence as well as equity and social justice. The 1986 policy also emphasizes the need to raise the level of investment in education from about 4 per cent of national income in 1986 to 6 per cent by 1990 and even higher thereafter.

Soon after assuming office in 1984, Prime Minister Rajiv Gandhi announced his decision to launch a National Literacy Mission (NLM) to bring functional literacy to some 80 million illiterate people in the 15 to 35 age group. The teaching of functional literacy is designed to achieve a variety of goals, including selfreliance in literacy and numeracy; the development of awareness among the poor and the illiterate of the causes of their deprivation; the acquisition of skills to improve economic status and general well-being; understanding of the values of national integration; conservation of the environment; women's equality; and the small family norm. NLM also stresses the importance of post-literacy and continuing education.

A number of important initiatives have been taken as a result of the new national policy on education:

— A nationwide programme for the improvement of primary education facilities, including reorganization of teacher training, is now under way.

— New curricula have been written for primary and secondary education and new textbooks and teaching materials have been prepared.

— Special programmes have been launched to improve science teaching, introduce computer literacy and promote awareness of environmental issues.

— By 1988, 256 Navodaya Vidyalayas had been established.

— Approximately 500,000 students and 500 voluntary agencies were involved in the National Literacy Mission in 1987-1988. Several districts and big cities such as Delhi, Bombay, Bangalore, Madras and Ahmedabad are launching campaigns to eradicate illiteracy by the end of 1990.

— A statutory body, the All India Council of Technical Education, has been created to maintain standards for institutions of technical education and to modernize technical education to prepare the workforce needed for rapid technological and scientific change.

2

10+2+3 System

The Educational and Training Enterprize in India which operates at all conceivable levels from pre-school to post doctoral is of a monumental size. In the formal education system, the preschool years range from 1 to 3 followed by 10 years of high school and 23 years of higher secondary. The tertiary education is of mostly 3 to 4 years for under-graduate studies followed by Masters, M.Phil and Ph.D degrees. There are many Universities and institutions for the post-doctoral research and training. On the non-formal side the age group addressed 9 to 40 under two separate programmes for school age children and adults, respectively. The Open learning system has also started functioning in the country with the establishment of the National Open School and National Open University to provide the leadership and direction. At present there are 5 Open Universities and 4 Open Schools in India.

There are more than 7,40,000 formal schools. More than 3.6 million teachers are working on full time basis. There are more than 175 Universities offering under graduate and post graduate courses and about 6000 colleges affiliated to these universities.

The educational structure in India is generally referred to as the Ten + Two + Three (10+2+3) pattern. The first ten years provide undifferentiated general education for all students. The +2 stage, also known as the higher secondary or senior secondary, provides for differentiation into academic and vocational streams and marks the end of school education. In some states, the plus two stage is located in intermediate, junior or degree colleges but is not regarded as a part of the tertiary stage of education. Besides, the technician educational programme has been shown to exist after the ten year of general education. The location of one year or two year programmes of the Industrial Training Institutes have been shown at VIII+ and X+ levels followed by the apprenticeship training. The non formal systems operating at elementary stage, secondary stage (open school) and tertiary stage (open university) have been shown as shaded portions.

In India education is in the concurrent list, meaning thereby that even though the broad guidelines and structures of education and its administration may be laid down by the Central Government, yet the States are free to evolve and frame their own policies and structures of education within a broad framework. India constitutes of 32 States and Union Territories. As would be expected, variations in content, quality and medium of education prevail. These variations influence the structures of education and its administration.

EDUCATIONAL POLICY

Educational policy and progress have been reviewed in the light of the goal of national development and priorities set from time to time. In its Resolution on the National Policy on Education in 1968, an emphasis on quality improvement and a planned, more equitable expansion of educational facilities and the need to focus on the education of girls was stressed. About a decade ago and a half later, the National Policy on Education (NPE-1986) was formulated which was further updated in 1992. The NPE 1986 provides for a comprehensive policy framework for the development of education upto the end of the century and a Plan of Action (POA) 1992, assigning specific responsibilities for organising, implementing and financing its proposals.

India's commitment to the spread of knowledge and freedom of thought among its citizens is reflected in its Constitution. The Directive Principle contained in Article 45 enjoins that " the State shall endeavour to provide within a period of ten years from the commencement of this Constitution, for free and compulsory education for all children until they complete the age of fourteen years". Article 29 (i) provides that any citizen having a distinct language, script, special care of the economic and educational interests of the underprivileged sections, particularly, the Scheduled Castes and Scheduled Tribes is laid down as an obligation of the State under article 46.

Though education is in the concurrent list of the Constitution, the State Governments play a very major role in the development of education particularly in the primary and the secondary education sectors.

NATIONAL SYSTEM OF EDUCATION

The concept of a National System of Education implies that, up to a given level, all students, irrespective of caste, creed, location or sex, have access to education of a comparable quality. To achieve this, the Government will initiate appropriately funded programmes. Effective measures will be taken in the direction of the Common School System recommended in the 1968 Policy.

The National System of Education envisages a common educational structure. The 10+2+3 structure has now been accepted in all parts of the country. Regarding the further break-up of the first 10 years efforts will be made to move towards an elementary system comprising 5 years of primary education and 3 years of upper primary, followed by 2 years of High School. Efforts will also be made to have the +2 stage accepted as a part of school education throughout the country.

The National System of Education will be based on a national curricular framework which contains a common core along with other components that are flexible. The common core will include the history of India's freedom movement, the constitutional obligations and other content essential to nurture national identity. These elements will cut across subject areas and will be designed to promote values such as India's common cultural heritage, egalitarianism, democracy and secularism, equality of the sexes, protection of the environment, removal of social barriers, observance of the small family norm and inculcation of the scientific temper.

All educational programmes will be carried on in strict conformity with secular values. India has always worked for peace and understanding between nations, treating the whole world as one family. True to this hoary tradition, Education has to strengthen this world view and motivate the younger generations for international co-operation and peaceful co-existence. This aspect cannot be neglected.

To promote equality, it will be necessary to provide for equal opportunity to all not only in access, but also in the conditions for success. Besides, awareness of the inherent equality of all will be created through the core curriculum. The purpose is to remove prejudices and complexes transmitted through the social environment and the accident of birth.

Minimum levels of learning will be laid down for each stage of education. Steps will also be taken to foster among students an understanding of the diverse cultural and social systems of the people living in different parts of the country. Besides the promotion of the link language, programmes will also be launched to increase substantially the translation of books from one language to another and to publish multi-lingual dictionaries and glossaries. The young will be encouraged to undertake the rediscovery of India, each in his own image and perception.

In higher education in general, and technical education in particular, steps will be taken to facilitate inter-regional mobility by providing equal access to every Indian of requisite merit, regardless of his origins. The universal character of universities and other institutions of higher education is to be underscored.

In the areas of research and development, and education in science and technology, special measures will be taken to establish network arrangements between different institutions in the country to pool their resources and participate in projects of national importance.

The Nation as a whole will assume the responsibility of providing resource support for implementing programmes of educational transformation, reducing disparities, universalisation of elementary education, adult literacy, scientific and technological research, etc.

Life-long education is a cherished goal of the educational process. This presupposes universal literacy. Opportunities will be provided to the youth, housewives, agricultural and industrial workers and professionals to continue the education of their choice, at the pace suited to them. The future thrust will be in the direction of open and distance learning.

The institutions which will be strengthened to play an important role in giving shape to the National System of Education are the University Grants Commission, the All India Council of Technical Education, the Indian Council of Agricultural Research and the Indian Medical Council. Integrated planning will be instituted among all these bodies so as to establish functional linkages and reinforce programmes of research and post graduate education. These, together with the National Council of Education Research and Training, the National Institute of Educational Planning and Administration, the National Council of Teacher Education and the National Institute of Adult Education will be involved in implementing the Education Policy.

A Meaningful Partnership

The Constitutional Amendment of 1976, which includes Education in the Concurrent List, was a far-reaching step whose implications-substantive, financial and administrative-require a new sharing of responsibility between the Union Government and the States in respect of this vital area of national life. While the role and responsibility of the States in regard to education will remain essentially unchanged, the Union Government would accept a larger responsibility to reinforce the national and integrative character of education, to maintain quality and standards (including those of the teaching profession at all levels), to study and monitor the educational requirements of the country as a whole in regard to manpower for development, to cater to the needs of research and advanced study, to look after the international aspects of education, culture and Human Resource Development and, in general, to promote excellence at all levels of the educational p yramid throughout the country. Concurrency signifies a partnership, which is at once meaningful and challenging; the National Policy will be oriented towards giving effect to it in letter and spirit.

STRUCTURE OF SCHOOL EDUCATION

The focus in on the broad dimensions and magnitude of the structure, organisation and progress in education. Further it also highlights growth and priority areas in education in India that point to the challenges of the future. There are about 888 thousands educational institutions in the country with an enrolment of about 179 millions. Elementary Education System in India is the second largest in the World with 149.4 millions children of 6-14 years enrolled and 2.9 million teachers. This is about 82% of the children in the age group.

A uniform structure of school education, the 10+2 system has been adopted by all the States and Union Territories of India. However, within the States and the UTs, there remains variations in the number of classes constituting the Primary,

Upper Primary, High and Higher Secondary school stages, age for admission to class I, medium of instruction, public examinations, teaching of Hindi and English, number of working days in a year, academic session, vacation periods, fee structure, compulsory education etc.

Stages of School Education in India

Primary Stage

The Primary Stage consists of Classes I-V, i.e., of five years duration, in 20 States/UTs namely Andhra Pradesh, Arunachal Pradesh, Bihar, Haryana, Himachal Pradesh, Jammu & Kashmir, Madhya Pradesh, Manipur, Orissa, Punjab, Rajasthan, Sikkim, Tamil Nadu, Tripura, Uttar Pradesh, West Bengal, Andaman & Nicobar Islands, Chandigarh, Delhi and Karaikal and Yanam regions of Pondicherry. The primary stage consists of classes I-IV in Assam, Goa, Gujarat, Karnataka, Kerala, Maharashtra, Meghalaya, Mizoram, Nagaland, Dadra & Nagar Haveli, Daman & Diu, Lakshadweep and Mahe region of Pondicherry

Middle Stage

The Middle Stage of education comprises Classes VI-VIII in as many as 18 States.Uts viz., Arunachal Pradesh, Bihar, Haryana, Himachal Pradesh, Jammu & Kashmir, Madhya Pradesh, Manipur, Punjab, Rajasthan, Sikkim, Tamil Nadu, Tripura, Uttar Pradesh, West Bengal, Andaman & Nicobar Islands, Chandigarh, Delhi and Karaikal region of Pondicherry; Classes V-VII in Assam, Goa, Gujarat, Karnataka, Kerala, Maharashtra, Meghalaya, Mizoram, Dadra & Nagar Haveli, Daman & Diu, Lakshadweep and Mahe region of Pondicherry and Classes VI-VII in Andhra Pradesh, Orissa and Yanam region of Pondicherry. In Nagaland Classes V – VIII constitute the upper primary stage.

Secondary Stage

The Secondary Stage consists of Classes IX-X in 19 States/UTs. Viz., Arunachal Pradesh, Bihar, Haryana, Himachal Pradesh, Jammu & Kashmir, Madhya Pradesh, Manipur, Nagaland, Punjab, Rajasthan , Sikkim, Tamil Nadu, Tripura, Uttar Pradesh, West Bengal, Andaman & Nicobar Islands, Chandigarh, Delhi and Karaikal region of Pondicherry. The High School stage comprises classes VIII to X in 13 States/UTs viz., Andhra Pradesh, Assam, Goa, Gujarat, Karnataka, Kerala, Maharashtra, Meghalaya, Mizoram, Orissa, Dadra & Nagar Haveli, Daman & Diu, Lakshadweep and Mahe & Yanam regions of Pondicherry. However, the Higher Secondary / Senior Secondary stage of school comprising classes XI-XII (10+2 pattern) is available in all the States/UTs though in some States/ UTs these classes are attached to Universities/Colleges.

Age Restriction for Admission

The minimum age for admission to class I of the Primary School stage is generally 5+ or 6+ years. In 22 States/UTs the minimum age for admission to Class I is 5+ years and in 7 States/UTs the minimum age for admission is 6+ years. There is no age restriction in the case of Mizoram. In Gujarat, the minimum age for admission is 5+ years (voluntary) and 6+ years (compulsory). In Lakshadweep, the minimum age for admission is 5 ½ years.

MEDIUM INSTRUCTION

Mother tongue or regional language is the medium of instruction at the primary stage of education in most of the States/UTs. Facilities for studying in a medium other than regional language vary considerable in different States and Union Territories.

Teaching of Hindi

Apart from Hindi speaking States, teaching of Hindi is

compulsory in most of the non-Hindi speaking States/UTs, though the classes from which the teaching of Hindi is compulsory differ from State to State. Teaching of Hindi is not compulsory in the States of Tamil Nadu, Tripura and Karaikal region of Pondicherry.

Teaching of English

Teaching of English is compulsory in all the States/UTs, except Bihar. However, the classes in which teaching of English is compulsory differs from State to State. In general, it is compulsory in Classes VI-X in most of the States/UTs.

Public Examinations

In all the States/UTs Public Examinations are conducted at the end of X an XII Classes by the respective State Boards of Secondary and Higher Secondary Education. The minimum age for the Secondary School Examination varies from 14+ to 16+ years in Andhra Pradesh, Arunachal Pradesh, Assam, Bihar, Gujarat, Jammu & Kashmir, Karnataka, Kerala, Maharashtra, Manipur, Orissa, Punjab, Tamil Nadu, Tripura, West Bengal, Andaman & Nicobar Islands, Delhi, Lakshadweep and Pondicherry. In Mizoram, the minimum age for secondary school examination is 13+ years.

Other States/UTs either do not have age restriction or have not prescribed any age restriction. The minimum age for higher Secondary School Examination varies from 16+ to 18+ years in Arunachal Pradesh, Bihar, Gujarat, Jammu & Kashmir, Kerala, Maharashtra, Punjab, Tamil Nadu, Tripura, Andaman & Nicobar Islands, Delhi, Lakshadweep and Pondicherry. In other States/UTs, either there is no age restriction prescribed or if it exists, it has not been indicated. In some of the States/ UTs, the first Public Examination is also conducted at the Middle stage of School Education.

Number of Working Days

The number of working days of School Education in a year is generally more than 200 days in all the States/UTs.

Academic Session

The academic session begins from different months of the year in the different States and Union Territories. However, in most of the States, the long vacation periods are availed in the summer season while in some of the hilly States, these fall in the winter months.

Compulsory Education

Compulsory education has been enforced in four States and Union Territories at the primary stage of education while in eight States/UTs there is compulsory education covering the entire elementary stage of education. As many as 20 States/ UTs have not introduced any measure of compulsion upto the year 1997-98.

Free Education

A majority of States and Union Territories have introduced free education in Classes I-XII of their schools.

Tution Fees per Annum per Child in Govt. Schools

In the States/UTs where education is not free for classes IX and above, the annual fee varies considerably from the highest level of Rs. 360/- for classes XI and XII in the case of Meghalaya to the lowest at Rs. 48/- in the case of Assam.

Administration and Funding

Education is divided into preprimary, primary, middle (or

intermediate), secondary (or high school), and higher levels. Primary school includes children of ages six to eleven, organized into classes one through five. Middle school pupils aged eleven through fourteen are organized into classes six through eight, and high school students ages fourteen through seventeen are enrolled in classes nine through twelve. Higher education includes technical schools, colleges, and universities.

Article 42 of the constitution, an amendment added in 1976, transferred education from the state list of responsibilities to the central government. Prior to this assumption of direct responsibility for promoting educational facilities for all parts of society, the central government had responsibility only for the education of minorities. Article 43 of the constitution set the goal of free and compulsory education for all children through age fourteen and gave the states the power to set standards for education within their jurisdictions. Despite this joint responsibility for education by state and central governments, the central government has the preponderant role because it drafts the five-year plans, which include education policy and some funding for education.

Moreover, in 1986 the implementation of the National Policy on Education initiated a long-term series of programs aimed at improving India's education system by ensuring that all children through the primary level have access to education of comparable quality irrespective of caste, creed, location, or sex. The 1986 policy set a goal that, by 1990, all children by age eleven were to have five years of schooling or its equivalent in nonformal education. By 1995 all children up to age fourteen were to have been provided free and compulsory education. The 1990 target was not achieved, but by setting such goals, the central government was seen as expressing its commitment to the ideal of universal education.

The Department of Education, part of the Ministry of Human Resource Development, implements the central government's responsibilities in educational matters. The ministry coordinates planning with the states, provides funding for experimental programs, and acts through the University Grants Commission and the National Council of Educational Research and Training. These organizations seek to improve education standards, develop and introduce instructional materials, and design textbooks in the country's numerous languages. The National Council of Educational Research and Training collects data about education and conducts educational research.

State-level ministries of education coordinate education programs at local levels. City school boards are under the supervision of both the state education ministry and the municipal government. In rural areas, either the district board or the *panchayat* oversees the school board. The significant role the *panchayats* play in education often means the politicization of elementary education because the appointment and transfer of teachers often become emotional political issues.

State governments provide most educational funding, although since independence the central government increasingly has assumed the cost of educational development as outlined under the five-year plans. India spends an average 3 percent of its GNP on education. Spending for education ranged between 4.6 and 7.7 percent of total central government expenditures from the 1950s through the 1970s. In the early 1980s, about 10 percent of central and state funds went to education, a proportion well below the average of seventy-nine other developing countries. More than 90 percent of the expenditure was for teachers' salaries and administration. Per capita budget expenditures increased from Rs36.5 in FY 1977 to Rs112.7 in FY 1986, with highest expenditures found in the union territories. Nevertheless, total expenditure per student per year by the central and state governments declined in real terms.

Several factors work against universal education in India. Although Indian law prohibits the employment of children in factories, the law allows them to work in cottage industries, family households, restaurants, or in agriculture. Primary and middle school education is compulsory. However, only slightly more than 50 percent of children between the ages of six and fourteen actually attend school, although a far higher percentage is enrolled. School attendance patterns for children vary from region to region and according to gender. But it is noteworthy that national literacy rates increased from 43.7 percent in 1981 to 52.2 percent in 1991 (male 63.9 percent, female 39.4 percent), passing the 50 percent mark for the first time.

There are wide regional and gender variations in the literacy rates, however; for example, the southern state of Kerala, with a 1991 literacy rate of about 89.8 percent, ranked first in India in terms of both male and female literacy. Bihar, a northern state, ranked lowest with a literacy rate of only 39 percent (53 percent for males and 23 percent for females). School enrollment rates also vary greatly according to age. To improve national literacy, the central government launched a wide-reaching literacy campaign in July 1993. Using a volunteer teaching force of some 10 million people, the government hoped to have reached around 100 million Indians by 1997. A special focus was placed on improving literacy among women.

A report in 1985 by the Ministry of Education, entitled *Challenge of Education: A Policy Perspective* , showed that nearly 60 percent of children dropped out between grades one and five. (The Ministry of Education was incorporated into the Ministry of Human Resources in 1985 as the Department of Education. In 1988 the Ministry of Human Resources was renamed the Ministry of Human Resource Development.) Of 100 children enrolled in grade one, only twenty-three reached grade eight.

Although many children lived within one kilometer of a primary school, nearly 20 percent of all habitations did not have schools nearby. Forty percent of primary schools were not of masonry construction. Sixty percent had no drinking water facilities, 70 percent had no library facilities, and 89 percent lacked toilet facilities. Single-teacher primary schools were commonplace, and it was not unusual for the teacher to be absent or even to subcontract the teaching work to unqualified substitutes.

The improvements that India has made in education since independence are nevertheless substantial. From the first plan until the beginning of the sixth (1951-80), the percentage of the primary school-age population attending classes more than doubled. The number of schools and teachers increased dramatically. Middle schools and high schools registered the steepest rates of growth. The number of primary schools increased by more than 230 percent between 1951 and 1980. During the same period, however, the number of middle schools increased about tenfold. The numbers of teachers showed similar rates of increase. The proportion of trained teachers among those working in primary and middle schools, fewer than 60 percent in 1950, was more than 90 percent in 1987.

However, there was considerable variation in the geographical distribution of trained teachers in the states and union territories in the 1986-87 school year. Arunachal Pradesh had the highest percentage (60 percent) of untrained teachers in primary schools, and Assam had the highest percentage (72 percent) of untrained teachers in middle schools. Gujarat, Tamil Nadu, Chandigarh, and Pondicherry (Puduchcheri) reportedly had no untrained teachers at either kind of school.

Various forms of private schooling are common; many schools are strictly private, whereas others enjoy government grants-in-aid but are run privately. Schools run by church and missionary societies are common forms of private schools. Among India's Muslim population, the *madrasa* , a school attached to a mosque, plays an important role in education. Some 10 percent of all children who enter the first grade are enrolled in private schools. The dropout rate in these schools is practically nonexistent.

Traditional notions of social rank and hierarchy have greatly influenced India's primary school system. A dual system existed in the early 1990s, in which middle-class families sent their children to private schools while lower-class families sent their children to underfinanced and underequipped municipal and village schools. Evolving middle-class values have made even nursery school education in the private sector a stressful event for children and parents alike. Tough entrance interviews for admission, long classroom hours, heavy homework assignments, and high tuition rates in the mid-1990s led to charges of "lost childhood" for preschool children and acknowledgment of both the social costs and enhanced social benefits for the families involved.

The government encourages the study of classical, modern, and tribal languages with a view toward the gradual switch from English to regional languages and to teaching Hindi in non-Hindi speaking states. As a result, there are schools conducted in various languages at all levels. Classical and foreign language training most commonly occurs at the postsecondary level, although English is also taught at the lower levels.

Since independence, the central and state governments have been expanding the provision of primary formal and non-formal education to realise the goal of Universilisation of Elementary Education (UEE). The challenge now is to sustain and deepen current reforms in education and encourage local planning and management of strategies for expanding and improving primary education. With a view to cushioning the impact of rising costs of text books and exercise books, the government has exempted writing and printing paper supplied to all State Text Book Corporations from excise duty. It is expected that this would make school text books more affordable for students from weaker sections of society.

Removal of systemic deficiencies in the implementation of UEE and forging ahead necessitates the creation of informed public opinion and a facilitative environment akin to that of the Total Literacy Campaign. This has to be achieved through effective and sustained advocacy, massive community mobilisation and consciousness building. With this perspective, a national programme of media publicity and advocacy has been planned. The programme will target: i) teachers and all those involved in education of children; ii) students and parents of students, particularly non-literate parents; and iii) community opinion leaders.

The Kasturba Gandhi Shiksha Yojana, a programme to establish residential schools for girls in all the districts which have a particularly low female literacy rate has been announced. A sum of Rs. 2500 million has been provided in this year's budget. The central government has also decided to grant financial incentives and scholarships for the girl child born in families living below the poverty line.

Several central and state level initiatives have been in operation from the early 1980s. While the design of these projects vary substantially, all of them address the objectives and strategies of the National Policy on Education 1986. They pay special attention to increasing girls' enrolment, improving educational outcomes, strengthening community involvement, improving teaching and learning materials and providing in-service teacher training.

Colleges and Universities

Receiving higher education, once the nearly exclusive domain of the wealthy and privileged, since independence has become the aspiration of almost every student completing high school. In the 1950-51 school year, there were some 360,000 students enrolled in colleges and universities; by the 1990-91 school year, the number had risen to nearly 4 million, a more than tenfold increase in four decades. At that time, there were 177 universities and university-level institutions (more than six times the number at independence), some 500 teacher training colleges, and several thousand other colleges.

There are three kinds of colleges in India. The first type, government colleges, are found only in those states where private enterprise is weak or which were at one time controlled by princes. The second kind are colleges managed by religious organizations and the private sector. Many of the latter institutions were founded after 1947 by wealthy business owners and politicians wishing to gain local fame and importance. Professional colleges comprise the third kind and consist mostly of medical, teacher-training, engineering, law, and agricultural colleges. More than 50 percent of them are sponsored and managed by the government. However, about 5 percent of these colleges are privately run without government grant support. They charge fees of ten to twelve times the amount of the government-run colleges.

The profusion of new engineering colleges in India in the late 1980s and early 1990s caused concern in official education circles that the overall quality and reputation of India's higher education system would be threatened by these new schools, which operated mainly on a for-profit basis. As the government tightened its support to higher education in the early 1990s, colleges and universities came under considerable financial stress.

The All-India Council of Technical Education is empowered to regulate the establishment of any new private professional colleges to limit their proliferation. In 1992 the Karnataka High Court directed the state government to rescind permission to nine organizations to start new engineering and medical colleges in the state. Gaining admission to a nonprofessional college is not unduly difficult except in the case of some select colleges that are particularly competitive. Students encounter greater difficulties in gaining admission to professional colleges in such fields as architecture, business, medicine, and dentistry.

There are four categories of universities. The largest number are teaching universities that maintain and run a large number of colleges. Unitary institutions, such as Allahabad University and Lucknow University, make up the second kind. The third kind are the twenty-six agricultural universities, each managed by the state in which it is located. Technical universities constitute the fourth kind. In the late 1980s, more technical universities, such as the Jawaharlal Nehru Technological University in the state of Hyderabad, were founded. There were also proposals to found medical universities in some states. By 1990 Andhra Pradesh and Tamil Nadu already had established such universities. Out of the 177 universities in the country, only ten are funded by the central government. The majority of universities are managed by the states, which establish them and provide funding.

There was a high rate of attrition among students in higher education in the 1980s. A substantial portion failed their examinations more than once, and large numbers dropped out; only about one out of four students successfully completed the full course of studies. Even those students who were successful could not count on a university degree to assure them employment. In the early postindependence years, a bachelor's degree often provided entrance to the elite, but in contemporary India, it provides a chance to become a white-collar worker at a relatively modest salary. The government traditionally has been the principal employer of educated manpower.

State governments play a powerful role in the running of all but the national universities. Political considerations, if not outright political patronage, play a significant part in appointments. The state governor is usually the university chancellor, and the vice chancellor, who actually runs the institution, is usually a political appointee. Appointments are subject to political jockeying, and state governments have control over grants and other forms of recognition. Caste affiliation and regional background are recognized criteria for admission and appointments in many colleges. To offset the inequities implicit in such practices, a certain number of places are reserved for members of Scheduled Castes and Scheduled Tribes.

Main players in the higher education system in the country are:

— University Grants Commission (UGC) is responsible for coordination, determination and maintenance of standards, release of grants.

— Professional Councils are responsible for recognition of courses, promotion of professional institutions and providing grants to undergraduate programmes and various awards. The statutory professional councils are:
  - — All India Council for Technical Education (AICTE),
  - — Distance Education Council (DEC)
  - — Indian Council for Agriculture Research (ICAR),
  - — Bar Council of India (BCI),
  - — National Council for Teacher Education (NCTE)
  - — Rehabilitation Council of India (RCI)
  - — Medical Council of India (MCI),
  - — Pharmacy Council of India (PCI)
  - — Indian Nursing Council (INC)
  - — Dentist Council of India (DCI)
  - — Central Council of Homeopathy (CCH)
  - — Central Council of Indian Medicine (CCIM)

Central Government is responsible for major policy relating to higher education in the country. It provides grants to the UGC and establishes central universities in the country. The Central Government is also responsible for declaration of Educational Institutions as 'Deemed to be University' on the recommendation of the UGC. Presently there are sixteen (16) *Central Universities* in the country. In pursuance of the Mizoram Accord, another Central University in the State of Mizoram is planned. There are 37 Institutions which have been declared as Deemed to be Universities by the Govt. of India as per Section of the UGC Act, 1956.

State Governments are responsible for establishment of State Universities and colleges, and provide plan grants for their development and non-plan grants for their maintenance. The coordination and cooperation between the Union and the States is brought about in the field of education through the Central Advisory Board of Education (CABE).

Special Constitutional responsibility of the Central Government: Education is on the 'Concurrent list' subject to Entry 66 in the Union List of the Constitution. This gives exclusive Legislative Power to the Central Govt. for co-ordination and determination of standards in Institutions of higher education or research and scientific and technical institutions.

ACADEMIC QUALIFICATION FRAMEWORK

There are three principle levels of qualifications within the higher education system in the country. These are:

— Bachelor / Undergraduate level

— Master's / Post-graduate level

— Doctoral / Pre-doctoral level

Diploma courses are also available at the undergraduate and postgraduate level. At the undergraduate level, it varies between one to three years in length, postgraduate diplomas are normally awarded after one year's study. Bachelor's degree in arts, commerce and sciences is three years of education (after 12 years of school education). In some places there are honours and special courses available. These are not necessarily longer in duration but indicate greater depth of study.

Bachelor degree in professional field of study in agriculture, dentistry, engineering, pharmacy, technology and veterinary medicine generally take four years, while architecture and medicine, it takes five and five and a half years respectively. There are other bachelor degrees in education, journalism and librarian-ship that are second degrees. Bachelor's degree in law can either be taken as an integrated degree lasting five years or three-year course as a second degree.

Master's degree is normally of two-year duration. It could be coursework based without thesis or research alone. Admission to postgraduate programmes in engineering and technology is done on the basis of Graduate Aptitude Test in Engineering or Combined Medical Test respectively. A pre-doctoral programme - Master of Philosophy (M.Phil.) is taken after completion of the Master's Degree. This can either be completely research based or can include course work as well. Ph.D. is awarded two year after the M.Phil. or three years after the Master's degree. Students are expected to write a substantial thesis based on original research. generally takes longer.

EDUCATION AND SOCIETY

Historically, Indian education has been elitist. Traditional Hindu education was tailored to the needs of Brahman boys who were taught to read and write by a Brahman teacher. During Mughal rule (1526-1858), Muslim education was similarly elitist, although its orientation reflected economic factors rather than those of caste background. Under British company and crown rule (1757-1947), official education policies reinforced the preexisting elitist tendencies of South Asian education. By tying entrance and advancement in government service to academic education, colonial rule contributed to the legacy of an education system geared to preserving the position and prerogatives of the more privileged.

Education served as a "gatekeeper," permitting an avenue of upward mobility to those few able to muster sufficient resources. Even the efforts of the nationalistic Indian National Congress faltered in the face of the entrenched interests defending the existing system of education. Early in the 1900s, the Congress called for national education, placing an emphasis on technical and vocational training. In 1920 the Congress initiated a boycott of government-aided and government-controlled schools; it founded several "national" schools and colleges, but to little avail. The rewards of British-style education were so great that the boycott was largely ignored, and the Congress schools temporarily disappeared.

Postprimary education has traditionally catered to the interests of the higher and upwardly mobile castes. Despite substantial increases in the spread of middle schools and high schools' growth in enrollment, secondary schooling is necessary for those bent on social status and mobility through acquisition of an office job. In the nineteenth century, postprimary students were disproportionately Brahmans; their traditional concern with learning gave them an advantage under British education policies. By the early twentieth century, several powerful cultivator castes had realized the advantages of education as a passport to political power and had organized to acquire formal learning.

"Backward" castes (usually economically disadvantaged Shudras) who had acquired some wealth took advantage of their status to secure educational privilege. In the mid-1980s, the vast majority of students making it through middle school to high school continued to be from high-level castes and middle- to upper-class families living in urban areas. A region's three or four most powerful castes typically dominated the school system. In addition, the widespread role of private education and the payment of fees even at government-run schools discriminated against the poor.

The goals of the 1986 National Policy on Education demanded vastly increased enrollment. In order to have attained universal elementary education in 1995, the 1981 enrollment level of 72.7 million would have had to increase to 160 million in 1995. Although the seventh plan suggested the adoption of new education methods to meet these goals, such as the promotion of television and correspondence courses and open school systems, the actual extended coverage of children was not very great.

Many critics of India's education policy argue that total school enrollment is not actually a goal of the government considering the extent of society's vested interest in child labor. In this context, education can be seen as a tool that one social class uses to prevent the rise of another. Middle-class Indians frequently distinguish between the children of the poor as "hands," or children who must be taught to work, and their own children as "minds," or children who must be taught to learn.

The upgraded curriculum with increased requirements in English and in the sciences appears to be causing difficulties for many children. Although all the states have recognized that curriculum reform is needed, no comprehensive plan to link curricular changes with new ways of teaching, learning, teacher training, and examination methods has been implemented. The government instituted an important program for improving physical facilities through a phased drive in all primary schools in the country called Operation Blackboard.

Under Operation Blackboard, Rs1 billion was allocated—but not spent—in 1987 to pay for basic amenities for village schools, such as toys and games, classroom materials, blackboards, and maps. This financial allotment averaged Rs2,200 for each government-run primary school. Additional goals of Operation Blackboard included construction of classrooms that would be usable in all weather, and an additional teacher, preferably a woman, in all single-teacher schools.

The nonformal education system implemented in 1979 was the major government effort to educate dropouts and other unenrolled children. Special emphasis was given to the nonformal education system in the nine states regarded by the government as having deficient education systems: Andhra Pradesh, Assam, Bihar, Jammu and Kashmir, Madhya Pradesh, Orissa, Rajasthan, Uttar Pradesh, and West Bengal. A large number of children who resided in these states could not attend formal schools because they were employed, either with or without wages. Seventy-five percent of the country's children who were not enrolled in school resided in these states in the 1980s.

The 1986 National Policy on Education gave new impetus to the nonformal education system. Revised and expanded programs focused on involving voluntary organizations and training talented and dedicated young men and women in local communities as instructors. The results of a late 1980s integrated pilot project for nonformal and adult education for women and girls in the Lucknow district of Uttar Pradesh provide important data for analyzing recent implementation trends and initial results of both the nonformal education system and adult education in India.

Under this project, 300 centers were opened in rural parts of the district with the approval of the Department of Education, the central government, and the state government of Uttar Pradesh with financial and advisory support from the United Nations Educational, Scientific, and Cultural Organization (UNESCO). Because of the shortage of women teachers in rural areas of Uttar Pradesh, in the pilot project nonformal education for girls aged six to fourteen was integrated with the adult education program for women aged fifteen to thirty-five, so that the same staff and infrastructure could be used.

Most of the families of the project participants were in subsistence farming or engaged as farmhands, clerical workers, and petty merchants. Often the brothers of female participants attended a formal school situated about one or two kilometers from their homes. Most of the 300 instructors for the 300 centers were young women between the ages of eighteen and thirty-five. Each center averaged twenty-five women and twenty girl participants. The physical facilities of the centers varied from village to village. Classes might be held on the balcony of a brick house, within a temple, in a room of a mud-walled house, or under open thatch-roof structures. Besides focusing on the acquisition of literacy skills, the project increased participant motivation by also offering instruction in household work, such as sewing, knitting, and preserving food.

In 1987 a UNESCO mission to evaluate progress in this project in the areas of functional literacy, vocational skills, and civic awareness observed that randomly chosen participants in both nonformal and adult education classes effectively demonstrated their reading and writing skills at appropriate levels. As a result of many such local programs, literacy rates improved between 1981 and 1991. Male literacy increased from 56.5 percent in 1981 to 64.2 percent in 1991 while women's literacy rate increased from 29.9 percent in 1981 to 39.2 percent in 1991.

Understanding India's health care and education systems contributes to the larger understanding of this complex nation's diverse society. General trends and averages concerning social conditions on a national level may not adequately describe how human activity is expressed spatially and temporally in specific areas. The great variations in local environmental and social conditions require that national and state or union territory programs aimed at improving the quality of life not adhere too strictly to any one standard plan.

Local climate, topography, and drainage patterns all need to be considered in terms of how they relate to local forms of land use and ethnic and linguistic groupings. Increasing urbanization in India also complicates efforts at monitoring local conditions. Only with the full support and understanding of India's many rural and urban residents will new ways of focusing India's immense human resources toward the goals of developing and conserving renewable natural resources, limiting population growth, providing increased health care, and achieving education for all be successful.

3

Common School System

The word 'common' in Common School System (CSS) refers to state-financed quality education, not a common syllabus-setting and examination board. The school system has to leave space for expressing the wide diversity of our people through locally developed context-specific syllabuses," says Virgil D'Sami, executive director of a Chennai-based NGO Arunodhaya and convener of the Tamilnadu Alliance for Right to Education and Equity, the local chapter of NAFRE.

The new government's higher priority to education is seeing experts and activists revisit the 40-year old Kothari Commission recommendations for a common school system. There is considerable excitement within the community of educationists, academics and social activists about the top billing education has received in the UPA government's Common Minimum Programme (CMP). In its CMP, announced on May 28, the UPA had pledged to raise public spending on education to at least 6 percent of the GDP, impose a cess on all central taxes to "universalise access to quality basic education" and to reverse the creeping communalisation of school syllabuses of the past five years.

Given this sudden and unexpected top-level commitment to education, particularly elementary education, academics and education non-government organisations (NGOs) believe this is a good time to press their long-standing demand for a common school system (CSS). First recommended 40 years ago by the Kothari Commission on Education and subsequently given lip sympathy in the National Education Policies of 1986 and 1992, the proposed CSS has remained a dead letter for almost half a century. "We are happy that the UPA coalition unlike many previous governments has made a public commitment to quality education for all children. Such purposefulness is new and a sign of changed priorities. In our letters to the drafting committee we had strongly recommended that the CMP should commit itself to a ten-year framework for developing a common school system up to high school.

The rationale of CSS is self evident: to provide education of equitable quality to all children and end the canalisation of children into private, government aided and government schools on the basis of parental ability to pay and social status. Though the CMP is silent on CSS, we are encouraged by the commitment the UPA has shown to education and will continue to press our demand for implementation of a common school system in India,".

Established in 1979, Child Relief and You (CRY). CRY is among the 2,400 non-government organisations which have joined hands to promote the National Alliance for the Fundamental Right to Education (NAFRE) which conceptualised and lobbied hard for the 86th Amendment to the Constitution of India unanimously approved by Parliament in November 2001. This constitutional amendment makes it mandatory for government to provide "free and compulsory education to all children of the age six to fourteen years".

With the 86th Amendment having mandated compulsory elementary education, educationists have discovered to their dismay that the constitutional amendment is silent about the type or quality of education to be provided, and that at ground zero level — in India's 600,000 villages and multiplying slum habitats of urbania — the "free and compulsory education" being dished out to hapless children is in fact basic literacy instruction dispensed by barely qualified 'para teachers' in lieu of education. Therefore the constituent members of NAFRE have somewhat belatedly turned their attention to "the right to equity in education".

In August last year, NAFRE launched a public campaign demanding the implementation of a common school system in India. Ignored by the mainstream media, the campaign of NAFRE's 2,400 member NGOs in 15 states across the country has drawn public attention to the pernicious segregation and class divide that characterises Indian education, especially its unique home-grown three/four-tier schooling system. Under this tiered system children of the rich and famous are typically enrolled in five-star English-medium schools affiliated to the upscale CBSE, CISCE and IB examination boards which offer globally accepted syllabuses and curriculums.

Next in the pecking order are English medium government aided schools affiliated to state-level examination boards to which the children of the middle class are sent. And at the base of the education pyramid are shabby, poorly managed government/municipal schools which shove dubious quality language education down the unprotesting throats of the children of the poor majority.

Way back in 1964, the Kothari Commission on Education roundly condemned this separate, unequal school system:

> "...education itself is tending to increase social segregation and to perpetuate and widen class distinctions. At the primary stage, the free schools to which masses send their children are maintained by government and local authorities and are generally of poor quality. Some of the private schools are, on the whole, definitely better, but since many of them charge high fees they are availed of only by the middle and higher classes. At the secondary stage, a large proportion of the good schools are private but many of them also charge high fees which are normally beyond the means of any but the top ten percent of people, though some of the middle class parents make

> great sacrifices to send their children to them. There is this segregation in education itself — the minority of private fee-charging, better schools meeting the need of the upper classes and the vast bulk of free, publicly maintained, but poor schools being utilised by the rest. What is worse, this segregation is increasing and tending to widen the gulf between the classes and the masses," commented the report of the commission.

Forty years after this searing indictment of the Kothari Commission, little has changed. Ninety percent of the estimated 112 million children who enroll in primary school annually have no choice but to attend ill-maintained government schools staffed by unmotivated teachers, where they receive vernacular language education disqualifying them ab initio for aspiring to the best jobs and the good life in a rapidly crystallising English-dominated order.

According to the Public Report on Basic Education, one-fifth of government primary schools in the country are single teacher institutions without proper buildings, 58 percent don't provide drinking water to students and over 70 percent lack toilet facilities. This open, continuous and blatantly inegalitarian divide within the formative school system is arousing considerable anger and anguish within the nation's intelligentsia.

The most deprived are rural, poor and socially disadvantaged communities which are increasingly marginalised and excluded from enjoying the exceptional economic resurgence taking place today. The way forward is not to restrict the expansion in choices, but to make them uniformly available to all children regardless of whether they are boys or girls, where they are born, who their parents are, where they study, or what caste they belong to. We have to develop zero tolerance for inferior education and a two-track schooling system. Even if all children are not born equal, they have the right to education of equally good quality.

The general consensus among intellectuals monitoring the nation's socio-economic development effort is that the consistent failure to evolve an egalitarian common school system — endorsed by national policies on education in 1964, 1986 and 1992 — is lack of "political will". In effect, lack of political will is the inability of the silent majority — who by virtue of a substandard education have been condemned to a perpetual subaltern status in the English-dominated national economy — to press for equal quality education for their children.

A Dubai-based economist and financial advisor to the National Resource Centre for Inclusion and child rights activist: "The fundamental reason for the national failure to develop a common school system is the lack of a political constituency for education. Those who attend government schools are powerless while the rest — middle and upper classes — have no stake in them. Dr. Manmohan Singh recall a conversation with the incumbent prime minister Dr. he some time ago. He agreed with the logic of a common school system for all children but expressed helplessness without a powerful lobby being created for a CSS."

Not a few of the more perceptive social scientists ascribe the national failure to create a lobby for equal quality education for all children — which is the norm in all industrially developed countries — to a deep-rooted bias within the nation's powerful middle class for a filtering process which offers subsidised quality education — especially higher education — to merit students while the rest of the child population is sentenced to serve as a pool of cheap, barely literate labour. "Some perceive the universalisation of elementary education as a threat to the opportunities of their own children. In their view the role of the schooling system is to act as a filtering process which picks the best and brightest and helps them to realise their potential. If too many children get on board, the prospects of those who currently enjoy the privilege of good schooling facilities will be threatened," observe the authors of PROBE.

Anil Sadagopal, the erudite dean and professor of education at Delhi University, agrees with this damning indictment of the nation's establishment. "India's Parliament has expressed its unambiguous commitment to the common school system three times by endorsing the NPEs (National Policy on Education) of 1968, 1986 and 1992. But yet this proposal has not been translated into practice because the political leadership and bureaucracy at all levels together with the intelligentsia have a convenient escape route for their own children viz, the private school system. This shift in commitment from the government to the private school system is the root cause of the lack of political, bureaucratic and social will to improve government schools," he says.

An ardent champion of the common school system, Sadagopal stresses that the most important feature of CSS is "equitable — not uniform — education for schools, be they government, government-aided, local body or private." "Most advanced economies including US, Canada, Britain and several European countries have been built on the foundation of a fully funded government school system providing education of equal or near-equal quality to all children. No country in the world has universalised elementary education without promoting a common school system. Therefore the lack of commitment to CSS implies that India will never be able to provide education to all children despite the rhetoric of the Sarva Shiksha Abhiyaan," says Sadagopal.

One factor which has been consistently ignored by Indian politicians, social scientists and educationists is that all developed nations of the first world including the UK and US have a very strong government funded school network which is on a par with private schools in terms of infrastructure, quality of education and testing.

For instance in Britain there are only two types of schools: government and private and all students in either stream follow a common syllabus and upon school leaving (classes X and XII) are tested by the common GSCE and 'A' level exams. On the other hand in India, students in private schools write the English-medium pan-India CISCE board exam; some private and all Central government-managed schools write the all-India

CBSE exam, and students of state government and aided schools write the school leaving exam of state examination boards. It's hardly disputed that the 28 state boards offer inferior infrastructure, sub-standard education and less rigorous syllabuses and examination assessment.

Though the formation of a single pan-India syllabus and examination board such as the GCSE in Britain would go a long way in establishing at least a common syllabus requiring near-equal academic inputs, this proposal is fiercely resisted by education NGOs and child rights activists. The general consensus among them is that India is a heterogeneous society and requires community-specific (read state-specific) syllabi. "Contrary to popular perception, a common school system is not synonymous with regimented, homogenised education across the country — a colonial legacy. It should guarantee equity in education and educational opportunities, not merely equal quality education. D'sami's argument in favour of several community-specific syllabuses is endorsed by Lucknow-based educationist and former director of basic education in the government of Uttar Pradesh, Dr. H.P.Pandey. "Syllabuses have to reflect the variations that exist in our country. In fact education rests on the belief that the greater the variety, the better for society.

The preference of schools to affiliate with all-India exam boards is for the snob value they represent and while such students may score over those from state boards in college admissions, children from state boards to equally well in competitive exams. What we need to really change is the system of evaluation to make it more reliable. This can be achieved through common training programmes for all evaluators," says Pandey.

While some opponents of a genuinely common school system with a common syllabus and school leaving examinations are driven by issues such as sub-nationalism and cultural diversity, critics of the "context specific" education system are inclined to look deeper for economically advantageous motivations. "When people reject tried and tested policies — such as the common school system in Britain with a national syllabus and school leaving exams — one should look for economic motivations. The regional particularism and professed love of regional culture which has prompted the setting up of state examination boards is essentially motivated by the compulsion of state level politicians and bureaucrats to derive rents, commissions and kickbacks from construction, teacher appointments and text book printing rackets in government schools.

The educated upper and middle classes who were certain to complain about the subaltern education dispensed in government schools have been mollified by the provision of CISCE and CBSE affiliated schools. As usual the poor and powerless have to suffer the third class state government school system," says Dilip Thakore founder-editor of *Business India* and *Business World* and currently editor of *Education World*.

Kothari Commission recommendations

In 1964 the Central government appointed a high-powered committee under the stewardship of Dr. D.S. Kothari, then chairman of University Grants Commission (UGC) to frame a national policy which would give shape and direction to newly independent India's school education system. The resultant Kothari Commission Report on Education, a learned critique of Indian education, four decades later is still regarded as the most in-depth study of primary and secondary education in Indian history. The commission report inter alia advocated a common school system. According to the commission the characteristics of a common school system (CSS) are:

— Publicly funded schools open to all children irrespective of caste, creed, community, religion, economic condition or social status

— Where access to good education will depend not on wealth or class

— Adequate standards in all schools and at least a reasonable proportion of quality institutions

— No tuition fee is charged

— It meets the expectations of average parents so that they would not ordinarily feel the need to send their children to fee-charging schools outside the system

The Kothari Commission also suggested some essential reforms to implement CSS effectively. The report called for:

— Significantly increased national outlay for elementary education to build required levels of infrastructure and provide quality education, thereby transforming government, local-body and aided schools into genuine neighbourhood schools

— Allocation of special funding for improvement of school systems in backward areas, urban slums, tribal areas, hilly tracts, desert and marshy areas, drought and flood-prone zones, coastal belts and islands

— Providing free instruction for all in the mother tongue at the primary level, particularly for linguistic minorities; active encouragement of teaching in regional languages at the secondary level and discontinuance of state aid to schools imparting education other than in the medium of mother tongue/ regional language

— Phased implementation of the common school system within a ten year time frame, and essential minimum legislation, particularly to dispense with early selection processes, tuition fees, capitation fees etc

— Exploring ways of including expensive private schools into the common school system through combinations of incentives, disincentives and legislation

Even if belatedly, there is growing awareness of the division of the school system into first and subaltern classes followed by a rising tide of public indignation. This is evidenced by the massive support NAFRE's 'Perspective paper on common school system' has received. Presented at the launch of the CSS campaign in August last year, this concept paper circulated among educationists, social activists, teachers and the public for debate, has resulted in a well argued blueprint for implementing a common school system based on the recommendations of the Kothari Commission. At the centre of this implementation strategy is rapid upgradation of state and local government schools to meet minimum physical infrastructure and academic quality standards to transform them into "genuine quality neighbourhood schools."

"A common school system requires every neighbourhood to have access to a good government school equipped with all the facilities available in private schools — qualified teachers, infrastructure and quality education. If children from rich and poor households attend the same school, its management and teachers would be accountable, as at least the rich will be a pressure group for quality education. Such institutional upgradation will result in an overnight transformation of government schools. I don't believe it's anybody's case to downgrade private, so-called elite schools. The proposal is to upgrade corporation and government schools to the highest level to engineer a social transformation," says V. Vasanthi Devi, former vice-chancellor of Gandhigram Rural University and Manonmaniam University and currently chairman of the Tamilnadu State Commission for Women.

Nor are the resources required to upgrade government schools to an acceptable level mountainous. The Tapas Majumdar Committee, constituted in 1999 observed that if an additional outlay equivalent to only 0.7 percent of GDP is allocated to education every year, the government will be able to provide education of satisfactory quality to all children in the six-14 age group within ten years.

But while NAFRE's all-India CSS campaign has undoubtedly helped to create public awareness about the inequities that exist within the Indian school system, it has also come under heavy criticism from education observers and liberal intellectuals for its 'utopian definition' of CSS as also for some of its recommendations such as the government takeover of private schools to integrate them with the common school system, and insistence of the child's mother tongue as the medium of instruction in primary school.

In the common school system recommended by NAFRE, there will be no private schools; the entire school education network will be controlled, financed and managed by the Central and state governments. This proposed incremental role in education of government which since independence has been responsible for the pathetic condition of India's 700,000 government schools, will intensify licence-permit-quota-raj and multiply opportunities for corruption and politicisation of education, say critics of the NAFRE common school system blueprint.

COMMON SCHOOL SYSTEM HURDLES

The Kothari Commission's recommendation of a common school system (CSS) across the country was endorsed by the National Education Policies of 1986 and 1992. However the recommendation has never translated into action. In 1990, the apex Central Advisory Board on Education (CABE), which appraises the extent to which the National Education Policy is implemented by the Central and state governments and other agencies appointed a committee to review NEP 1986. The CABE constituted Acharya Ramamurti Committee in its analysis, outlined the following reasons for the common school system proposal not having made headway:

— Economic and social disparities; the well-to-do communities send their children to schools with better infrastructure, teachers and teaching standards; ordinary schools are not sought after and in turn this results in low investment in them.

— The constitutional protection given to minorities to establish and administer their own educational institutions is incompatible with a common school system

— In government schools, the quality of education dispensed has remained poor
— Lack of political will
— Public schools, privately managed English medium schools, schools charging capitation fees and those offering expensive coaching have proliferated
— Proliferation of exclusive Sainik schools and Kendriya/ Navodaya Vidyalayas in the government schools sector

The CSS will create more centralisation of authority and anybody with a bit of sense would oppose it, as it would vest powers in the hands of a few and nourish corruption," says Dr. Parth J. Shah, a former professor of economics at the University of Michigan and currently president of the Delhi-based NGO think tank Centre for Civil Liberties. According to Shah, developed countries such as the USA which have been built on the foundation of efficient public-funded school education systems are gravitating towards a charter system where the state funds only a part of student fees. "Rather than a common school system we too should opt for a voucher system under which the state can issue vouchers of varying denominations to all students.

The local community could determine school fees payable by vouchers and cash. Under such a scheme, a villager would be entitled to low denomination vouchers whereas those living in expensive metros would receive higher denomination vouchers as the cost of living is higher in urban areas. This is the ideal system for India," says Shah.

Given the continuously low priority given to elementary education by the Planning Commission and the Indian establishment in general, a US-style voucher scheme is likely to prove too ambitious. The Central and state government are hard put to mobilise 4 percent of GDP for education and only half of the Rs.9,800 crore committed by the Centre has been allocated to fund the Sarva Shiksha Abhiyaan initiative. Moreover to meet SSA targets, perennially deficit-running

Central and state governments have begun trading off quality to attain quantitative targets. Disturbing evidence of promotion of non-formal education centres and appointment of para teachers under SSA indicates a further dumbing down of already sub-standard education provided by government schools to the children of the under-privileged.

That's why perceptive social scientists believe that the NAFRE concept paper is a levelling-down blueprint when the requirement is to raise infrastructure, teaching and learning standards in government schools in particular, upward. They are well aware that contemporary India boasts an estimated 10,000 independent schools providing globally accepted primary and secondary education. These independent schools constitute a valuable national resource and educationists warn of the dangers of a common school system which would level their academic standards downwards.

Comments Madhav Chavan, the Mumbai-based director of Pratham, an NGO which since its promotion in 1994 has educated over one million children through its pre-school, in-school and out-of-school programmes:

> "Currently we have a four-five tiered system of government, government-aided, slum and shanty private schools, private schools affordable by the middle class and super private schools plus the unique Jawahar Navodaya Vidyalaya schools. Breaking this system down will result in chaos. However it is possible to devise a long-range plan to upgrade and improve government schools and eliminate at least three of the five tiers over a decade. As parents witness improved infrastructure and academic standards in government schools, the demand for admission into private, independent schools will decrease. I believe this is a possible and positive methodology to build an equitable school education network. On the other hand demolishing the existing system without having devised a provenly better one will result in chaos and confusion."

Refreshingly, even as a national consensus on the need for a common school system — in effect a consensus on upgrading pathetic government school standards — is gathering steam, the newly elected Congress-led United Progressive Alliance government at the centre is exhibiting new resolve to attain the Education For All ideal. The coalition government's CMP promises to double national expenditure on education to 6 percent of GDP within the next five years and specifically makes a commitment to providing access to "quality basic education" to all child citizens.

IT is now well understood globally that the threshold of 75 per cent expansion of basic education and literacy is essential to become self-sustaining. Official statistics in India put the literacy figures at around 65 per cent. The basic question of the quality of education at the level of universalisation of education and also that of higher education, technical education, medical education and management remains a matter of concern. In each of these, what makes the prime difference is the training and professional preparedness of those who teach. The situation deserves a thorough scrutiny of the quality of education.

It must be conceded that great expansion has taken place as a consequence of the efforts made to extend the outreach of elementary education to 'all'. Alternative strategies like open schooling, non-formal education, alternative education and others have been attempted. One concern that has emerged over the years is — what are our children learning in schools in the first five or eight years? Those putting their children in high-fee charging air-conditioned schools may just not be aware of such a concern. More than 50 per cent of children drop out before completing eight years in school. Needless to say, most of these children are from the weaker sections of the society, from rural areas and urban slums. This was the group that deserved special attention not only at the policy and planning stage but also at the implementation level.

One often comes across the real situation face-to-face when one visits schools for the children of the 'common man'. We had a concept of 'common school system'. If implemented, it could have changed the very face of school education in India. It was one of the most powerful recommendations of the Kothari Commission (1964-66). It received scant attention both at the level of policy and implementation. The result is before us: a majority of the schools are still in the same situation of deprivation and deficiency as they were 30 years ago. There has been expansion and upgradation in quality and efficiency, but only sporadic visibility could be claimed.

The dropout rates remain alarming, non-enrolments are substantial and failures at the matriculation level remain pegged at around 50 per cent. While everyone from policy planners to teachers are contributing to this failure, the blame is put squarely on the 'child'. Books may be in short supply, teachers may not be available or may not be teaching due to other assignments, but the failure is the learner's. How can this continue? Even the ever-increasing suicides after the declaration of Board results and pre-exam tensions and stresses are not making any dent in our approach to the entire issue. We are persisting with a treacherous examination system and continue to award marks — a practice discarded decades ago by educationally sensitive and conscious countries.

Quality depends not merely on the percentage of marks obtained in public examinations. We need to learn from experience and be prepared for changes without avoidable delay. Suggestions made to reduce curriculum load, change evaluation pattern and enhance emphasis in growth and development of the integral personality of the learner deserve much greater attention. Do people have a role? What are their rights as citizens and parents? What are their responsibilities and duties towards the education of their children? Can the State afford not to provide teachers in the specified teacher-student ratio or can it shun away from providing the basic facilities in every school? If a school does not function properly even for a day, why does it not become front-page news? Why is the community not worried?

The traditional Indian system of community ownership of education was destroyed by the British in a planned manner. Gandhiji repeatedly pleaded for its restoration. In Champaran, he opened three schools with community support. His later experiments in education are well known. These are, of course, quietly ignored. In 1931, he had warned the nation against continuation of the existing system of education. He wanted to open schools in every village, both for boys and girls, managed and sponsored by the people and the community. What happened after independence was just the reverse. Schools became government run schools for most of the children. The community withdrew itself from their functioning.

The dependence of schools on bureaucracy increased. Expansion meant fewer resources, less time with functionaries in education departments and inordinate delays. We are indeed moving fast towards an unenviable situation — the best equipped schools and the worst equipped schools are increasing in number, and dividing society. While some may have their hopes soaring high, others are being thrown into a world of gloom, despondency and darkness.

Today, there is considerable excitement within the community of educationists, academics and social activists about the top billing education has received in the UPA government's Common Minimum Programme (CMP). In its CMP, announced on May 28, the UPA had pledged to raise public spending on education to at least 6 percent of the GDP, impose a cess on all central taxes to "universalise access to quality basic education" and to reverse the creeping communalisation of school syllabuses of the past five years.

Given this sudden and unexpected top-level commitment to education, particularly elementary education, academics and education non-government organisations (NGOs) believe this is a good time to press their long-standing demand for a common school system (CSS). First recommended 40 years ago by the Kothari Commission on Education (1964-66) and subsequently given lip sympathy in the National Education

Policies of 1986 and 1992, the proposed CSS has remained a dead letter for almost half a century.

"We are happy that the UPA coalition unlike many previous governments has made a public commitment to quality education for all children. Such purposefulness is new and a sign of changed priorities. In our letters to the drafting committee we had strongly recommended that the CMP should commit itself to a ten-year framework for developing a common school system up to high school. The rationale of CSS is self evident: to provide education of equitable quality to all children and end the canalisation of children into private, government aided and government schools on the basis of parental ability to pay and social status. Though the CMP is silent on CSS, we are encouraged by the commitment the UPA has shown to education and will continue to press our demand for implementation of a common school system in India," says Illa D. Hukku, the Bangalore-based director, development support, Child Relief and You (CRY).

Established in 1979, CRY is among the 2,400 non-government organisations which have joined hands to promote the National Alliance for the Fundamental Right to Education (NAFRE) which conceptualised and lobbied hard for the 86th Amendment to the Constitution of India unanimously approved by Parliament in November 2001. This constitutional amendment makes it mandatory for government to provide "free and compulsory education to all children of the age six to fourteen years".

With the 86th Amendment having mandated compulsory elementary education, educationists have discovered to their dismay that the constitutional amendment is silent about the type or quality of education to be provided, and that at ground zero level — in India's 600,000 villages and multiplying slum habitats of urbania — the "free and compulsory education" being dished out to hapless children is in fact basic literacy instruction dispensed by barely qualified 'para teachers' in lieu of education. Therefore the constituent members of NAFRE have somewhat belatedly turned their attention to "the right to equity in education".

In August last year, NAFRE launched a public campaign demanding the implementation of a common school system in India. Ignored by the mainstream media, the campaign of NAFRE's 2,400 member NGOs in 15 states across the country has drawn public attention to the pernicious segregation and class divide that characterises Indian education, especially its unique home-grown three/four-tier schooling system. Under this tiered system children of the rich and famous are typically enrolled in five-star English-medium schools affiliated to the upscale CBSE, CISCE and IB (International Baccalaureate) examination boards which offer globally accepted syllabuses and curriculums.

Next in the pecking order are English medium government aided schools affiliated to state-level examination boards to which the children of the middle class are sent. And at the base of the education pyramid are shabby, poorly managed government/municipal schools which shove dubious quality language education down the unprotesting throats of the children of the poor majority. Way back in 1964, the Kothari Commission on Education roundly condemned this separate, unequal school system: "...education itself is tending to increase social segregation and to perpetuate and widen class distinctions.

At the primary stage, the free schools to which masses send their children are maintained by government and local authorities and are generally of poor quality. Some of the private schools are, on the whole, definitely better, but since many of them charge high fees they are availed of only by the middle and higher classes. At the secondary stage, a large proportion of the good schools are private but many of them also charge high fees which are normally beyond the means of any but the top ten percent of people, though some of the middle class parents make great sacrifices to send their children to them.

There is this segregation in education itself — the minority of private fee-charging, better schools meeting the need of the upper classes and the vast bulk of free, publicly maintained, but poor schools being utilised by the rest. What is worse, this segregation is increasing and tending to widen the gulf between the classes and the masses," commented the report of the commission. Forty years after this searing indictment of the Kothari Commission (endorsed by the National Education Policies of 1986 and 1992), little has changed.

Ninety percent of the estimated 112 million children who enroll in primary school annually have no choice but to attend ill-maintained government schools staffed by unmotivated teachers, where they receive vernacular language education disqualifying them ab initio for aspiring to the best jobs and the good life in a rapidly crystallising English-dominated order. According to the Public Report on Basic Education (1999), one-fifth of government primary schools in the country are single teacher institutions without proper buildings, 58 percent don't provide drinking water to students and over 70 percent lack toilet facilities.

EQUALS IN EDUCATION

The widening gap between the learning opportunities available to the haves and have-nots is creating a kind of apartheid in education. The most deprived are rural, poor and socially disadvantaged communities which are increasingly marginalised and excluded from enjoying the exceptional economic resurgence taking place today. The way forward is not to restrict the expansion in choices, but to make them uniformly available to all children regardless of whether they are boys or girls, where they are born, who their parents are, where they study, or what caste they belong to. We have to develop zero tolerance for inferior education and a two-track schooling system. Even if all children are not born equal, they have the right to education of equally good quality.

The general consensus among intellectuals monitoring the nation's socio-economic development effort is that the consistent failure to evolve an egalitarian common school system — endorsed by national policies on education in 1964, 1986 and 1992 — is lack of "political will". In effect, lack of political will is the inability of the silent majority — who by virtue of a substandard education have been condemned to a perpetual subaltern status in the English-dominated national economy — to press for equal quality education for their children.

Says Sathi Alur, a Dubai-based economist and financial advisor to the National Resource Centre for Inclusion and child rights activist: "The fundamental reason for the national failure to develop a common school system is the lack of a political constituency for education. Those who attend government schools are powerless while the rest — middle and upper classes — have no stake in them. He agreed with the logic of a common school system for all children but expressed helplessness without a powerful lobby being created for a CSS."

Not a few of the more perceptive social scientists ascribe the national failure to create a lobby for equal quality education for all children — which is the norm in all industrially developed countries — to a deep-rooted bias within the nation's powerful middle class for a filtering process which offers subsidised quality education — especially higher education — to merit students while the rest of the child population is sentenced to serve as a pool of cheap, barely literate labour. "Some perceive the universalisation of elementary education as a threat to the opportunities of their own children. In their view the role of the schooling system is to act as a filtering process which picks the best and brightest and helps them to realise their potential. If too many children get on board, the prospects of those who currently enjoy the privilege of good schooling facilities will be threatened," observe the authors of PROBE.

Anil Sadagopal, the erudite dean and professor of education at Delhi University, agrees with this damning indictment of the nation's establishment. "India's Parliament has expressed its unambiguous commitment to the common school system three times by endorsing the NPEs (National Policy on Education) of 1968, 1986 and 1992. But yet this proposal has not been translated into practice because the political leadership and bureaucracy at all levels together with the intelligentsia have a convenient escape route for their own children viz, the private school system. This shift in commitment from the government to the private school system is the root cause of the lack of political, bureaucratic and social will to improve government schools," he says.

An ardent champion of the common school system, Sadagopal stresses that the most important feature of CSS is "equitable — not uniform — education for schools, be they government, government-aided, local body or private." "Most advanced economies including US, Canada, Britain and several European countries have been built on the foundation of a fully funded government school system providing education of equal or near-equal quality to all children. No country in the world has universalised elementary education without promoting a common school system. Therefore the lack of commitment to CSS implies that India will never be able to provide education to all children despite the rhetoric of the Sarva Shiksha Abhiyaan," says Sadagopal.

One factor which has been consistently ignored by Indian politicians, social scientists and educationists is that all developed nations of the first world including the UK and US have a very strong government funded school network which is on a par with private schools in terms of infrastructure, quality of education and testing. For instance in Britain there are only two types of schools: government and private and all students in either stream follow a common syllabus and upon school leaving (classes X and XII) are tested by the common GSCE and 'A' level exams. On the other hand in India, students in private schools write the English-medium pan-India CISCE board exam; some private and all Central government-managed schools write the all-India CBSE exam, and students of state government and aided schools write the school leaving exam of state examination boards. It's hardly disputed that the 28 state boards offer inferior infrastructure, sub-standard education and less rigorous syllabuses and examination assessment.

Though the formation of a single pan-India syllabus and examination board such as the GCSE in Britain would go a long way in establishing at least a common syllabus requiring near-equal academic inputs, this proposal is fiercely resisted by education NGOs and child rights activists. The general consensus among them is that India is a heterogeneous society and requires community-specific (read state-specific) syllabi. "Contrary to popular perception, a common school system is not synonymous with regimented, homogenised education across the country — a colonial legacy. It should guarantee equity in education and educational opportunities, not merely equal quality education. The word 'common' in CSS refers to state-financed quality education, not a common syllabus-setting and examination board. The school system has to leave space for expressing the wide diversity of our people through locally developed context-specific syllabuses," says Virgil D'Sami, executive director of a Chennai-based NGO Arunodhaya and convener of the Tamilnadu Alliance for Right to Education and Equity, the local chapter of NAFRE.

D'sami's argument in favour of several community-specific syllabuses is endorsed by Lucknow-based educationist and former director of basic education in the government of Uttar Pradesh, Dr. H.P.Pandey. "Syllabuses have to reflect the variations that exist in our country. In fact education rests on the belief that the greater the variety, the better for society. The preference of schools to affiliate with all-India exam boards is for the snob value they represent and while such students may score over those from state boards in college admissions, children from state boards to equally well in competitive exams. What we need to really change is the system of evaluation to make it more reliable. This can be achieved through common training programmes for all evaluators," says Pandey.

While some opponents of a genuinely common school system with a common syllabus and school leaving examinations are driven by issues such as sub-nationalism and cultural diversity, critics of the "context specific" education system are inclined to look deeper for economically advantageous motivations. "When people reject tried and tested policies — such as the common school system in Britain with a national syllabus and school leaving exams — one should look for economic motivations. The regional particularism and professed love of regional culture which has prompted the setting up of state examination boards is essentially motivated by the compulsion of state level politicians and bureaucrats to derive rents, commissions and kickbacks from construction, teacher appointments and text book printing rackets in government schools. The educated upper and middle classes who were certain to complain about the subaltern education dispensed in government schools have been mollified by the provision of CISCE and CBSE affiliated schools. As usual the poor and powerless have to suffer the third class state government school system," says Dilip Thakore founder-editor of *Business India* and *Business World* and currently editor of *Education World*.

Kothari Commission recommendations

In 1964 the Central government appointed a high-powered committee under the stewardship of Dr. D.S. Kothari, then chairman of University Grants Commission (UGC) to frame a national policy which would give shape and direction to newly independent India's school education system. The resultant Kothari Commission Report on Education (1964-66), a learned critique of Indian education, four decades later is still regarded as the most in-depth study of primary and secondary education in Indian history. The commission report inter alia advocated a common school system. According to the commission the characteristics of a common school system (CSS) are:

— Publicly funded schools open to all children irrespective of caste, creed, community, religion, economic condition or social status

—Where access to good education will depend not on wealth or class

— Adequate standards in all schools and at least a reasonable proportion of quality institutions

— No tuition fee is charged

— It meets the expectations of average parents so that they would not ordinarily feel the need to send their children to fee-charging schools outside the system

The Kothari Commission also suggested some essential reforms to implement CSS effectively. The report called for:

— Significantly increased national outlay for elementary education to build required levels of infrastructure and provide quality education, thereby transforming government, local-body and aided schools into genuine neighbourhood schools

— Allocation of special funding for improvement of school systems in backward areas, urban slums, tribal areas, hilly tracts, desert and marshy areas, drought and flood-prone zones, coastal belts and islands

— Providing free instruction for all in the mother tongue at the primary level, particularly for linguistic minorities; active encouragement of teaching in regional languages at the secondary level and discontinuance of state aid to schools imparting education other than in the medium of mother tongue/ regional language

— Phased implementation of the common school system within a ten year time frame, and essential minimum legislation, particularly to dispense with early selection processes, tuition fees, capitation fees etc

— Exploring ways of including expensive private schools into the common school system through combinations of incentives, disincentives and legislation

Even if belatedly, there is growing awareness of the division of the school system into first and subaltern classes followed by a rising tide of public indignation. This is evidenced by the massive support NAFRE's 'Perspective paper on common school system' has received. Presented at the launch of the CSS campaign in August last year, this concept paper circulated among educationists, social activists, teachers and the public for debate, has resulted in a well argued blueprint for implementing a common school system based on the recommendations of the Kothari Commission. At the centre of this implementation strategy is rapid upgradation of state and local government schools to meet minimum physical infrastructure and academic quality standards to transform them into "genuine quality neighbourhood schools."

"A common school system requires every neighbourhood to have access to a good government school equipped with all the facilities available in private schools — qualified teachers, infrastructure and quality education. If children from rich and poor households attend the same school, its management and teachers would be accountable, as at least the rich will be a pressure group for quality education. Such institutional upgradation will result in an overnight transformation of government schools. I don't believe it's anybody's case to downgrade private, so-called elite schools. The proposal is to upgrade corporation and government schools to the highest level to engineer a social transformation," says V. Vasanthi Devi, former vice-chancellor of Gandhigram Rural University and Manonmaniam University and currently chairman of the Tamilnadu State Commission for Women.

Nor are the resources required to upgrade government schools to an acceptable level mountainous. The Tapas Majumdar Committee, constituted in 1999 observed that if an additional outlay equivalent to only 0.7 percent of GDP is allocated to education every year, the government will be able to provide education of satisfactory quality to all children in the six-14 age group within ten years. But while NAFRE's all-

India CSS campaign has undoubtedly helped to create public awareness about the inequities that exist within the Indian school system, it has also come under heavy criticism from education observers and liberal intellectuals for its 'utopian definition' of CSS as also for some of its recommendations such as the government takeover of private schools to integrate them with the common school system, and insistence of the child's mother tongue as the medium of instruction in primary school.

In the common school system recommended by NAFRE, (which, it bears reiteration, has the support of 2,400 NGOs across the country) there will be no private schools; the entire school education network will be controlled, financed and managed by the Central and state governments. This proposed incremental role in education of government which since independence has been responsible for the pathetic condition of India's 700,000 government schools, will intensify licence-permit-quota-raj and multiply opportunities for corruption and politicisation of education, say critics of the NAFRE common school system blueprint.

Common school system hurdles

The Kothari Commission's recommendation of a common school system (CSS) across the country was endorsed by the National Education Policies of 1986 and 1992. However the recommendation has never translated into action. In 1990, the apex Central Advisory Board on Education (CABE), which appraises the extent to which the National Education Policy is implemented by the Central and state governments and other agencies appointed a committee to review NEP 1986. The CABE constituted Acharya Ramamurti Committee in its analysis, outlined the following reasons for the common school system proposal not having made headway:

— Economic and social disparities; the well-to-do communities send their children to schools with better infrastructure, teachers and teaching standards; ordinary schools are not sought after and in turn this results in low investment in them.

— The constitutional protection given to minorities to establish and administer their own educational institutions is incompatible with a common school system

— In government schools, the quality of education dispensed has remained poor

— Lack of political will

— Public schools, privately managed English medium schools, schools charging capitation fees and those offering expensive coaching have proliferated

— Proliferation of exclusive Sainik schools and Kendriya/ Navodaya Vidyalayas in the government schools sector

"I'm resolutely against a common school system because I believe it will be far worse than the existing system. If implemented it will encourage schools to operate as instruments of the state and authorise bureaucrats to determine education policies and parents' choice. This is a retrogressive proposal. In the proposed CSS there won't be any private schools, so it will snatch away the right of parents to decide the choice of school for their children. In my opinion government should simply get out of the business of running education and leave it to forward-thinking progressive individuals, trusts, NGOs, etc. The CSS will create more centralisation of authority and anybody with a bit of sense would oppose it, as it would vest powers in the hands of a few and nourish corruption," says Dr. Parth J. Shah, a former professor of economics at the University of Michigan and currently president of the Delhi-based NGO think tank Centre for Civil Liberties.

According to Shah, developed countries such as the USA which have been built on the foundation of efficient public-funded school education systems are gravitating towards a charter system where the state funds only a part of student fees. "Rather than a common school system we too should opt for a voucher system under which the state can issue vouchers of varying denominations to all students. The local community could determine school fees payable by vouchers and cash. Under such a scheme, a villager would be entitled to low denomination vouchers whereas those living in expensive metros would receive higher denomination vouchers as the cost of living is higher in urban areas. This is the ideal system for India," says Shah.

Given the continuously low priority given to elementary education by the Planning Commission and the Indian establishment in general, a US-style voucher scheme is likely to prove too ambitious. The Central and state government are hard put to mobilise 4 percent of GDP for education and only half of the Rs.9,800 crore committed by the Centre has been allocated to fund the Sarva Shiksha Abhiyaan (Education for All between six-14 years of age) initiative. Moreover to meet SSA targets, perennially deficit-running Central and state governments have begun trading off quality to attain quantitative targets. Disturbing evidence of promotion of non-formal education centres and appointment of para teachers under SSA indicates a further dumbing down of already sub-standard education provided by government schools to the children of the under-privileged.

That's why perceptive social scientists (such as Parth Shah) believe that the NAFRE concept paper is a levelling-down blueprint when the requirement is to raise infrastructure, teaching and learning standards in government schools in particular, upward. They are well aware that contemporary India boasts an estimated 10,000 independent schools providing globally accepted primary and secondary education. These independent schools constitute a valuable national resource and educationists warn of the dangers of a common school system which would level their academic standards downwards.

Comments Madhav Chavan, the Mumbai-based director of Pratham, an NGO which since its promotion in 1994 has educated over one million children through its pre-school, in-school and out-of-school programmes: "Currently we have a four-five tiered system of government, government-aided, slum and shanty private schools, private schools affordable by the middle class and super private schools plus the unique Jawahar Navodaya Vidyalaya schools. Breaking this system down will result in chaos. However it is possible to devise a long-range plan to upgrade and improve government schools and eliminate at least three of the five tiers over a decade. As parents witness improved infrastructure and academic standards in government schools, the demand for admission into private, independent schools will decrease. I believe this is a possible and positive methodology to build an equitable school education network. On the other hand demolishing the existing system without having devised a provenly better one will result in chaos and confusion."

Refreshingly, even as a national consensus on the need for a common school system — in effect a consensus on upgrading pathetic government school standards — is gathering steam, the newly elected Congress-led United Progressive Alliance government at the centre is exhibiting new resolve to attain the Education For All ideal. The coalition government's CMP (common minimum programme) promises to double national expenditure on education to 6 percent of GDP within the next five years and specifically makes a commitment to providing access to "quality basic education" to all child citizens.

With 59 million children out-of-school and another 90 million in school learning very little, the common school system is not a utopian ideal dug out from the archives of the Kothari Commission, but an imperative that will decide India's place in the comity of nations. ?

NPERC Perspective

The NPERC considered the development of Common School System to be a very vital component of the overall strategy for securing equity and social justice in education. The Common School System was originally advocated by the Education Commission (1964-66), under the chairmanship of Dr. D.S. Kothari (hereafter referred to as Kothari Commission). NPE, 1968 accepted the recommendation of the Kothari Commission for bringing about the Common School System. In the context of the national system of education, NPE, 1986 restated the determination of the Government to take effective measures in the direction of the Common School System.

The concept of national system of education would imply, according to NPE 1986, that, upto a given level, all students, irrespective of caste, creed, location, or sex, have access to education of comparable quality. The NPERC noted that the Common School System still remained a concept even though mooted by the Kothari Commission over a quarter of a century ago and expressed the view that the educational disparities are being further accentuated by the failure to implement the Common School System. The NPERC advocated concrete steps to translate the concept into a reality.

Upgradation of Schools

According to the NPERC, the Common School System cannot become a reality unless the government and local body schools are upgraded through the provision of adequate infrastructural facilities and academic inputs. Without such upgradation educational disparities would persist and the well-to-do would continue to send their children to the expensive private schools. The NPERC, therefore, recommended significant increase in the outlay on elementary education and provision of special allocations for improvement of the school system in backward areas, urban slums, tribal areas, hilly tracts, desert and marshy areas., drought and flood-prone zones, coastal belts and islands.

The prime objective of the Common School System is equalisation of educational opportunities; equalisation cannot be achieved without bridging the yawning gap between the few expensive private schools and the multitude of government and local body schools, at least in regard to primary education,, to begin with. The NPERC advocated a ten-year time-frame to achieve the Common School System.

The NPERC also put forth the view that as a step towards achievement of the Common School System the existing government, local body and government-aided schools have to be transformed into genuine neighbourhood schools; over a course of time private schools should also get transformed into such neighbourhood schools by making them freely accessible. The NPERC's conception of neighbourhood schools is at variance with that of the Kothari Commission as well as the normal usage. As is understood in the Western countries and as delineated by Kothari Commission, the term 'neighbourhood schools' implies that this school is attended by all the children in the given locality.

In contrast to neighbourhood schools, the public schools are residential and draw children from far and near. According to the NPERC's conception, the neighbourhood school is a school which is closely concerned with the concerns of the community around, serves the community and establishes linkages with the community by, inter alia, connecting subjects and curricula of the schools with the situation and demands of the community. Unlike the NPERC, which envisages neighbourhood schools as an intermediate stage in the progress towards the common schools, the Kothari Commission considered the neighbourhood schools to be the ultimate objective.

Quoting the Kothari Commission, the NPERC had indicated that one of the features of the Common School System was that access to education will depend on talent. We find that the correct position is that the Kothari Commission did not link talent with access to education in common schools and had instead advocated special schools for talented children.

Mother Tongue as Medium of Instruction

Towards achievement of Common School System, the NPERC had also recommended that it would be necessary to ensure instruction for all through the medium of mother tongue at the pre- primary and primary levels, particularly for linguistic minorities; active encouragement of teaching the regional languages at the secondary level; and discontinuance of state aid to the schools imparting education otherwise than through the medium of mother tongue/regional languages. This recommendation, excepting the part relating to state aid is a restatement of Article 350-A of the Constitution and the Three-Language Formula. It is universally accepted that adequate provision should be made for instruction in the mother tongue in the pre-primary and primary levels for all children including those of minorities' and for instruction in regional language in the secondary stage.

Knowing that medium of instruction is a major hurdle in the achievement of the Common School System, we have given a great deal of thought to the feasibility of presuming that only mother tongue should be the medium of instruction at the pre-primary and primary levels. That is to say, use of English as medium of instruction at the pre-primary and primary levels should be prohibited except for those children whose mother tongue is English.

Use of a foreign language for the medium of instruction at the pre-primary and primary levels does not make any sense' and does enormous harm to the creativity of children and to our national identity. However, the majority view is that given the objective conditions time is not ripe for stipulating that only mother tongue shall be the medium of instruction in the preprimary and primary levels.

To sum up, effective measures need to be taken to implement the provisions of NPE 68 and NPE in regard to Common School System. To this end, disparities between schools should be ended as early as possible by upgrading the quality of ordinary schools and providing amenties for achieving minimum levels of learning. Both the Centre and the State should take determined action in this regard. The privileged schools should accept social accountability by sharing their facilities and resources with other institutions, taking up community activities, and facilitating access to children of the disadvantaged groups.

4

NEIGHBOURHOOD SCHOOL

The present school system, inherited from the colonial ruler, was developed on the principle of homogeneity in the late 19th century to respond to the needs of an industrial and hierarchical society in the west. England embarked upon universal elementary education in 1870s, but it took over 90 years to end the "two nations in education" divided by grammar and secondary modern schooling, and bring in the school system for all children to learn together. There is empirical evidence to confirm that mixing children has improved overall education standards.

In the same period, the first education commission (1964-66) in India had recommended the common school system, and the concept of neighbourhood schools, which have been looked upon contemptuously by policy makers resulting in "many nations in education". The nature of society and the workplace has changed. Students live in an interdependent world; the workplace challenges would demand more collaboration and teamwork in coming years. A change in pedagogy would be possible only in heterogeneous classrooms, which have children with diverse interests, abilities and backgrounds. Schools in the 21st century are to be built upon the notion of "differences and diversities".

In the west a separate special school system was created for children with disabilities and learning difficulties. They are now trying to phase them out by creating inclusive school settings built on the principle of diversity and mixed abilities. In 1994, countries of the world assembled in Salamanca in Spain and declared that inclusive schools "are the most effective means of combating discriminatory attitudes, creating welcoming communities, building an inclusive society and achieving education for all".

India is a signatory of the Salamanca Statement. We have cultural advantages vis a vis the west with "unity in diversity" as part of our heritage. We have not created a separate special school system for the "disabled" and there is a process of "casual integration" in India's ordinary schools. In terms of building up an egalitarian school system this country was ahead of the west when Gandhi presented his Basic Education scheme in 1937, aimed at breaking the hierarchical order of "world of knowledge" over "world of work" by interweaving the two pedagogically. The Basic Education scheme continued to influence education policy during the early years of independent India until 1966, when the Education Commission replaced it by "work education" as one of the subjects in the school curriculum.

While arguing in favour of the concept of neighbourhood schools, the education commission (1964-66) advanced two reasons for a "good" education by eliminating social segregation in schools. First, it said, "a neighbourhood school will provide good education to children because sharing life with common people is... an essential ingredient of good education". Secondly, "the establishment of such schools will compel rich, privileged and powerful classes to take an interest in the system of public education and thereby bring about its early improvement". The "rich, privileged and powerful classes" never took interest in government schools, despite accepting the commission's recommendations on the common school system in 1968, and later in the 1986 national education policies.

The Ramamurti committee while reviewing the 1986 policy asked for implementing the neighbourhood school concept as the "first step in securing equity and social justice". The CABE (central advisory board of education) committee on policy (1992) while examining the Ramamurti committee report asked the "privileged schools" to accept "social responsibility by sharing their facilities and resources with other institutions and facilitating access to children of the disadvantaged groups." Some private schools in the metropolis are running "centres" for the "underprivileged" in the afternoon or in their outhouses — thus doing "excellence" in the forenoon and equity in the afternoon, devoid of the principle of addressing excellence and equity simultaneously.

Nobody can prevent an idea whose time has come, says the prime minister. The idea of achieving excellence and equity together in schools was conceived by Gandhi in pre-Independence days. It is be to be seen if the time for all children learning together and elimination of "many nations in education" has come.

NEIGHBOURHOOD SCHOOL SUGGESTED TO END INEQUALITY

Growing segmentation of society because of dual schooling system catering differently to the needs of the rich and the poor has become a cause of serious concern for education planners, educationists and social activists here. Experts feel that the system hardly allows equalisation of educational opportunities and something needs to be done to provide the same quality of education to all students up to the age of 14 years.

The education policy, formulated after the Education Commission (1964-66) submitted its recommendations,had stressed the concept of equalisation of opportunities for all. The Commission had recommended development of a common school system which should cover every part of the country, education at all levels and for all categories of children. It was recommended that neighbourhood schooling was the only means to bridge the gap between education provided to the rich and the poor.

The neighbourhood school plan envisages that every school would admit children living in its vicinity without consideration of caste, creed or economic and social status. Besides ensuring social unity, the concept is also likely to help children receive good education as participation in the life of common people itself is a necessary part of this.

There are other factors also which hinders development of such a system. Presently knowledge is increasing in an exponential fashion.This explosion of knowledge had not only created an urban-rural divide but also a state-to-state divide. This divide would have to be bridged by taking steps for equalisation of educational opportunities.

The so-called public schools rarely follow the neighbourhood admission policy. While these schools deprive children living in the neighbourhood, they provide admission to others who reach there from a distance of up to 20 km. Growing competition in life had made children as well as parents conscious of the quality of education. They wanted to be served by any school which they think was best for them. This made it necessary to improve the standards of common schools which catered mainly to the poor.

The government should take legal measures to implement the neighbourhood school system and common school system. A public awareness programme should be launched to encourage the concept.Cooperation of persons interested in the cause of education should be sought and a practical approach adopted to make the system a success. Experts recommends that an "education cess" to generate resources to provide sufficient material facilities in common schools which should be developed as centres of excellence. A common syllabous should be formulated for all schools as far as possible. The syllabus should also have sufficient elasticity to meet specific needs, experts felt.

BENEFITS OF NEIGHBOURHOOD SCHOOLS

In US, the concept of neighbourhood schools, located in the middle of residential areas in all parts of the city, which can be reached easily by foot or by bike (with special routes set up as necessary for younger children) is widely welcomed by student, parents teachers and health professionals. The oppose policies that direct urban children to schools that are located so far from their homes as to make walking or cycling too dangerous or completely impractical (other than to permit certain specialized programs).

Today, when new subdivisions are being approved, the proximity and capacity of the neighbourhood schools are also being considered. If the schools aren't within walking/cycling distance, the school boards must have plans and schedules to build new schools that meet these needs. In addition, to the extent that these schools remain open for after-school and evening activities, they allow children to walk or cycle to reach their recreational destinations, again eliminating unnecessary car trips.

Most people opposes closing neighbourhood schools if these closures will force many children to take the bus or be driven to school, rather than being Able to cycle or walk. The health and other disadvantages to the students, as well as the blow to the neighbourhoods which will no longer be anchored by a school, will more than outweigh any cost savings. When a school is opened or closed, the zone boundaries should be re-examined so as to maximise the number of students within walking/cycling distance of their school. This may increase number of students disrupted by the school closure, but it is our belief that the long term benefits to the students and the environment outweigh the short term costs.

Benefits of cycling and walking

Cycling is an appropriate means of transportation for all ages, barring physical limitations. In particular, we strongly encourage children to cycle to schools and other destinations, once they have achieved the cognitive skills and training needed to safely navigate a bicycle in traffic, and with the understanding that the nature and length of their trips not exceed their physical stamina and abilities.

When children cycle, they:

— become physically fit and avoid obesity, at a time when health professionals are warning that many children are at risk for obesity;

— are assured of the daily moderate activity they need for health, an activity they may or may not get at school owing to physical education cutbacks;

— improve their ability to learn in school, through increased fitness and increased concentration made possible by reducing their excess physical energy by exercising beforehand;

— become more aware of their surroundings and more confident in navigating through their neighbourhoods;

— gain new experiences and knowledge not available through the windows of a car or bus;

— learn to consider cycling part of one's daily life, setting a pattern for lifelong bicycle use and fitness;

— learn how to navigate in traffic and respect other vehicle operators from an early age;

— gain confidence in their daily lives from having mastered a useful skill, and from improving their skill and endurance over time.

Most of these benefits also apply to walking; cycling is faster than walking, can provide more vigorous exercise, and allows the child to travel longer distances. However, children could combine these modes by walking to school in the winter and cycling in better weather.

Increasing the number of children who cycle or walk to school also reduces the number of parents dropping their children off at school by private automobile, which endangers other children, wastes fuel, worsens air pollution, and reduces the quality of life in the neighbourhoods driven in.

Changes in School Desegregation

One of the most prominent current trends is the increasing number of court cases which release school districts from court supervision of their desegregation efforts (known as granting "unitary" status). The result has been that many urban school districts are moving toward increasing resegregation of their schools as students return to neighborhood schools.

A second important trend in school desegregation is increased attention to access to education and academic performance of minority students. Both school districts involved in court cases and those involved in desegregation planning have shifted attention away from a focus on desegregation efforts, which primarily concern student assignment to achieve racial integration, and toward increased attention to issues related to within-school equity and integration.

During the 1970s and 1980s, the focus of desegregation was on the physical integration of African American and white students through such measures as busing, school choice, magnet schools, use of ratios, redrawn school district boundaries, mandatory and voluntary intra- and interdistrict transfers, and consolidation of city districts with suburban districts. While many of these efforts are continuing in school districts across the nation, courts are declaring more and more large urban districts unitary.

In Board of Education of Oklahoma v. Dowell, the U.S. Supreme Court ruled that formerly segregated school districts could be released from court-ordered busing once they have taken all "practicable" steps to eliminate the legacy of segregation. This meant that districts could be freed from court oversight if they had desegregated their students and faculty and met the other requirements of mandatory desegregation, such as transportation and facilities. The court further ruled that school districts are not responsible for remedying local conditions, such as segregated housing patterns. In essence, with this ruling, the Supreme Court made it easier for districts to be declared unitary, or to be released from desegregation orders.

In the case of Freeman v. Pitts, the 1992 Supreme Court ruling held that Federal district courts can have discretion to order incremental withdrawal of court supervision over school districts. In other words, a school district does not need to achieve unitary status in all six of the "Green factors"—student assignment, faculty, staff, transportation, extracurricular activities, and facilities—before being released from court supervision. The Green factors, codified by the Supreme Court decision in Green v. School Board of New Kent County, are typical components of a school system where desegregation is mandatory. Thus, the Freeman decision effectively weakened the Green standards by allowing schools to desegregate incrementally, although it did not release districts from their obligation to desegregate.

Missouri v. Jenkins is one of the most complex desegregation cases to date in the United States. Since 1985, the state of Missouri has spent $1.4 billion on the court-ordered desegregation plan for the Kansas City school district. In 1995, however, the U.S. Supreme Court ruled that a desegregation plan does not have to continue just because minority student achievement scores remain below the national average. The state of Missouri could not be required to provide funding for programs and various kinds of school improvement activities, or to pay for a plan aimed at attracting white students from suburban districts for an undetermined amount of time, simply because minority student achievement scores remained below the national average.

The state could only be required to do what is practicable for remedying the vestiges of past discrimination; it was not responsible for remedying inequities that may exist between students within schools. Recently, a Federal judge ruled that the state be freed from financial responsibility by approving a settlement paying $315 million that would cut out $100 million in annual state subsidy for school desegregation efforts after 1999. The court ordered that the district narrow the gap in test scores between black and white students by the end of 1998-99.

Many educators, parents, community members, and politicians are relieved to see an end to the desegregation orders that for years heavily influenced decisions about educational and fiscal policies. Conversely, critics and civil rights advocates argue that the current trend toward dismantling court-ordered desegregation in many school districts is a step backwards toward segregated schooling. Recent studies indicate that school segregation and the creation of school districts with numerous poor students, which have been increasing during the 1990s, are also affecting Latino students. Latino students are increasingly isolated from whites, and are more highly concentrated in high poverty schools, than any other group of students.

When a school district is released from court supervision, it is often free to send students back to their neighborhood schools. Community members, parents, and educators often support a return to neighborhood schools because they believe that desegregation is costly, that it has not accomplished what it was intended to do many years ago, and that it has resulted in meager improvements. They also hope that whites and middle-class residents who fled during desegregation will return to the schools closer to their homes. Other people claim that African American children would be better off staying in neighborhood schools rather than being transferred out of their communities to unfamiliar and often unwelcoming places.

Despite this belief in the value of neighborhood schools, the reality is that many urban students return to schools that are segregated and inferior. Often new funding for upgrading school facilities and educational programs is promised but not delivered. However, as is the case with many large urban schools, even an infusion of extra funds is often not enough to transform a school, as schools must struggle with the profound and increasing poverty and joblessness in their local communities.

School Resegregation

Gary Orfield and his colleagues at the Harvard Project on School Desegregation have reported that school segregation has increased steadily over the past 15 years, particularly in non-southern states. The increase in school segregation has profound consequences for urban minority students. For example, while only 5 percent of segregated white schools face conditions of poverty among their students, more than 80 percent of segregated African American and Latino schools do.

This means that a student who moves from an integrated school back to a segregated neighborhood school will most likely exchange the resources of a middle-class school for a poverty-stricken one, the result of the end of court-mandated busing or desegregation choice plans. High poverty schools have generally lower levels of educational performance and are less likely to prepare students for college than more affluent schools.

Impact on Academic Performance

It is clear that desegregation has little relevance for many of the nation's largest cities: a number of the biggest urban districts are one- sixth or less white, and thus lack a sufficient number of white students to meaningfully desegregate. Desegregation plans in many smaller cities are becoming increasingly ineffective with the tremendous growth of white suburbs and the expansion of inner-city neighborhoods without adjustments to racial balance mandates. Even within desegregated schools, claims persist that segregation still continues under the guise of school tracking and grouping practices. Because of these trends in the 1990s, desegregation planners across the country are increasingly turning their attention from desegregation remedies such as student transfer and reassignment to achieve racial balance to a focus on access, equity, and the academic performance of minority students.

As more school districts have fulfilled their responsibilities insofar as the above-described Green factors are concerned, plaintiffs in desegregation cases have shifted their focus to what are sometimes referred to as "educational vestiges." They argue that the educational achievement of racial and ethnic minority students continues to lag behind that of white students in the school district, and that this achievement gap, a vestige of legalized segregation, must be eliminated before a school district can be released from court orders. This argument is critical, and it will most likely be the subject of further Supreme Court decisions.

The gap in performance on standardized test scores between white students and African American and Latino students, and differences in the choice of courses and curriculum available to different groups of students, is leading to serious examination of what happens to minority students within individual schools and classrooms. It will most likely lead to an era of desegregation cases that focus on within-school integration.

Within-School Integration

Currently, several school districts across the country are engaged in desegregation planning and are focusing on provisions that address internal integration rather than the more conventional desegregation measures such as student assignment. Willis uses the term "within-school integration" to mean "the elimination of all vestiges of segregation from all policies, practices, programs, and activities within a district's school". The focus of within-school integration is provision of the greatest possible integration and interaction among students and staff regardless of the student composition of the school.

Such a situation sparked a desegregation case in Rockford, IL, People Who Care, et al. v. Rockford Board of Education. The school district was under District Court order to address within-school integration in its high schools, all of which are racially balanced. The district was also ordered to implement a student assignment plan utilizing controlled choice; to develop programs for significant improvement in instruction and achievement in a subset of elementary schools that for a short period of time will remain minority, racially identifiable; and to integrate all courses and other educational services offered in middle and high school. The court had found the level of internal segregation within racially integrated schools severe, as the district had maintained separation of white and minority students in most courses and in extracurricular activities.

For many school districts engaged in desegregation planning, the emphasis on within-school integration addresses both integrated schools and racially identifiable schools (segregated schools) since a school district often has a combination of both schools. For integrated or racially balanced schools, plans are developed to address equitable participation and performance of minority students compared to white students attending the same schools.

Monitoring equity within schools in the implementation of desegregation plans has often been difficult, in part because of the reliance on inadequate data from school districts. In the past, school districts were not required by the courts to provide discrete information on different groups of students. At best, statistical indicators such as achievement and attendance data were provided for only two student categories: white and minority. More recently, this limited categorization has been considered inadequate as the demographics in school districts change, and as school officials, plaintiffs, and court monitors ask for a more extensive breakdown of data. Going beyond simple separation by race, they seek data disaggregated by poverty status and fluency of English, and equity indicators such as information on enrollment levels in special education, extent of mainstreaming, courses and grades of students, grade retention rates, graduation rates, access to services, participation of parents, etc.

Racial Diversity as an Educational Goal

As desegregation cases come to a close, many educators are questioning the extent to which they should attempt to promote racial and ethnic integration without court orders to do so. As the nation becomes more multicultural, educators argue that public school diversity is more important than ever, since many school districts have retained or implemented school policies, such as the institution of selective admissions criteria to special schools or magnet programs, which sometimes adversely impact minority students.

It is, however, unclear how the judicial system will respond to desegregation efforts, as advocates argue that diversity policies are in the national interest and critics respond that they are unnecessary unless there are specific wrongs to be righted. Legal challenges have already been brought against two top high schools in the nation: Lowell High School in San Francisco and Boston Latin School in Massachusetts. In San Francisco, Chinese American students who were denied admission brought a lawsuit against the school district, particularly centered on Lowell High School, challenging the 40 percent cap on Chinese American students. Before the court could rule, the school changed its quota policy. Subsequently, a judge upheld the cap but left open the possibility that it might be time to end the policy.

SOCIAL EDUCATION THROUGH URBAN HISTORY AND NEIGHBORHOOD STUDIES

Urban studies courses, often accompanied by field experiences, have largely disappeared from the curriculum, especially in secondary schools. But, as is often the case with good ideas from the past, community studies and an urban focus are returning to the social studies. In the decades of acute urban crisis in the United States, especially the 1960s and 1970s, scholars and educators paid a lot of attention to helping students connect with urban settings. Schools were to be a part of the battle to save Americas cities and to build strong local communities everywhere in the nation.

Then a series of forces changed the direction of American education. The back to basics movement, with its increasing public insistence on academic standards, often narrowly focused on factual knowledge or academic skills; and the increasing detachment of schools from their communities, with the eclipse of the neighborhood school, turned the social studies toward reliance on basic textbooks. Field trips and study outside the school walls became less frequent in the 1980s and 1990s.

Courses in urban studies, local history, and the built environment faded away, but never completely disappeared. Now, in the new century, old questions are being asked once again. How can we make a community interesting to itself? In which ways can schools best help their students prepare for a lifetime of learning? Why are cities so appealing? How should schools connect to their communities?

The core of the issue is that, in 2001, cities are back. It is now fashionable to live downtown and to have roots in old neighborhoods. Even the new suburbs, founded in the 1960s and 1970s, are realizing that they have a history, distinctive elements worthy of preservation. The aging baby boom generation is discovering that on the old crabgrass frontier a local character has emerged which should be handed on to the next generation.

A movement called the New Urbanism has brought a new appreciation for the virtues, social, cultural, and ecological, of the old urban neighborhoods. Schools are beginning to react to the newfound interest in cities, hoping to find curricular space in history and geography courses for in-depth study of the local environment. Indeed, schools are now considering how much time they should devote to the study of local places and community institutions.

Rural School Busing

The familiar image of the yellow school bus making its way over a winding country road serves as an emblem of rural education in the United States. At the same time, its nostalgic connotations may contribute to the tendency to accept at face value the centralizing and standardizing agenda that rural school busing enacts. Policymakers and school administrators have routinely attached positive connotations to this agenda—improvement of school conditions, a higher quality of instruction, and robustness of outcomes. But do the projected improvements actually materialize? And, when they do, is there a hidden price tag?

Even before the 1800s, families in small rural towns began to establish schools so that their children could learn to read and write. For much of the 1800s, these schools were organized informally, provided with little support or supervision from states, and positioned to address community interests and needs. The school year was short and attendance poor. Children, of course, walked to these schools, and many children who lived in the countryside were unable to attend. For many rural children, therefore, instruction—mostly practical in nature—came from parents, nearby relatives, or neighbors.

These circumstances did not, however, mesh well with states' interests in compelling student attendance. Policymakers and education leaders saw considerable value in using the system of common schools to accomplish national political and economic aims. To do so, they were willing to structure schooling in ways that would affect the routines of family life and farm production, at a time when most Americans farmed or lived in the country. As early as the 1880s, policymakers began to call for school consolidation as a way to improve the conditions of rural schools. Without innovations in the mechanics and infrastructure of transportation, however, these proposals had comparatively little impact.

By the 1930s, transportation technologies had caught up with proposals to create new consolidated schools, and the smallest rural schools began to close. Since that time, rural students have been bused to increasingly larger schools, located at greater and greater remove from their homes. In fact, consolidation has cut the number of U.S. school "districts" by 91 percent since about 1930, and the number of "schools" by 67 percent, while the number of "students" has simultaneously increased by 83 percent. The effect on rural school transportation budgets is seldom appreciated. Today, school districts in rural areas spend more than twice per pupil what urban districts spend on transportation.

Despite the fact that for more than half a century generations of rural children have been riding school buses, educators know very little about that experience from the perspective of communities, families, or students. Important questions, however, concern the length of rides experienced by rural students, the effects of those rides on school participation and academic achievement, and the impact of widespread school busing on rural ways of life. Rural educators, of course, know that many of their students board buses early in the morning and arrive home in the very late afternoon. Still, as Killeen and Sipple note, "on the national level .... no data or statistics exist which account for the bus ride time for children".

A recent study, however, provided some rudimentary comparisons between ride times for elementary students in rural and suburban schools. Overall, the study showed that rural schoolchildren were more likely than their suburban counterparts to have bus rides of 30 minutes or longer. Their rides also tended to be more arduous, traversing poorer roads and more hilly or mountainous terrain than those experienced by suburban students. In addition—for good or ill—rural elementary children were quite likely to be "double-routed," an efficiency measure placing them on buses with middle and high school students.

These circumstances may seem to some educators a fair price for rural children to pay in order to derive benefits from larger, more centralized schools. Certainly costs in academic terms would offer serious cause for concern. In the absence of more recent studies on achievement impacts, the most reasonable basis for evaluating the costs and benefits of long bus rides comes indirectly from research addressing the effects of large scale schools on the achievement of low-socioeconomic-status (SES) students. Low-SES students makes particular sense in rural locales, where so many families' incomes fall below the national median.

A preliminary picture of the rural school bus ride has been provided in a recent study by Howley. Based on a five-state survey of elementary school principals, the researcher discovered that most rural children experience rides of excessive length. Whereas almost all such children (85 percent) experience one-way bus rides of more than 30 minutes, approximately one quarter of them experience one-way rides of more than 60 minutes.

Not only do long bus rides extend the length of the school day for many rural children, so too do long wait times at school (i.e., before the start of and after the conclusion of the instructional day). On average, the morning wait time for rural students in the responding schools was an estimated 14 minutes. Their average afternoon wait time was 13 minutes. Rural students also travel to school over relatively rough roads. Although there is considerable variation by state, approximately 36 percent of rural bus routes traverse paved major roads, about 43 percent paved minor roads, and about 20 percent unpaved minor roads. Moreover, in many rural locales, sizable proportions of the roads used to transport children cross hilly and even mountainous terrain.

Given the challenging bus rides that rural students face, many districts appear to be taking steps to ensure the safety and effectiveness of their transportation systems. Approximately 50 percent of rural districts employ a full-time transportation director. Sixty-nine percent provide regular first-aid instruction to bus drivers, and about 77 percent equip all of their buses with two-way communication devices.

5
THREE LANGUAGE FORMULA

In the multilingual context, 'language law' is one of the most important forms, which empowers a language and its speakers too. Language law in India may be comprehensively described and discussed under such themes as the following: Language law in education, Language law in administration, Language law in legislation, Language law in judiciary, Language law in mass communication, etc.

EARLY CODIFICATION OF RIGHTS

In India, earliest documented codification of various sorts of rights should be traced to Manusmriti, written perhaps two thousand years ago. In the colonial period, the first codification of rights as such began with the codification of the ownership of land by the East India Company and the other rights followed this codification. These "...followed the principle of equality before the law - a very strange concept in a society structured by caste". The formal system of justice in India was further institutionalized through appropriate Constitutional provisions. Adjudication or judicial review of rights relating to language and other cultural institutions naturally formed part of this process.

LANGUAGE RIGHTS IN INDIA

The history of language rights in India can be traced back to the period of the Emperor Ashoka (268 - 226 BC). He was the first ruler to recognize the language rights of the people. He ordered that his edicts and directions relating to governance and righteous living be communicated to the people in their language, and not in his language only. Hence, today we see his inscriptions in the languages of the people in different parts of the country. That was the time when the 'law' was normally not written, but was mainly conventional and practiced by the people as given tenets of life for the community and individuals to follow.

Although executive orders and decisions were recorded, written law or codification of laws as a body of literature that was intended to be adhered to and interpreted in judicial proceedings is almost an innovation, in spite of the widespread knowledge of Manu's Dharma Shastra, and Islamic Shari'at. This was a contribution of the British rule, and it had its own impact.

In the literature, the term language right is treated synonymously with linguistic rights and linguistic human rights. Some scholars consider these as individual rights and some others consider them as collective rights. Different scholars and different countries treat them differently. There are overt primary rights, often formulated explicitly, and secondary rights that are covert in nature because these secondary rights are the consequences of some other right.

The Epicenter of Language Rights

The epicenter around which the discussion of language rights normally revolves is mainly the rights of the linguistic minorities. The sources of these rights in general are: the international declarations, constitutions of the countries, legislation, policy statements, the official communiqués issued by the countries for the promulgation and implementation of language-related orders and declarations, reports of the committees or commissions, and the judgments of the courts relating to language use in different domains. Formulation of language policy in this manner, and any modification(s) of the existing policy affect the character of 'language rights of the people'. Language rights have to be discussed in the social, economic and pedagogical contexts and not in isolation.

GLOBALIZATION AND LANGUAGE RIGHTS

The wind of globalization blowing across the world is bringing changes in every sphere of life in many countries. The acceptance of globalization as a dominant economic model has introduced certain urgency to modify even language loyalty and identity questions in the minds of the citizens of various countries, because, in these nations, English is fast replacing other languages as the lingua franca.

Paulston writes that, "Language rights is an important new topic for us, because their existence usually reveals past and present injustice or exploitation against the weak in the world. Our responsibility as academics is the careful exploration of the nature of language rights and their consequences".

As language rights relate to the status and use of languages, from a linguistic point of view, the Rights relating to language education at all levels of education as enshrined in the Constitution of India; Rights bestowed through official orders in continuation of the provisions in the Constitution; the interpretation of the Rights relating to language by the courts of law, and the Rights applicable as part of the declaration of the human rights. These include primarily, the right to learn a language, the right to learn through a language of choice, and secondarily, the rights of users of various languages, the rights of languages themselves to exist and develop in some sense, and the actual language education scenario in India in the context of all these language education rights.

LANGUAGE EDUCATION

The States Reorganization Commission had asked the Union

Government to elucidate a policy outline for education in mother tongue at the Secondary stage. The All India Council for Education recommended the adoption of the Three Language Formula (TLF) in September 1956. The endorsement for this formula came from various directions. It was adopted by the Chief Ministers' conference.

The National Policy on Education of 1968 spoke about the regional languages and the Three Language Formula. The 1986 Policy reiterated the earlier stand. The National Policy on Education 1968 recommended the inclusion of the TLF 'which includes the study of a modern Indian language, preferably one of the Southern languages, apart from Hindi and English in the Hindi speaking states, and of Hindi along with the regional language and English in the non-Hindi speaking states,' at the Secondary stage. This was reiterated in the Education Policy 1986 and was adopted as the Programme of Action by the Parliament in 1992. These are major attempts to arrive at a language policy for education.

Since education is in the concurrent list of the Seventh Schedule of the Constitution, the language policy formulation for education and its implementation is left to the State governments under the Constitutional safeguards, recommending the broad guidelines cited above. However, the TLF did not come into practice in all the states consistently. Also, whatever was termed and practiced as TLF was not uniform in all the states that accepted it as a norm. The National Curriculum Framework for School Education: A Discussion Document that was released on January 1, 2000, while reviewing the Three Language Formula, states that:

> In a number of states/organizations/ boards, however, the spirit of the formula has not been followed and the mother tongue of the people has been denied the status of the first language ... because of the changed socio-economic scenario, the difference between the second and the third languages has dwindled. Thus, in reality, there may be two-

> second languages for all purposes and functions. Some states follow only a two-language formula whereas in some others classical languages like Sanskrit and Arabic are being studied in lieu of a modern Indian language. Some boards/institutions permit even European languages like French and German in place of Hindi. In this scenario, the three-language formula exists only in our curriculum documents and other policy statements.

According to this document, the three languages are: (i) the home language/the regional language, (ii) English, and (iii) Hindi in non-Hindi speaking states and any other modern Indian language.

The Universal Declaration of Human Rights states, 'Every one has the right to education. Education shall be free, at least in the elementary and fundamental stages. Elementary education shall be compulsory... Parents have a prior right to choose the kind of education that shall be given to their children'. The Constitution of India also makes provision for '... free and compulsory education for all children until they complete the age of fourteen years'.

Right to Learn Language(s)

A language survives when it is learnt as a mother tongue by its native speakers, grows and develops when it is used in more and more new domains by the people. During the Pre-British period, and during the British period, it was the political power that decided the kind of education to be taught and pursued, and the language in which the education was to be imparted. Individuals had no right to decide, the ruler assisted by his advisors, or according to his whim and fancy, used to decide about the education of their people. People were hardly a party to such decisions. The Indian society was governed by varnashrama, and education was not for all but only for a few. For example, women and Shudras were prohibited from learning. The impact of such a situation on this language - the general public do not use it, and many a time, people consider it as a "dead" language. If all the people had equal right to learn it, probably it could have survived as a widely current and spoken language.

Also, in pre-British India, education per se was not as formal as it became in due course of time. It was not also open to all the people. The social stratus decided the kind of education that one can get. There is direct link between language of administration and languages in/of education. English entered the field of education in India in 1792. It became the language to be taught as part of schooling and also a medium of instruction. So, during the British regime English became the official language in India around 1830. Even then the education was not for all, it was for a few privileged classes of people.

CONCEPT OF LINGUISTIC MINORITY

In the post-independence India, the Constitution of India in its 'Cultural and Educational Rights' Article 29(1) protects the interests of the minorities, by providing certain language rights to them such as:

> Any section of the citizens residing in the territory of India or any part thereof having a distinct language, script or culture of its own shall have the right to conserve the same.

The concept of linguistic minority/majority is the result of the re-organization or re-creation of the Indian States on the basis of language as one of the criteria to draw geographic boundary. When the question as to what shall be the unit, either the state or the country, to consider a group that qualifies for the linguistic minority status, came before the Supreme Court of India, the Court gave the verdict that "Linguistic minority can, therefore, logically only be in relation to a particular State". According to the same judgment "Article 29(1) gives the right to all sections of citizens, whether they are in a minority or the majority religions, to conserve their language, script or culture. With this background of 'right to learn language,' we can look at its realization in the society.

The Constitutional Intent

Other than the protection assured to linguistic minorities mentioned above, the Constitution has no explicit statements regarding the language(s) to be taught in education or the language(s) through which education has to be imparted (except in the case of linguistic minorities). This may have been a tactical compromise or decision on the part of the Constitution makers, because every one could sense the great linguistic complexity of free and democratic India. So, it is left to the wisdom of the Government(s) to frame a suitable language policy for education. Hence the policy is outlined in Policy statements for education, and, many a times, such policy statements were framed based on the guidance or the recommendations of various committees constituted for the specific purpose.

LANGUAGE RIGHTS IN KARNATAKA

Karnataka is one of the most multilingual states in India. The linguistic demography, according to the 1991 Census, is as follows:

Kannada	66.2
Urdu	9.96
Telugu	7.39
Tamil	3.84
Marathi	3.64
Tulu	3.06
Hindi	1.96
Konkani	1.57
Malayalam	1.68
Kodagu	0.21

Majority/Minority Syndrome

In India, we see that both the majority and the minority assert their language rights as far as language in education is concerned. The linguistic minorities are afraid that the language of the majority will be used as a tool of oppression against them. In Karnataka, most of the time the minorities perceive threat from Kannada, the Official Language of the State, and try to find shelter under English. They perceive a threat to the existence of their community as a distinct group. They fear the loss of their home language. And they like to assert their linguistic rights.

Sometimes the majority perceives some threat to the existence and continuation of their language (Kannada) from Hindi, some other times from Sanskrit, and at other times from English. The Constitution has given right to the regional languages to become official languages of the concerned states.

The major challenge towards the implementation of the language policy and its relation to language rights was faced when there was a conflict between the majority and the minority in Karnataka. It continued for more than a decade as a legal battle for language rights. The Kannada majority began to fear that their language has been deprived of the pride of place in all walks of life as it deserved. This fear forced the majority to agitate for such a place for their language in Karnataka.

In the multilingual setup that prevails in Karnataka, the desire to retain and preserve Kannada (and Kannadiga) interests as the dominant linguistic group, and the fear of loss of stature in the state that the Kannadigas consider to be their traditional homeland shape and guide the responses of the majority mother tongue group (Kannada) and to assert their linguistic rights. But the minority, most of the time, perceives a threat from Kannada, the Official Language of the State, and tries to find shelter under English. Often social, economic, political, legal, and other issues not related to education came to influence the language choice for education purposes.

THE THREE LANGUAGE FORMULA IN KARNATAKA

Karnataka had adopted TLF for education in schools since the linguistic reorganization of states in 1956 for more than two decades. The late sixties and the early seventies witnessed strong opposition to Hindi since it was perceived as a threat to the existence, use, and development of Kannada. This had forced the Kannada speakers to lean towards English. However, many among them also felt that Kannada faced a threat to its continuation as the dominant school language from Sanskrit. It was possible to pass the SSLC State Board examination without passing the Kannada course in the scheme outlined above. It was but inevitable, then, that this scheme created and widened the incompatibility between the policy of language choice for administration and the languages chosen for the purposes of education.

Linguistic Movements for Language Rights

Linguistic movements initiated by various political parties, groups of Kannada teachers, students, college and university professors, literary critics, playwrights, and creative writers created an awakening among the Kannada speaking majority to seek a place of pride or pre-eminent place for Kannada in the affairs of the State. Their dream was to restore the primacy and the lost glory of their language as the only medium of governance in the linguistically re-organized Kannada state. This awakening in favor of using Kannada as the language of administration was a consequence of many factors including linguistic movements, political agitations, and the general political awakening among the backward classes. This description of the linguistic situation in Karnataka can be easily applied to many other linguistically re-organized Indian states also.

Inter-twining of Socio-economic and Political Factors with Language Rights

Spread of literacy mainly in Kannada, and the spread of general education among the people, had led to a new awakening. The large-scale migration of people, mainly from adjacent Tamil Nadu, for jobs that opened up through fast industrialization of the state was perceived to be curtailing the job opportunities for the Kannada majority. All these needed an avenue for the expression of their anger and disgust among the people. The language choice in education in 1979 provided an avenue to meet the challenge thrown up by industrialization and consequent migration of people from other linguistic groups.

The government decided to delete Sanskrit from the first language list in 1979 and included it in the second/third language list. But the government that took this decision did not remain in power to implement its decision. The subsequent government reconsidered the stand of the previous government, and decided to maintain the status quo. Pro-Kannada groups protested against this decision.

Gokak Committee's Landmark Report

This agitation against retaining Sanskrit in the first language list made the government to think afresh about the language choice in school education.

Government Order on the Gokak Committee Report

The order issued by the Government of Karnataka on the basis of this report prescribed the following pattern for language study:

— At the secondary school level First Language Kannada or Mother tongue: Urdu, Tamil, Telugu, Marathi, English, or Hindi.

— Two other languages Kannada, Hindi, English, Sanskrit, Arabic, Persian, Urdu, Tamil, Telugu, or Marathi.

— The Kannada-speaking majority did not find this solution adequate to meet their demand to accord a pre-eminent place to Kannada. Up to this point, in the debate or agitation over the choice of languages for school education, only the Kannada protagonists were in the forefront.

Reconsideration of the Order

The linguistic or religious minorities did not participate in the debate actively. The Government, after reconsidering its order, issued the notification (on July 20, 1982) detailing the language choice for school system and modus operandi for its implementation through the circular, dated the August 11,1982.

According to this order: At the secondary school level, the language pattern to be adopted shall be as follows (from the academic year 1987-88) A. First language: Kannada shall be the sole first language (to carry 125 marks) B. Two other languages from the following: Urdu, Tamil, Telugu, Marathi, English, Hindi, Sanskrit, Arabic, Persian, Malayalam or Kannada. (To carry 100 marks each).

Students coming from outside the State and joining VIII or IX Standard in the State of Karnataka and who did not study Kannada earlier may be permitted to take English or Hindi as first language. The teaching of Kannada from the Ist standard in non-Kannada schools will commence from the academic year 1983 itself and the language pattern for High School prescribed in Para (1) above will come into force from the academic year 1987-88.

Inadequate Understanding of the Concepts such as Mother Tongue, First Language, etc.

An analysis of this language formula reveals an inadequate understanding of the concepts like mother tongue, first language, and the strategy adopted for choosing languages for education. Also this formula stands out as an exceptional case where a regional (majority) language/Official Language of the State is ascribed a special status of sole first language in the secondary school, and this language is made a compulsory language for all students irrespective of their mother tongue with the same syllabus.

This formula does not grade languages as first language, second language, etc., either in terms of pedagogical concepts, or in terms of chronology of their introduction in the school system. In this formula, the Kannada mother tongue student had an advantage over the students of other mother tongues.

A mother tongue Kannada speaker has Kannada as first language. The Urdu or other mother tongue student has to take Kannada as the first language. He might select Urdu or another language as one of the other two languages. The third language may be English. Thus Hindi, one of the languages of the three language formula is not included as part of his education. If he desires to take Hindi, his mother tongue is not included as part of his education.

Agitation by the Minorities and the Decisions by the Karnataka High Court

The Linguistic Minorities Protection Committee and others challenged the order and the relevant circular of the Director of Public Instruction in the High Court of Karnataka.

The following three questions came up before the Full Bench. Whether the Government Order dated July 20, 1982 or any part of it is void being violative of the fundamental rights guaranteed to the petitioners under Articles 29(1) and 30(1) of the Constitution Whether the Government Order dated July 20, 1982 or any part of it is violative of the pledge of equality guaranteed under Article 14 of the Constitution.

Whether, on the facts and in the circumstances of the case, the Circular dated August 11, 1982 issued by the Director of Public Instruction of the State Government is violative of Article 14, 29(1) and 30(1) of the Constitution? This became a classic case and formed a basis for wider debate on the role of the Regional language/Official Language in the school curriculum and on the question of student's mother tongue as medium of instruction. This case did not have any analogy to the cases decided by the Courts hitherto in the country.

The Position of the Litigants - Linguistic Minorities

In this case, the litigants argued as follows:

There is no rational basis for making Kannada as the sole first language; it is unreasonable for the State to compel the students to study the official or regional language if they do not have aptitude and if they intend to reside in the state only temporarily; providing opportunity to study their language is as much in the national interest as is the study of the regional language; to achieve primacy for Kannada, minorities need not be compelled to study it from the first standard in the schools; the parents and students should choose whatever they want to study and the State cannot 'indulge in regimentation' in the matter relating to the study of languages; children must have the benefit of having education in their mother tongue; children whose mother tongue is not Kannada get a discriminatory treatment and they cannot study Kannada and compete with Kannada mother tongue students; the right to equality under Article 14 is affected; the linguistic minorities have the right under Article 29 to take steps to conserve their language and also a right under Article 30 to establish institutions of their choice, which right includes a right to take a decision as to what language should be studied as first language; it is for them to decide in what manner their language should be conserved, preserved, produced and it is not for the Government to decide and the Government under the guise of public interest cannot impose conditions.

The Position of the State Government

The State, while arguing in favor of its policy, said: it has the power and right to take steps for the development of Kannada, including making the study of Kannada compulsory to all the children from the primary school stage and as the sole first language in the secondary school since Kannada is the declared Official Language of the State, and hence it is rational to make it compulsory; this is necessary to give primacy to Kannada in the affairs of the State; also 'the State has power to make regulations in the interest of excellence in education and any regulations so made by the Government cannot be regarded as infringing on the rights of the minority groups; the usefulness of a language is measured in terms of its use in administration, trade, industry, defense, managerial decision-making and such other wide variety of a range of domains and in social and family affairs. Such domains can be covered by more than one language used complimentary to each other. Language development is central to educational advancement on a mass scale. Educational development is central to economic, cultural, and political developments.

Language development is corollary to national development. India is a country with a population of sizable numbers, speaking and using different languages and therefore the problem becomes difficult and complex,' and 'a child belonging to a minority section of the community in any State speaking a language other than the regional or the local language will thus develop its personality with two languages; one spoken at home, the other spoken beyond the threshold of his home, for, in the absence of knowledge of the local language an individual would be at a severe disadvantage in participating in the daily life of the State. When a child or person learns two languages, one as his mother tongue and the other as the language spoken by the people around, both become his language. Therefore, it cannot be said that a child speaking a language other than the regional language at home is totally alien to the regional language'.

The Judgment

The Judges examined the submissions made before them. The majority opinion of the Bench on the teaching of Kannada compulsorily in the primary stage, and as the sole first language in the secondary schools considered that such insistence led to the violation or otherwise of various Constitutional provisions. Their opinions can be summarized as follows:

— The Government order compelling all children to learn Kannada in the primary schools in the State including those established by minorities is arbitrary and violative of Article 14, because, this Article 'incorporates an injunction both to the Legislature and Executive not to deny equality before law and equal protection of the laws'. The children with Kannada mother tongue and others are dissimilarly placed because the children with Kannada mother tongue will not study any additional language, whereas the children with other mother tongues are forced to study the regional or the Official Language causing additional burden. This burden may cause dropouts. Curtailing the periods allotted to other subjects to accommodate Kannada is irrational and arbitrary.

The order prescribing Kannada as the sole first language at the secondary school level is also discriminatory because it prevents the students from having a language of his choice as first language. This will place him in a disadvantageous position from the student who comes with Kannada as first language from the first standard. The grace marks to be awarded to bridge the gap itself accepts this discrimination. Since grace marks are awarded only to the students who fail to secure minimum marks for pass and not to others, the order places everyone in unequal position.

Since Kannada mother tongue students can study Kannada both as first language and as other language gives them an advantage over others who have to study three different languages in high school. This is against the three language formula. Also from the point of view of Kannada, even the Kannada mother tongue children are denied an opportunity to take any other language as first language and enhance their knowledge. The students coming from other States for VIII to

X standards cannot opt for their mother tongue and have to opt for Hindi or English. This is a clear case of discrimination and is against all other regional languages. It is the opinion of various committees and commissions that children should not be burdened with an additional language in the primary school itself.

The issue of medium of instruction and first language is intimately connected. In most of the cases, the language chosen by the student as first language happens to be his medium of instruction also. So 'it would be incongruous to say that a linguistic minority's choice for medium of instruction is absolute but the choice of first language is not'. Prescribing the study of the Official Language of the State as one of the three languages in the high schools under the three language formula will not violate Article 14. The language and script can be conserved through educational institutions. The rights guaranteed under Article 29 and 30 are not subject to restrictions.

The State cannot either directly or indirectly take away or abridge, infringe or impart the right guaranteed by these articles. This language rule is not in the interests of the minority. Here the choice is of the minority groups themselves. The Government has only the right to prescribe the general standards to secure excellence in education in each of the subjects. People in this country have one citizenship and under Article 16 have right to employment in service anywhere in the country. Since no other State has such a language policy, this policy will be inconsistent with personal liberty and equality guaranteed under the Constitution.

In Karnataka, minorities are not opposed to the use of Kannada fully in administration. Even then Kannada has failed to replace English. It is fancy for English that has retarded the progress of Kannada and its replacement in different walks of life. The judges felt that this 'does not mean that Kannada, the Official Language, cannot be made compulsory subject for study for the students in this State'. They made it clear 'that the State which has, subject to the provisions of the Constitution, the power to prescribe the syllabus to regulate education, can prescribe Kannada as one of the compulsory subjects. It is also the duty of every citizen who is a permanent resident of this State to study Kannada. But the regulations made in this behalf must be of general pattern and should apply uniformly to all'.

They agreed that 'there are no two opinions on the primacy for Kannada in the affairs of the State and its occupation of pride of place in the affairs of the State' and 'that position must be accorded to regional/Official Language of each and every State of our country'. However, in the process of arguments, the possibility that the minority language speaking students who have already accepted Kannada as mother tongue may try to misuse the provision of grace marks by reverting back to their minority mother tongue, and that the allocation of grace marks is likely to condone under-achievement in Kannada, and thus frustrate the very purpose were ignored.

Based on the majority opinion, the court directed that the Government of Karnataka will be at liberty:

— To introduce Kannada as one of the two languages from that primary school class from which the study of another language in addition to mother-tongue is made obligatory as part of the general pattern of primary education;

— To make the study of Kannada compulsory as one of the three languages for study in secondary schools, by making appropriate order or Rules, and make it applicable to all those whose mother tongue is Kannada and also to linguistic minorities who are and who become permanent residents of this State, in all primary and secondary schools respectively, whether they are Government or Government recognized, including those established by any of the linguistic minorities.

Thus, as the proceedings show, in language-related litigation academic issues take a back seat and the legal issues come to the forefront.

A New Policy Promulgation by the State Government

On the basis of the direction of the court, the Government of Karnataka elucidated the language policy for school education in its order pending the decision of the Supreme Court. This is the first time that the government used the word language policy for education in its official document. Accordingly:

> From 1st standard to 4th standard, mother tongue will be the medium of instruction, where it is expected that normally only one language from the group of languages, namely, Kannada, Tamil, Telugu, Malayalam, Marathi, Hindi, Urdu, or English will be the compulsory subject of study. From 3rd standard Kannada will be an optional subject for non-Kannada speaking students. This will be taught on a purely voluntary basis and it will not be at the cost of any other instruction imparted in the school or any other school activity in which all school children participate. There will be no examination at the end of the year in Kannada language.

From the 5th standard onwards, where, in the normal course a second language is introduced, the child has to study a second language selected from the group of languages, namely, Kannada, Tamil, Telugu, Malayalam, Marathi, Hindi, Urdu, English, Persian, Sanskrit, or Arabic, which will be other than the First language, subject to the condition that the child who has not taken Kannada as the First language will have to take Kannada as the Second language.

From 5th standard, provision will be made for the study of the third language which will be other than the languages studied by the student as First and Second language. This has to be chosen from the group of languages, namely, Kannada, Tamil, Telugu, Malayalam, Marathi, Hindi, Urdu, English, Sanskrit, Arabic, or Persian. Attendance in the third language class will be compulsory, writing of the examination in the third language will also be compulsory, but from 5th to 7th standards it will not be obligatory to pass the third language examination.

No extra credit will be given in rank, division, class, etc., on account of the marks obtained in the third language examination from 5th to 7th standard.

At the secondary stage, i.e., from 8th to 10th standards, three languages will be compulsory. First language carrying - 125 marks, Second language - 100 marks and the Third language carrying - 100 marks. It will be obligatory to pass the examinations conducted in all these three languages, and one of them shall be Kannada. The standard expected in second and third languages at the end of 10th standard will be what would have been achieved at the end of 6 years of study, if the language subject had been chosen as First language.

As contemplated in Government Order No. ED 113 SOH 79, July 20, 1982, Kannada-speaking students will not be given any grace marks in Kannada. Non-Kannada speaking students will be awarded up to a maximum of 15 grace marks to enable the students to pass the Kannada language examination. Exemption from studying Kannada as a compulsory language can be given to the students whose parents have come to the state on temporary transfer.

CURRICULUM GUIDELINES

Meanwhile, the government, in order to implement the Education Policy 1986, issued curriculum guidelines to be adopted from 1992-93. According to this order, the students could opt for mother tongue Kannada, English, Telugu, Tamil, Hindi, Marathi, or Urdu in the 5th, 6th and 7th standards. The second language will be English for Kannada mother tongue students, and Kannada for all others.

The third language can be one of the following: Hindi, Sanskrit, Persian, Arabic or English. Here each language carries 100 marks. Learning Kannada is made compulsory. The students opting for Sanskrit should answer in Sanskrit only. In the secondary school, the first language consists of Kannada, Sanskrit, Telugu, Tamil, Urdu, Marathi, English, or Hindi. The second language list has Hindi, English or Kannada. The third language list has Hindi, English, Sanskrit, Persian, Kannada, or Arabic. One of the three languages should be Kannada. Here the first language is for 125 marks, and other two 100 marks each.

Medium versus Language as a Subject

The question of language through which education has to be imparted always gets entangled with the issue of language(s) to be taught in the schools. The same thing happened in case of Karnataka too. The choice of medium of instruction in Karnataka was also based on the statements in the Constitution and the Grant-in- Aid Code of the State government since Oct 19, 1969. According to this arrangement, 'in all primary schools, the medium of instruction shall ordinarily be the Regional Language or mother tongue of the child'. The English medium schools or English medium sections in the primary schools were permitted by the Director of Public Instruction to cater to the needs of migratory groups and 'students whose mother tongue is a minority language for which there is no provision in the schools of the locality.'

English Gains Ground

The anti-Hindi stand of earlier decades, instead of supporting the regional languages, gave rise to the fast growth of education in the English medium. This gave an added advantage to the linguistic minorities who could opt for English due to their perceived threat from the regional language. Thus, the microscopic minority of English mother tongue succeeded in providing a universal umbrella for all the elites in all categories, the minorities as well as the majority, by creating a common avenue for education through the English medium.

So, the primary and secondary education in the English medium, like engineering and medical education, has become donation/capitation-oriented, and ultimately a tradable commodity. The legal provisions that were framed to protect minority rights became an effective means for every section of Karnataka society to make capital out of the very same legal provisions. There were institutions of the linguistic minorities imparting higher education and primary education in English medium but not through their mother tongue.

The Division Bench of the High Court heard the Linguistic Minorities Protection Committee and others on languages to be taught in schools and medium of instruction. The minority litigants had argued on the basis of the opinions of experts that the child has fundamental right to have education only in his or her mother tongue in the primary schools and found no justification to introduce Kannada in addition to mother tongue at that level.

Government was directed to 'to provide and ensure that primary education up to first four years including pre-primary education is imparted in mother tongue of the children concerned, in Government schools as also schools established by any private agency including linguistic minorities which are recognized, whether receiving financial aid or not, subject to the existence of the prescribed minimum number of children having a common mother tongue who have got themselves admitted to the school concerned '. This order of June 19, 1989 while elucidating the language policy had said, "From 1st standard to 4th standard mother tongue will be the medium of instruction, where it is expected that normally only one language ... will be the compulsory subject of study".

Arguments Before the Supreme Court: The Verdict of the Supreme Court

The validity of this judgment was questioned in the Supreme Court on the ground that the linguistic minorities are discriminated and they cannot be forced to study Kannada (violation of Article 14); linguistic minorities can not be prevented from an opportunity to choose languages(violation of Article 350-A). Finally, the Supreme Court did uphold the High Court judgment and ruled that (a) there is no element of compulsion because mother tongue of the child is medium of instruction, (b) only one of the languages is a compulsory subject of study, (c) Kannada is optional from 3rd standard for non-Kannada mother tongue speakers and it is taught on voluntary basis and there is no examination. Study of Kannada does not throw any burden on children. There is no violation of Article 350 -A.

Orders of the Government of Karnataka, 1994

In pursuance of this judgment, the Government issued the order of April 29, 1994 wherein it made a comprehensive policy relating to language choice for education and medium of instruction in Karnataka. Accordingly, from 1st to 4th standards, the child's mother tongue will be the medium of instruction. It will be Kannada, Tamil, Telugu, Malayalam, Marathi, Hindi, Urdu, or English. From 3rd standard Kannada will be an optional subject.

There is no examination in it at the end of 3 or 4th standard. From the 5th standard, the student has to choose second and third languages. They can be one of the following: Kannada, Tamil, Telugu, Malyalam, Marathi, Hindi, Urdu, English, Sanskrit, Arabic, or Persian. The student, who is not studying Kannada as first language, has to study it as second language. Attendance for classes and appearing for examination for third language is compulsory and it is not an examination (a student need not pass this) subject.

In the secondary schools three languages have to be studied compulsorily. The first language will be any one of the following: Kannada, Tamil, Telugu, Malayalam, Marathi, Hindi, Urdu, or English. The second and third languages can be any two of the following: Kannada, Tamil, Telugu, Malayalam, Marathi, Hindi, Urdu, English, Sanskrit, Arabic, or Persian. One of these should be Kannada.

STRATEGIES OF THE MAJORITY

During the evolution of this language policy, The Kannadigas (the majority group) adopted two strategies: the path of persuasion to persuade the government, and the path of agitation to pressure the government.

Most of the minority language speakers followed the paths of representation and litigation. But the minority groups of Kodagu, Tulu, Konkani, Lambani/Banjari, Yerava and smaller pre-literate groups did neither, because their mother tongues and Kannada are complementarily distributed in non-formal and formal domains respectively. Their mother tongues are historically restricted to home domains. Almost all the speakers are in areas where they are exposed to Kannada from their birth.

In this context one can raise the question of rights and the exercising of such rights by these people. These communities have found that Kannada/English is/are adequate to satisfy their needs and welfare. In this case, they seem to have exercised their right not to exercise their language right. Their language and culture are protected and groomed by academies, institutions and well meaning individuals in Karnataka. And these groups did not see any threat to the continuation of their identity from Kannada.

Tulu-speaking political leaders have asked that, in their mother tongue speaking area, the moral stories from their language and culture be made part of schooling in 1st and 2nd standards. When the Literacy campaign was conducted in the South Canara district, where Tulu is the majority language, the primers prepared in Tulu using Kannada script were introduced. The adult learners were not enthusiastic about this experiment. The DPEP prepared a draft Soliga (a preliterate language) 1st standard primer in Kannada script for use in the BR Hills region where it is spoken. But it was reported that '...the community leaders and the State Project Officer have expressed reservations about the need for textbooks in Soliga language ...'

TWO IMPORTANT ISSUES: INDIAN LANGUAGES AS MEDIA OF INSTRUCTION

Two important aspects relating to the issue of medium of instruction are,

— Number of students opting for a medium. The success rate in the chosen medium.

— The number of students opting for the Kannada medium at the SSLC stage is on the so also. Other language media are not that competitive. As regards Marathi, the number of students has actually decreased.

The rate of success in the examinations in the regional language medium is not also encouraging, whereas the English medium education has greater rate of success in the examination.

In fact, the regional language medium is rural-based and is preferred mostly by the poorer sections of Karnataka society. The regional language medium prevails mostly in government schools. The English medium is prominently found in the urban areas, preferred by those who could afford it, and is mainly offered by the schools that are run by private organizations.

Now, the supporters of the Kannada medium of instruction see a threat to Kannada and its development from English/ English medium education. All attempts to have new English medium sections in schools/new schools in the government sector are prevented. This has further allowed the private English medium schools to flourish without competition from the schools run by the government. Although it is compulsory to have mother tongue/regional language medium from 1 to 4 standards, it is often reported that many private and unaided schools, even sometimes some of the aided schools, do not follow this rule.

The Resultant Scenario

Due to the assertion of rights by majority/minority about the school languages, the following scenario emerges:

— Earlier, the Mother tongue list at the primary education level was open-ended. Now the list defines them, with specific mention of languages.

— From the 3rd standard, Kannada is made compulsory for non-Kannada mother tongue students. But this is not an examination subject.

— From the 5th standard, the students can change their medium of instruction to English or any other medium.

— From the 5th to 7th standards, the number of languages which can be opted as first language is reduced from 10 to 8. Gujarati and Sindhi are dropped. Sanskrit, Persian, and Arabic are added to the II and III language list. Kannada is one of the two compulsory languages if it is not opted as the first language.

Passing in III language is compulsory

— The students who take Sanskrit as a subject, should write the examination in that language only.

— From the 8th to 10th standards, pass in all the three languages is compulsory.

— Malayalam is added to the first language list, and Sanskrit is deleted.

— The second language list is expanded by adding Sanskrit, Malayalam, Arabic, and Persian.

— The medium of instruction is Mother tongue or Kannada. Implications.

The judgments of the High Court and the Supreme Court on the choice of languages in education and medium of instruction have many implications for language education in multilingual India. They are,

The three-language formula, which was so far designated as a strategy, and which had no direct Constitutional status and was totally dependent on the governmental and institutional support, has now been given a legal sanction and status from the Apex court of the country for its implementation.

Teaching a regional language, the Official Language of the concerned state as a compulsory language in the schools, more specifically at the secondary stage, is recognized as legally acceptable. It may even be considered as a must.

Earlier research had claimed that learning more languages is not a load. The same is reinforced by the judgment that teaching more languages as subjects from primary schools is not a burden imposed on the students. A government need not wait up to the 5th standard to introduce a second language. It can be introduced from the 3rd standard itself.

The Constitutional safeguard for the linguistic minorities to have education through their mother tongues in the primary schools is made obligatory for all the mother tongue groups, irrespective of their majority or minority status. Kannada is now recognized by the courts as the 'second mother tongue' of the indigenous speakers of the minority languages in Karnataka.

RIGIIT TO LEARN THROUGH A LANGUAGE

Right to learn through a language is an important issue in any multilingual situation. Most of the time teaching languages and teaching through a language gets mixed-up since they are interrelated. So, we saw in the case of Karnataka the way the issue started with 'which language to be taught and when' but ended up in getting a judgment about teaching through a language too from the courts of law.

Tamil Nadu Linguistic Demography

The linguistic demography of Tamil Nadu according to 1991 Census is as follows:

Language	*Percentage of speakers*
Tamil	86.7

Telugu	7.12
Kannada	2.15
Urdu	1.85
Malayalam	1.17
Gujarati	0.43
Hindi	0.28
Marathi	0.12
Others	0.9

Move Toward English as the Choice Medium of Instruction

In the late nineties, Tamil, the Official Language of Tamil Nadu, also faced a peculiar situation, wherein the Tamil mother tongue students, for a few decades, moved in the direction away from their mother tongue as their medium of instruction in the schools. The apprehension started to grow in the Tamil society that the students studying through the English medium and not studying in their mother tongue were in great number as a product of this trend and they are alien to their culture.

The Government of Tamil Nadu Order and the Madras High Court

So, the Government of Tamil Nadu issued an order on January 13, 1999 stating that "... at least two out of three subjects, that is, Social Studies (History and Geography), Math, and Science shall be taught through the medium of Tamil, apart from teaching Tamil as a subject in Nursery and Elementary Schools." A single Judge of the Madras High Court, in his judgment on June 7, 1999, held that "... this order is valid only for those students, whose mother-tongue is Tamil. Or in other words ... Government order is not applicable to the pupils, whose mother-tongue is not Tamil."

Justice Mohan Committee

The back drop for the government order was a representation from a Tamil Association which, apart from the above, had demanded that "the priority in employment shall be given to those who have studied through Tamil Medium of Instruction in the Government/Government Undertaking Departments." In June 1999, a high level five member committee headed by Mr. Justice Mohan, a former Supreme Court Judge, was set up to "...frame guidelines for introducing Tamil as medium of instruction at all levels in the Educational sphere from Nursery to Higher education." On the recommendations of the committee, the Government issued another order on November 19, 1999. The summary of the order is that - In all schools Tamil or mother tongue shall be the first language; in all schools from class 1 to 5, Tamil or mother-tongue shall be the medium of instruction.

Contention About What Constitutes a Mother Tongue

Here, what constitutes a mother tongue became an important item for adjudication. On behalf of the government it was argued that "...mother-tongue of a child should only be understood for the purpose of these cases as the language which the child is most familiar with ... mother-tongue need not be the mother's tongue or father's tongue. Generally, the parents are the proper persons who can assess and say as to which is the language, that child is most familiar with." In 1949, the Provincial Education Ministers had resolved and the Central Advisory Board of Education had approved that "the mother-tongue will be the language declared by the parent or guardian to be the mother-tongue."

The Court Order

The court ruled that the order issued by the government was illegal on many grounds like the following:

— The order could have been made through proper legislative sanction.

— The constitution of the Justice Mohan Committee was not proper.

— Since the matriculation schools had English medium for the past 50 years, now they can not be forced to change over to Tamil medium.

— Proper application of mind is not there formulating the order as far as its implications are concerned.

— Notion of mother tongue is not properly understood while making the order.

— Principle of natural justice is not followed.

— The rule is not uniformly applicable.

— The rule does not take mobility of parents of the students into account.

One will not lose his culture by studying in English medium, etc.

Important Issues Relating to Language Rights as Exemplified in the Court Order

Issues discussed in the judgment from the point of view of language rights are important to us. They are:

— The mother-tongue will be the language declared by the parent or guardian to be the mother-tongue.

— The parents have the right to choose the kind of education that will be given to their children.

— Right to education is a fundamental right, which also includes the right to choose the medium of instruction, and it can be exercised by the parents on behalf of their children, and they have absolute and exclusive right in this regard.

— Citizens shall have the freedom of speech and expression, which would include the right to educate and to be educated.

The fundamental right guaranteed to the minority institutions under Article 30(1) of the Constitution of India includes "... right to teach the subjects in the medium of their own choice." Career opportunities will be more advantageous to those who have studied in the English medium than using the Tamil medium. Compelling the students to study in Tamil will affect their career, and doom their future prospects.

The Universal Declaration of Human Rights - is also applicable in the Indian context since India. India is a signatory to the document.

LANGUAGE RIGHTS - THEORY AND PRACTICE

It is interesting to note that in case of Karnataka, it was the linguistic minorities who challenged the modification in the language policy for education, and, in the case of Tamil Nadu, the schools teaching in English medium knocked at the doors of justice. The students in the latter schools were mostly students with Tamil as their mother tongue.

As we saw in both the cases, the pedagogical aspects of language education have taken a back seat and the issues are fought mainly from the legal angle. The issues became very handy for the political parties in some sense. Political interests have counted more than any thing else in the decision-making about language use in education. Practicality of existence of a right and practical utility of such a right under specific socio-economic conditions still remains to be examined. The economic issues are driving the parents/students towards one or the other language normally other than their own mother tongue (Indian language).

Though it looks as if the parents have the right to choose the kind of education they need for the children, the government has the power to decide on the options to be provided about language choice available for the parents and children. The parents have to exercise their choice within the broad framework made available to them. Indian Census 1991 counts 216 mother tongues within its territory. Through merging of many mother tongues into languages, 114 languages were arrived at. The rights to learn language(s) and the right to learn through languages as already discussed are bestowed on the citizens. In this context, let us see the actual practice of these language rights as recorded in the Third, Fifth, and Sixth All India Education Surveys.

With this evidence it is noticed that there is a reduction in number of languages being used in the schools as school languages and also as medium of instruction. It may be noticed that as the country goes higher and higher in the educational ladder, the number of languages being used too becomes less.

The languages will continue to be used in the schooling process either as a subject or as a medium of instruction or both only if the students/parents exercise their right to learn their mother tongue and through their mother tongue. Seeking, and fighting for recognition of the language rights is different from practicing or exercising them. If we are asked whether linguistic rights are misused or abused, undoubtedly we can say that they are not used for the purpose for which they exist.

Today the consequence of these explanations, clarifications, and adumbrations of Language rights by the courts is that people use their language rights to get education of their choice driven by market forces and not in the letter and spirit as codified in the Constitution, or in the statutes framed for that purpose. There is a paradigm shift. So, English which should have been an additional language in education in India has become a substitute language.

6

Navodaya Vidyalaya and Kendriya Vidyalaya

The educational system in India has faced a basic dilemma ever since its introduction by the British. The essence of this problem was summed up by Mahatma Gandhi in his historic statement at Chatham House, London, in 1931. The British administrators when they came to India, instead of taking hold of things as they were, began to root them out. They scratched the soil and began to look at the root and left the root like that and the beautiful tree perished.

The village schools were not good enough for the British administrator so he came out with his own programme. Every school must have so much paraphernalia, building and so forth. Well, there were no such schools at all — ancient schools have gone by the board — and the schools established after the European pattern were too expensive to fulfil a programme of compulsory primary education of these inside of a century. This very poor country of mine is ill able to sustain such an expensive method of education.

Free India did not have the will to fulfil Mahatma Gandhi's dream of reviving the ancient tradition of the village schoolmaster, supported by the community, his status and survival as a *guru* being embedded within the culture and ecology of his immediate environment. Instead the government chose to continue with efforts to educate the masses through a vast, centralised machinery and superstructure of staff, infrastructure and resources. Successive efforts at universalisation of primary education, ranging from Operation Blackboard to DPEP and Education For All, have only reinforced the strength of the challenge posed by Mahatma Gandhi in his statement at Chatham House. The Adult Literacy Campaign and, more recently, the investment thrust on primary education to produce the literate child, carries within itself the hidden suspicion that the goal of universal education for the masses may even be quietly set aside one day, planners having perhaps finally realised that the goal is unattainable within the present system.

As pointed out by the Mahatma, the success of this system depends solely on expenses and affordability. It thus gives rise to a situation where a mass of underprivileged and under-educated children face a largely urban elite population of privileged schoolchildren. Needless to say, it is the latter who get into the universities. While the tax-payer pays for both government schools as well as universities, the poor man pays for both but benefits from neither. The per capita public cost of university education is exorbitant when compared with school education. In the words of Ivan Illich, School is a perfect system of regressive taxation where the privileged graduates ride on the back of the entire paying public.

Every poor Indian who can manage to make both ends meet thus strives to join the ranks of far better schools, because only these can form the gateway to subsidised higher education. The past two decades have seen a phenomenal growth of two types of private schools outside the system of government schools. These are the so-called elite schools where education is sold to the highest bidder, and the plethora of petty teaching shops against which it is fashionable for the educated elite to occasionally raise a hue and cry. In between there do exist a large number of institutions, often run by charitable or religious organisations, which seek to make as many compromises as possible within the given system.

It is not surprising that the government of a democratic state would also be compelled to join this race for providing more expensive schools for quality education. The Kendriya Vidyalayas, Sainik Schools, Railway Schools, Tibetan Schools and Navodaya Vidyalayas are responses to the basic dilemma facing the existing system. The KVs and NVs together run about 1,200 schools. The KVs, which were set up to cater to children of government servants having All-India transfer liability, have now increasingly opened their doors to the children of upwardly mobile, less privileged urban families. While 'political pressure' is ostensibly to blame, the trend basically reflects a sensible popular response of the underprivileged.

In the public perception, the system of mass government-sponsored education appears to have failed to deliver the goods, increasing expansion having led apparently to decreasing quality. Hence the upwardly mobile social classes are aggressively latching on to whatever better education is available at public cost.

As regards rural India, it needed a statesman like Rajiv Gandhi to visualise that the day was not far off when the rural elite would also grow restive and clamour for expensive quality education at par with quality schools set up in urban areas serving predominantly urban populations. Hence Navodaya Vidyalayas were set up as residential schools with 75 per cent reservations for rural candidates, all candidates being selected on the basis of a nation-wide talent test. No doubt the Navodaya system has made the best possible compromises within the given contradictions of the existing social system.

There is a 30 per cent reservation for girls and reservation for scheduled castes and scheduled tribes commensurate with their population strength in the district. Elitism of merit is the hallmark of the system. While the talent test is open to all rural children studying in class V of rural schools, the admissions are also structured so as to ensure that all geo-economic regions within the district are proportionately and equitably represented and no single region dominates.

NAVODAYA VIDYALAYAS

Navodaya Vidyalayas have sometimes been sarcastically described as the Doon School alternative for rural areas. But this can mean different things to different people. From the urban point of view it is often a derisive comment implying that by the very nature of the socio-economic set-up of the country, Doon Schools can hardly be relevant for country bumpkins. For the rural elite it is viewed as an optimistic statement, since they would naturally like to have the best for themselves, the urban elite invariably furnishing the role model.

There is a third point of view put forth by planners and educationists who feel that these rural elite schools are being set up at the cost of improvements in mass universal education. Such expensive schools set up in the rural environment only bring into focus the deprivation suffered by the rural masses. Setting aside expenditure on construction, which is quite heavy (each school complex costing over Rs.4 crores), the average cost per Navodaya student comes to about Rs. 9,900 per annum. Is such heavy investment on as few as 500-odd students per district justified? These are the questions raised by the Acharya Ramamurti Report, as also by the CPI(M) government of West Bengal, which has steadfastly refused to introduce the Navodaya Vidyalaya Scheme in its state purely for ideological reasons.

The Acharya Ramamurti Report indicts the NV Scheme on the grounds that it is very costly, it caters to a microscopic minority of the total school population and perpetrates an exclusive system inconsistent with the 'long cherished common school system of public education'. These educationists, however, seem to have overlooked the main problem pointed out by Mahatma Gandhi with the 'cherished system of public education', namely, that if at all schools are to be established after the European pattern they will inevitably be too expensive for the people.

If rural areas are not to follow the pattern of more and more exclusive and expensive schooling mushrooming in urban areas, rural talent will never get a chance to compete for higher education unless it migrates to the urban environment. This is a hard fact of life which this point of view does not face but which could be realised. By initiating the Navodaya Vidyalaya Scheme, government simply brought the process of handling contradictions inherent within the system to its logical climax. To the urban elite, however, what is sauce for the goose is definitely not sauce for the gander.

In the trend towards exclusive and increasingly expensive education the residential school stands at the apex of the school system and is sought to be duplicated for educationally underprivileged and rural children by the Navodaya Vidyalayas. As regards day schools, it is no secret that home tuition is embedded in the system of even the best public schools today. Both schools as well as parents find themselves unable to cope with the existing syllabus as well as an increasingly competitive environment without the aid of home tuitions, which today comprise a flourishing business. In government schools the underprivileged may also suffer since the temptation to earn more as a side business tends to retard optimum contribution of government teachers within school.

Thus even the expensive day school has ended up in total dependence on a parallel and equally expensive system of home coaching. A recent development in the private sector has now led to the opening of even more exclusive elite schools which restrict the number of students per class. While sixty students are replaced by twenty students only in these super schools, the costs of sixty are naturally paid for by the twenty privileged families. School has, therefore, become a flourishing and money-guzzling industry. Children exist for schools, not schools for children, and this is as true for private paying schools as it is for government schools.

While the seeds of spiralling expenses have grown into monstrous weeds, the seeds of alienation spread in a more subtle manner. The residential school is an apt symbol of alienation not only from its cultural and social environment but also from society itself. It stands at the apex of a system which rests on this artificial separation that seeks to inculcate values of exclusivity and elitism. Within the day schools the system alienates the teacher from the taught through the weight of sheer numbers and the cumulative burden of learning and measuring up to academic standards. It also alienates the student community as a whole from the socio-cultural matrix which surrounds it.

The accent on competition and the constant stress on the individual as against the group and the community further alienates children from one another. Seeds of alienation are embedded in the examination system, which lays a premium on a system of marking that is the sole determinant of individual achievement, the costs of which are paid for by the under-achievers. In its mildest form the under-achievers pay for it by being relegated to 'non-ability' as against 'ability' sections in public schools, alienation from one's immediate peers being thus glorified and institutionalised. At its worst the system is scarred by student suicides.

Universities like Taxila and Nalanda flourished and attained international acclaim. In the ancient systems of learning the *guru* invariably utilised the older boys to teach the younger ones. Their roles were supportive, not exploitative. How unlike the system of public schools, where the exploitation of younger boys by older boys is dubbed respectably as 'ragging'. While the school tie and similar indicators of superior status may still hold them together at school, these tenuous bonds no longer operate in the universities. University students in India in particular are in essence a mob, whether it be a passive mob or a mob on the rampage.

There are often deaths of students in which their peers are indirectly or directly involved through ragging. It is not a mere coincidence that these incidents have generally occurred in professional institutions for engineering or medical students.

While at first glance this phenomenon may appear to be incomprehensible, once the seeds of alienation present in the whole system are exposed it could also be seen as an offshoot of the system itself. The idea and essence of peace and universal harmony, of oneness with nature and association with the earth, of education as a pursuit in the arts of living in an interconnected universe is entirely missing from the system. Instead to the fore are values of individual achievement, branding and typing young persons as bright, mediocre, elite, poor, underprivileged. Divisive forces predominate over harmony. Products dominate over people. Competition dominates over brotherhood.

That this system is giving rise to problems entirely of our own making is being realised in many parts of the world. Radical thinkers, sociologists and educationists have raised voices in protest. Everett Reimer in *School Is Dead* and Ivan Illich in *Deschooling Society* have asked some of the profoundest questions about education today. They have recognised that most countries in the world can only afford to give their children the barest minimum of education while the costs of schooling are rising everywhere faster than enrolments and faster than national incomes. While regarding schools as institutional props for privilege for most people, Everett Reimer also recognises the fact that they are at the same time major instruments of social mobility. But he questions the cost in terms of true learning, true creativity and true democracy.

The search for alternatives in education has already begun. Some, like Everett Reimer, search for alternatives in terms of content, organisation and finance. At the other end of the spectrum, *Letter to a Teacher*, written by eight young Italian village boys from the school of Barbiana, is a minor classic which reveals with devastating clarity how the school system oppresses and marginalises the rural poor by divorcing them completely from their ecological base and their cultural environment. It also presents a radical alternative.

In India today the government's and NGOs' search for alternatives has led to greater support and funding for non-formal schools, the most dramatic example being that of the Charvaha Schools of Bihar. However, this experiment suffers from all the general weaknesses of the state system. In Bihar there are other alternatives developed with more success, such as the model 'Sidh', started by Pawan Kumar Gupta, an NGO, in and around about 15 villages surrounding Kempty, near Mussoorie.

Many other examples of rural-based education centres can be documented where the initiative for establishment and management has vested with communities themselves. Craft-oriented training and basic education have been outstanding successes of Dwarko Sundrani's Bodh Gaya Ashram, where schooling on the Gandhian pattern is made available to the poorest of the poor in Bihar. These non-formal schools, being beyond the pale of the state boards, are also free from the usual bureaucratic supervision of school inspectors, but by their very nature they are limited to the class V level.

The Yashpal Committee was set up specifically for suggesting ways to reduce the academic burden on students in recognised schools. The Committee strongly recommended toning down of individual competitiveness and introduction of group activity in schools. Simultaneously it advocated decentralisation of curriculum formation, textbook writing and much greater involvement of teachers in these processes, particularly textbook formation. In general the Yashpal Committee came out strongly against textbooks, syllabi and examinations which together form a system that inflicts upon the children the 'tyranny of rote memorisation.

The Department of Education has taken up these suggestions for serious review. The CBSE pattern of education will be set aside or modified in the near future. Sir Thomas Munro, who set in motion the process of establishment of schools after a new pattern in Madras Presidency in the 1820s, aptly summarised the aims of the new education as being 'to facilitate the acquisition of wealth or rank'.

As long as society accepts these as the aims of schooling, the CBSE syllabus and the emphasis on science and commerce streams will continue regardless of the Yashpal Committee report or any other similar reports. There are a few notable public schools which have departed from the mainstream and yet retained eminence within the general delivery system.

The difficulties of innovating within over three hundred and seventy government residential schools such as the Navodaya Vidyalayas would be apparent to any educational administrator. Being wholly funded by government, there is an even greater compulsion for these schools to deliver and perform as per the marks-oriented examination system laid down by the CBSE. Not only do residential schools allow for more investment in time, but the Vidyalayas themselves, with their resource pool of talented rural students, stand Janus-like between two worlds — with one hand they can reach out to grasp the best of scientific and technical skills, while with the other they can gather easily the ancient wisdom of the east enshrined in the oral tradition and rituals of their immediate cultural environment. Hence the Samiti has started a small venture to give schooling a human face through a carefully planned programme of Art in Education, based firmly on the indigenous *guru-shishya* tradition of learning.

Workshops in theatre, folk music, folk arts, epics and ballad singing can very easily slip into the groove of consumerism and assembly-line production that has come to characterise our school system. Again, overemphasis on achievement and the accent on the individual could vitiate the cathartic experience, the flowering of creativity, the realisation of a deep harmony between man and nature which these workshops should generate.

Hence every workshop in Navodaya Vidyalayas is designed around an activity with a cluster of groups working on the theme in accordance with their own particular talent. Thus a Pandawani workshop held in Durg was not just an exercise to locate another Teejan Bai amongst the students and project her on the stage. It was an experience in which the literary group interviewed Teejan Bai, wrote up reports and poems, while the visual art group was busy drawing and painting the scenes she depicted.

Those who had talent for dramatic performances learnt the art and performed on the stage, but it was a holistic experience through which the Chhattisgarhi children of Durg moved towards a joyous self-attainment, a recognition of an abiding and ancient identity which was derived from sources that stand apart from and are superior to their school and their schoolmasters.

The richness of rural roots and traditions gave them a sense of pride and psychological reassurance which no success in examinations could ever give. By honouring notable rural artists in this fashion the Samiti was able to bridge the gulf between teacher and taught, urban and rural, so-called literate and so-called illiterate. To put it in the works of Dharampal, the present system "has kept most educated Indians not only ignorant of the society they live in, the culture which sustains this society and their fellow beings, but yet more tragically, for over a century it has induced a lack of confidence and loss of bearing amongst people of India in general".

It is ultimately left to each one of us in the educational field to move one small step forward towards this transformation of vision towards reorientation of values and objectives of education. Not only in India, but in the entire world, education places an overriding value on products over people, on achievement over harmony.

NAVODAYA VIDYALAYA SAMITI

In order to provide good quality modern education to the talented children predominantly from the rural areas,

Government of India launched in 1985-86 a scheme to establish Navodaya Vidyalayas on an average one in each district. Two hundred and seventy-five Navodaya Vidyalayas covering 22 States and 7 Union Territories have so far been established in the country. Five Navodaya Vidyalayas have been sanctioned recently.

Admission to Navodaya Vidyalaya is at the level of Class VI. In view of the fact that most of the students so admitted would have been taught earlier through the medium of the mother-tongue/regional language, instruction is provided through the same medium up to Class VI or VIII, during which time intensive teaching of Hindi/English both as a language subject and co-media is undertaken. Thereafter, the common medium would be Hindi/English. At this stage, there is a migration of 30 per cent students from each Navodaya Vidyalaya to another Navodaya Vidyalaya in a different linguistic region. The migration is mainly between Hindi and non-Hindi speaking districts. Navodaya Vidyalayas are co-educational and primarily for children from rural areas. Hence admission of children from urban areas is restricted to a maximum of one-fourth. Efforts are made to ensure that atleast one-third of the students in each Navodaya Vidyalaya are girls.

Reservation of seats in favour of children belonging to the Scheduled Castes and Scheduled Tribes is provided in proportion to their population in the concerned district, provided that in no district such reservation is less than the national average.

The Main stay of the Navodaya Vidyalay Samiti is the administration of the residential schools all over the country and various other activities centring around the school education. The Schools run by the Samiti are called Jawahar Navodaya Vidyalaya (JNV). Four hundred and fifty such Schools have been sanctioned in States and Union Territories except Tamil Nadu and West Bengal (one state level JNV on the memory of Choudhari Devi Lal has been sanctioned at village Shergarh (Debwali) District Sirsa, Haryana

Objectives

The objectives of the Navodaya Vidyalaya Scheme are as follows:

— To provide good quality modern education, including a strong component of culture, inculcation of values, awareness of the environment, adventure activities and physical education - to the talented children predominantly from rural areas, without regard to their family's socio-economic condition.

— To ensure that all students of Navodaya Vidyalayas attain a reasonable level of competence in three languages as envisaged in the three language formula.

— To serve, in each district, as focal points for improvement in quality of school education in general through sharing of experiences and facilities.

Scouting and Guiding, and NCC

Navodaya Vidyalaya Samiti is recognised as a State for Scouting and Guiding activities by the Bharat Scouts and Guides. Navodaya students regularly and actively participate in various programmes of BSG.

NCC is being introduced in JNVs in a phased manner. Samiti had a total cadet strength of 9150 during 2000-2001. As part of NCC training, students of the JNVs attended several camps and excelled themselves.

Games and Sports

Games and Sports are encouraged in the JNVs to develop fitness, physical and neuro-muscular skills and promote the spirits of co-operation and sportsmanship. Vidyalayas organize National Sports Meets to identify talented children in sports. Specialised sports like archery, Judo and Gymnastics are encouraged in some of the JNVs situated in tribal areas in the country.

Migration : An Experiment In National Integration

One of the important features of the Navodya Vidyalaya Scheme is a scheme of exchange of students from one Navodaya Vidyalaya in a particular linguistic region to another Vidyalaya in a different linguistic region to promote understanding of the diversity and plurality of India's. cultures and people. According to the Scheme 30% of children from one Navodaya Vidyalaya are migrated to another Vidyalaya at Class IX level. The migration lakes place generally speaking, between Hindi and Non-Hindi speaking districts. As per this policy during the academic year 2000-2001, migration of 30% of students from 371 Vidyalayas has taken place. The students to be migrated are selected by the district magistrates who are ex-officio Chairmen of the Vidyalayas, on the basis of students' voluntary willingness and by a lottery, where sufficient number is not forthcoming on voluntary basis.

The Migration Scheme had a modest beginning during 1988-89 with only two JNVs and 31 migrated children. In a span of ten years, migration is taking place on a large scale. 5015 students were on migration during 2000-2001. Due precautions are taken in transporting the children from the remotest parts of the country between JNVs located in North, South, East or West India.

The officers from the Headquarters as well as Regional Offices of the NVS during their visits to JNVs make it a point to see that the migrated children are happily adjusted in the Vidyalayas they have migrated to . By and large, migrated children are well adjusted but for a few exceptions. The Principals have been instructed to ensure that the children under migration are made to feel at home to the extent possible by giving them special care and attention.

Facilities

Education in the JNVs including boarding and lodging as well as expenses on uniform, textbooks, stationery, rail/bus fare from to the homes etc. are free for all students. The present norms in respect of expenditure on students are as under:

Items	Rates	Total (Rs)
Boarding	@ Rs 500/-per month per child for 9 months	5000.00
Uniform	@ Rs 600/-per child per year (To be provided one in two years).	600.00
Text Books	@ Rs 100/-per year per child	100.00
Toilet Articles	@ Rs 300/-per year per child	300.00
Other items (Stationary, Travelling, Medical Expenses etc.)		500.00
Total expenses per child per year		6500.00

Mess Facilities

Being residential schools proper mess arrangements are of great importance in our Navodaya Vidyalayas. The Mess is run by the Vidyalaya itself under the overall direction of the Principal and with the help and guidance of the Chairman of the Vidyalaya Management Committee. The Mess Committee consists of the Principal as Chairman and two House Masters (one male and one female) two boys and two girls as members and the Catering Assistant as Member Secretary. Where there is no Catering Assistant one male House Master is the convener of the Committee. The Samiti has sanctioned posts of Cook and Mess Helpers for Vidyalayas. Principals are free to appoint a few more helpers on part time/ casual basis.

Opening Of NVS

The original objective of providing one Navodaya Vidyalaya in each district, has been actively pursued. 450 Vidyalayas are sanctioned at present in 33 states and UT's including one State Level JNV sanctioned at Sirsa (Haryana).

10 new JNVs have been sanctioned in the year 2001-2002. It is proposed to open 33 new JNVs during the rest of 9th Plan period, bringing the total coverage to 482 districts..

The opening of a Navodaya Vidyalaya is based on the proposal from the concerned State/UT Governments offering 30 acres of suitable land free of cost, sufficient temporary building and other infrastructure free of rent or on permanent basis.

The coverage of Navodaya Vidyalaya in educationally backward districts has been considerably high.Out of the States with literacy rate below 50%, 100% coverage has been made in Orissa, Jammu & Kashmir, Karnataka, Manipur, Dadra & Nagar Haveli, Madhya Pradesh, Meghalaya and Rajastan with the reference to the number of districts existing at the commencement of VIIIth plan.

Statewise Details of JNVs Sanctioned/Uncovered Districts and their percentage as on 15st October, 2001

S. NO.	Name of State/UT	Total No. of districts	JNVs Sanctioned	Balance Districts	Percentage Coverage
(1)	(2)	(3)	(4)	(5)	(6)
1	ANDHRA PRADESH	23	22	01	96%
2	ARUNACHAL PRADESH	14	09	05	64%

3	BIHAR	37	34	03	92%
4	GUJARAT	25	17	08	68%
5	HARYANA	19	15+1 #	04	79%
6	HIMACHAL PRADESH	12	11	01	92%
7	KERALA	14	13	01	93%
8	MAHARASHTRA*	37	29	08	78%
9	RAJASTHAN	32	31	01	97%
10	SIKKIM	04	03	01	75%
11	NAGALAND	07	05	02	71%
12	UTTAR PRADESH	70	54	16	77%
13	DELHI* (Educational 9)	04	02	02	50%
14	ASSAM	23	20	03	87%
15	CHHATISH-GARH	16	09	07	56%
16	JHARKHAND	19	16	03	84%
17	UTTRANCHAL	13	08	05	62%
18	ORISSA	30	18	12	60%
19	KARNATAKA	27	26	01	96%
20	MIZORAM	08	03	05	38%
21	MADHYA PRADESH	45	42	03	93%
22	MEGHALAYA	07	06	01	86%
23	TRIPURA	04	03	01	75%

100% COVERAGE

1	GOA	02	02	--	100%
2	JAMMU & KASHMIR	14	14	--	100%
3	MANIPUR	09	09	--	100%
4	ANDAMAN & NICOBAR	02	02	--	100%
5	DADRA & NAGAR HAVELI	01	01	--	100%
6	DAMAN & DIU	02	02	--	100%
7	LAKSHDWEEP	01	01	--	100%
8	PONDICHERRY	04	04	--	100%
9	CHANDIGARH	01	01	--	100%
10	PUNJAB	17	17	--	100%
	TOTAL	543	449+1	94	

* 3 extra JNVs have been sanctioned by the Govt. for Bombay and Delhi. Actual districts in Maharashtra 35 and Delhi 9 # One State level J.N.V. sanctioned at Sirsa (Haryana)

The National Policy on Education 1986 envisaged establishment of a Navodaya Vidyalaya in each District of the country. The first two schools were started in 1985-86 on experimental basis. The number of schools have now grown to 482 spread over 34 Union States and Union Territories. These schools have over 1.41 lakhs students on rolls. Navodaya Vidyalayas are fully residential and co-educational schools covering classes VI to XII.

Education in the Vidyalayas is free for all enrolled students including lodging, boarding, text books, uniforms etc. The Vidyalayas seek to promote and develop talented, bright and gifted children predominantly from rural areas who may otherwise be denied good educational opportunities.

The Vidyalayas are affiliated to Central Board of Secondary Education (CBSE) and impart the CBSE curricula.Admission to Vidyalayas is made at the class VI level through open test conducted at District level by CBSE. About 35,000 students are admitted every year.

NVS has sanctioned 14 new schools during 2002-2003(as on 25/11/2002) in different Union States except Tamil Nadu and West Bengal, who have so far opted out of the Navodaya Vidyalaya system of schooling.

The NavodayaVidyalayas envisage a new style of growth and development aimed at identification and development of talented, bright and gifted children predominantly from rural areas who are denied good educational opportunities. These institutions are envisaged as model and pace-setting institutions to lead the secondary education system in India as need based productive and paving the way for the realization of national goals.

Distribution of JNVs in Eight Regions

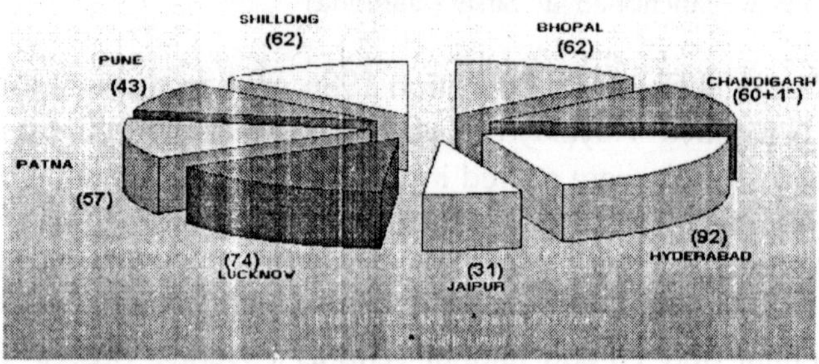

These Vidyalayas have been conceived as an idea, a progressive forward looking concept, making modern India the focal area of development through educational excellence. Objectives of quality education with a strong component of culture, inculcation of values, promotion of National Integration, adventure activities, physical education, reasonable level -of competence as envisaged in Three Language Formula and serving the respective districts as focal points for improving quality of education through sharing of experiences and facilities have been some of the main alms of these institutions.

Management

The chain of Navodaya Vidyalayas is managed by Navodaya Vidyalaya Samiti which is an autonomous organization of the Ministry of Human Resource Development, Department of Secondary Education and Higher Education.

The Samiti functions through an Executive Committee under the Chairmanship of the Union Minister of Human Resource Development. Union Minister of State for Education is the Vice- Chairman of the Samiti. The Executive Committee is assisted by Finance Committee ,and Academic Advisory Committee in its functions.

The Samiti has eight Regional Offices and eight Sub-Regional Offices for administration of Vidyalayas under their respective regions. These offices are located at places in different States. For each Vidyalaya, there is a Vidyalaya Advisory Committee and a Vidyalaya Management Committee for the general supervision of the Vidyalaya. District Magistrate of the concerned district is the Chairman of the Vidyalaya level Committees with local educationists, public representatives and officials from the District as members. NVS headquartered is presently located at Indira Gandhi Stadium, I.P.Estate, New Delhi.

Admissions

Admission in Navodaya Vidyalaya are made at level of Class VI through a test conducted by CBSE on all India basis. Till 1998, the Jawahar Navodaya Vidyalaya Selection Test (JNVST) was conducted by the National Council Of Educational Research and Training (NCERT). The medium of the test is in 20 Indian languages and is largely non-verbal and objective in nature and is so designed that talented children from rural areas are able to compete without suffering a disadvantage. All the children who have studied in and passed from Class V from any recognized school of that district and are between 9 to 13 years of age are eligible to appear.

As per the Scheme, a maximum of 80 students can be admitted in Class VI per year in a JNV. However, in view of shortage of accommodation in some Vidyalaya, it is restricted to 40 only. There is proposal to have a 50 % expansion in the intake of students.

Year	Registered	Appeared	Selected
1999	5,20,392	4,63,150	26,850
2000	5,83,243	5,33,333	27,813
2001	6,32,924	5,83,530	29,632

Procedure For Admission

Admissions to Jawahar Navodaya Vidyalayas take place on the basis of a selection test designed and conducted by the CBSE. The test , called the Jawahar Navodaya Vidyalayas Selection Test (JNVST) is of nonverbal nature, class neutral and so designed as to ensure that talented children from the rural areas are able to compete without facing any disadvantages.

Because of the poor communication facilities in rural areas special care is taken to ensure that children from far flung rural areas get admission forms free of cost without any problem. Sufficient publicity is done through Doordarshan, All India Radio, local newspapers, pamphlets, visits of Principals and teachers of Navodaya Vidyalayas to the local schools of the district. As a result rural areas are becoming aware of the Navodaya Vidyalaya Scheme.

Eligibility Conditions

To appear at the Selection Test, a candidate has to fulfill the following eligibility conditions:

— A candidate appearing for the Selection Test must be studying in Class V in a recognized school in that district where he/she is seeking admission in the just preceding academic session for which Selection Test is conducted. Actual admission in Class VI in the session is, however, subject to the condition of having passed Class V before admission.

— A candidate seeking admission must be between the age group 9-13 years on 1st May of the year of admission for which the Selection Test is conducted. This applies to all categories of candidates including those who belong to the Scheduled Castes and Scheduled Tribes.

— A candidate must have studied and passed Class III, IV & V from recognized school/schools in the preceding three continuous academic sessions for which the Selection Test is conducted spending one full academic session in each class through the formal system of education, without any repetition of class, gap and/or break in attendance.

— A candidate who is not promoted to Class V before November of the preceding academic year for which. the test is conducted is not eligible to apply.

— No candidate is allowed to appear in the selection test, for the second time under .any circumstances.

— A candidate seeking admission under the rural quota must have studied and passed III, IV & V from recognized school (s) located in the rural areas.

— The above conditions are applicable to all the candidates irrespective to their caste or gender.

Reservation

At least 75% of the seats in a district are filled by candidates selected from rural areas and remaining seats are filled from the urban areas of the district. A candidate who has studied in a school located in an urban area, even for a part of session in any of the classes III, IV, and V or passes any one or more of these classes from such a school as above is considered as an urban candidate. Urban areas are those which are so defined in the 1991 census or in subsequent Government notification. All other areas are considered rural.

Reservation of seats in favour of children belonging to Scheduled Castes and Scheduled Tribes is provided in proportion to their population in the concerned district provided that no district, such reservation will be less than the national average (15% for SC and 7.5% for ST) but subject to maximum of 50% for both the categories (SC & ST) taken together. These reservations are interchangeable and over and above the candidates selected under open merit.

Efforts are made to ensure that one-third of the total seats are filled up by girls.

Activities

The thrust on academic excellence in the classroom has been accompanied by an effort to build up the Vidyalayas as co-educational residential institutions. The House System of Jawahar Navodaya Vidyalayas, functions as an effective instrument for the development of the personality of the students. It furthers team spirit, by involving students in a variety of co curricular and extra curricular activities. The inter house competitions, organisational responsibilities, games, sports & art in education activities help students to groom themselves into competent & self-confident individuals.

The value of dignity of labour & concern for environment is sought to be incorporated by self help activities that are part & parcel of the daily schedule of all Vidyalayas. Teachers who stay in residence provide teaching help after class hours through remedial teaching sessions held in the afternoons. Teachers as House Masters or House Mistress maintain a close association with students and provide the necessary support to children.

Games & Sports

Games and Sports are encouraged in the Jawahar Navodaya Vidyalayas to develop fitness, physical and neuro-muscular skills and to promote the spirit of co-operation and sportsmanship. The Navodaya Vidyalaya Samiti organises cluster level, regional level and national level sports meets to identify talented children in sports.

NCC in JNVs

NCC is being introduced in JNVs In a phased way. Samiti has a total cadet strength of 9150 (7200 Boys + 1950 Girls) in 138 JNVs. As a part of NCC, training. Cadets of JNVs attended several NCC camps and excelled themselves. NCC cadets took part in Republic Day parades in several districts. Important days like NCC Diwas, Quami Ekta Diwas were celebrated by our cadets. Activities like tree plantation, Shramdaan, Adult Literacy Programme were taken up.

Youth Parliament

Ministry of Parliamentary Affairs, Govt. of India, has introduced Youth Parliament Competitions for Jawahar Navodaya Vidyalayas to prepare the youth with added skills and competencies to Cater to the needs of the fast changing world scenario and to enable them to understand the democratic values in all spheres of life: These programmes were started in JNVs in 1997-98.

Art In Education Programme

The Art in Education programme is an expansion of the Samiti's pace-setting activities. Besides providing an opportunity for students to inculcate nationalistic values through cross cultural interchange, it also emphasizes upon education enrichment and integration with the community in which the Vidyalaya is located.

Eminent personalities from the fields, of' the letters, arts and sciences are invited to interact with students. Students have received -training in traditional art under the tutelage of traditional Gurus and contemporary theatre directors. Under this programme, a National Integration Meet is organised every year in which about one thousand children, and teachers, from Navodaya Vidyalayas all over the country participate.

The Art in Education programme also aims at enriching the curricula of the formal education system. It also aims at strengthening universal values and promoting group activities whereby joy of learning is achieved. It aims at personality development of students by emphasizing child centred and result oriented activity:

Pace setters

The founding fathers of the Navodaya Vidyalaya Scheme assigned a specific role to Navodaya Vidyalayas. They hoped that these rural area schools would play the role of pace-setting Institutions in the district by achieving high levels of excellence. The indicators of excellence are the quantity and the quality of the results, communicative and linguistic ability of the children, competitive spirit and capability, innovative learning practices, developing correct attitudes and values that help them to groom themselves tom become useful, active and patriotic citizens of the country while achieving these goals , adequate care is taken to ensure that the children keep their linkages with the local community around them and contribute their help for furthering these values in the neighborhood and community.

Students of Navodaya Vidyalaya have been participating in several projects and programmes relating to the eradication of illiteracy, adoption of a village for creation of general awareness about the development programmes being undertaken by the Government Of India and respective States, sanitation and cleanliness drives and shramdaan.

Students Profile

About 1.27 lakh students were on the rolls of Navodaya Vidyalayas at the end of the academic session 1999-2000. The percentage of students belonging to SC/ ST categories, girls and rural areas in the Navodaya Vidyalayas is well above national norms (15 % SC & 7.5 % ST)

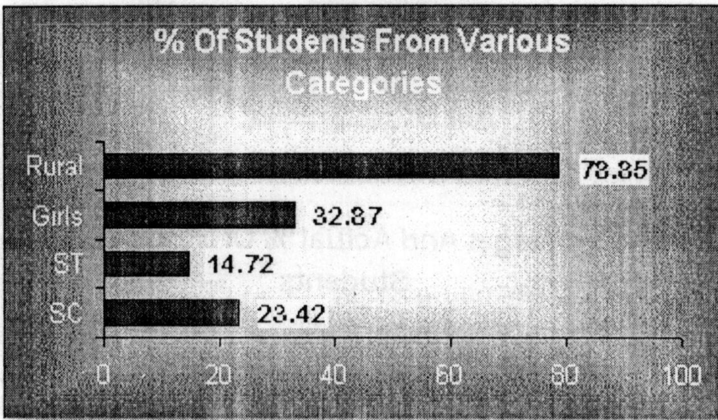

Thus the JNVs are serving rural students, specially girls, SC & ST students in excess of national averages. For this they have also been commended by the Standing committee of Parliament for the Ministry of Human Resource Development In April, 1997 as follows:

> "The Committee is happy to note that various norms made for reservation of seats for SC's and ST's are fulfilled and hopes that this practice would continue in future also."

Navodaya is the only scheme providing quality education to students from the rural areas and weaker sections of the society with a 75% reservation of seats for students from rural areas, 1/3 seats for girls, and reservation for SC and ST students in proportion to their population in the district.

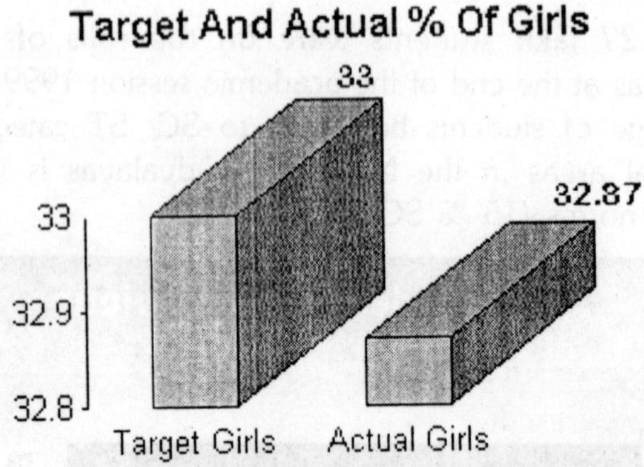

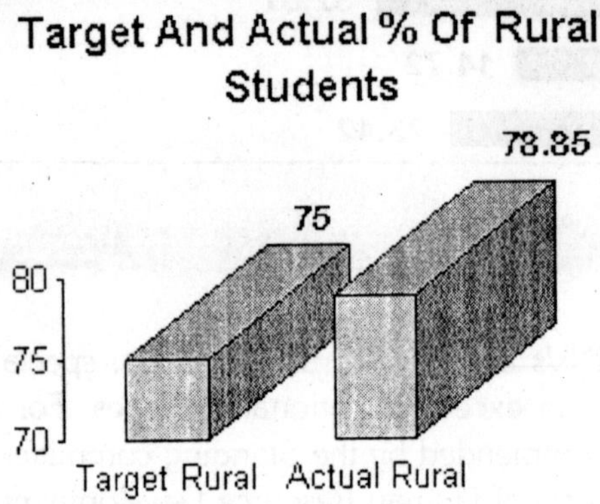

A socio-economic survey of Navodaya Vidyalaya students was carried out in 221 Vidyalayas in the year 1989-90. Another sample survey was carried out in 94 Vidyalayas in four select Union States and the findings of the survey confirmed that over the years socio-economic profile of the students remained the same with minor variations.

Construction programme

Out of the 280 Navodaya Vidyalayas 160 Vidyalayas have been shifted to permanent site. Construction work is almost completed in ill and 35 Vidyalayas under phase I and Phase Zero respectively. Sanction for additional buildings, Phase-II for 187 Vidyalayas, amounting to Rs. 150.45 crores has also been issued during the year 1991-92.

Incentives to Teaching Staff

Since all Navodaya Vidyalayas are residential and located in remote areas, the following incentives have been provided to attract good teachers/principals:

i) Rent free, partly furnished, accommodation as available at site.

ii) Children education allowance at the rate of Rs.150/p.m. per child subject to maximum of two children.

iii) Free boarding facilities to House masters and teachers staying with the students.

iv) Free lunch to all teachers.

v) Facility for the appointment of spouse as per Samiti's rule.

vi) Admission of children in the Navodaya Vidyalayas where teachers are posted without admission test and free boarding facility to such children.

vii) Teaching Allowance of Rs.100/-p.m.

Professional Growth of Staff

Navodaya Vidyalaya Samiti has given training and orientation their due importance, to have committed and competent staff in the system. Navodaya being a new system by itself, the Samiti had so far organised for its staff (Principals, teachers and non-teaching staff) one hundred and sixty-five in-service courses of various types, namely orientation course, induction courses, subject-wise course, work- shops, etc. The duration of the courses had varied from a minimum of one week to a maximum of one month. These courses have been organised in collaboration with NIEPA, CCRT, NCERT, KHS, CIEFL and CIIL, etc. Samiti has also encouraged the teachers to join the correspondence course in "Reading Skills".

KENDRIYA VIDYALAYAS

Kendriya Vidyalayas are opened at stations having a sizable concentration of Central Government employees. The vidyalayas in defence establishments are opened on the recommendation of the Ministry of Defence. Those in civil sector are sponsored by various Ministries of Government of India Employees Welfare Associations. Kendriya Vidyalayas are also opened in the campuses of public sector undertakings and institutions of higher learning. The number of Kendriya Vidyalayas, sector-wise, is as under:

a)	Defence Sector	:	343 +6
b)	Civil Sector	:	251 +14
c)	Public Sector Undertakings	:	134 +2
d)	Institutions of Higher Learning	:	15 +1
			743 +23 = 766

Admission Policy

In view of the objectives of the scheme of Kendriya Vidyalayas, the first priority in admission in civil/defence sector schools is given to the children of transferable Central Government employees. In Kendriya Vidyalayas in public sector undertakings and institutions of higher learning, however, the first priority in admission is given to the children of employees of the concerned organisation.

Fifteen per cent and seven and a half per cent of fresh admissions in every Kendriya Vidyalaya are reserved for the children of transferable employees belonging to SC, ST communities respectively. In the event of such children not being available, the vacancies are thrown open to children belonging to general category.

Examination Results

Kendriya Vidyalayas have made a mark of themselves in the educational system at the school level in the country.

Achievement in co-curricular activities

Kendriya Vidyalayas have also distinguished themselves in co-curricular activities including games and sports, out-door activities, environmental educational programmes and fine and performing arts. Kendriya Vidyalaya students have been winning prizes every year in international and national competitions such as Soviet Land Nehru Award, Shanker's Children's Painting Competitions and Essay Competitions held by the Department of Environment, Government of India, besides awards and prizes in local and regional competitions.

Most of the Kendriya vidyalayas run nature and adventure clubs which are affiliated to the World Wild Life Fund of India and the National Adventure Foundation of India, respectively. About 10,000 students are trained in rock-climbing and about 550 are sent for trekking to glaciers every year. Kendriya Vidyalaya Sangathan is a member of the School Games Federation of India and also of the Bharat Scouts & Guides. Special emphasis is also laid on mass participation of students in cultural activities and games and sports for which periods are provided in the school time- table for all classes in all Kendriya Vidyalayas.

National Integration

Every Kendriya Vidyalaya is a miniature India where teachers and students belonging to different language groups with different faiths and following different customs are seriously engaged in the process of teaching and learning. The students take the same oath, sing the same songs under the same flag in the same uniform and follow the same curriculum and co-curricular programmes.

Kendriya Vidyalayas have been in the lead in community singing programmes. Inter-Vidyalaya contests leading to regional competitions are held annually. Cultural activities such as dramatics, variety shows, declamations, debates, poetry recitations, story-telling with a view to fostering social, cultural and national values form an integral part of school curriculum in every Vidyalaya.

National integration and international understanding have been taken as projects at all India level by the Kendriya Vidyalaya Sangathan. Under these projects, exhibitions are held every year.

Personality Development through activities, games & Sports

Vigorous and sustained efforts are made every year in the field of Games & Sports with a view:-

i) to ensuring mass participation;

ii) to spotting out talent and to nurture it; and

iii) to developing spirit of sportsmanship and qualities of leadership.

To achieve these objectives, the following steps are undertaken:-

Coaching Camps

Coaching camps are organised every year in which about 400 students (both boys and girls) receive specialised coaching and training in various games and sports during summer vacation as well as in the co-ordination-cum-coaching camps organised before the participation of the KVS teams in the tournaments organised by the School Games Federation of India.

Organisation of KVS meets at various levels

A year-long plan is drawn up and implemented for organising games and sports meets at Vidyalaya, Sub-regional, Regional and National levels in KVS. In all these meets about 35,000 students participate every year.

Sports

The KVS also runs four sports hostels at Kendriya Vidyalaya, IIT, Madras (for basket ball and volley ball), KV, Kirki, Pune (for Hockey), and KV No. 1, Gwalior (for Cricket). The entire expenditure on board and lodging, playing kit and nutritious diet is borne by the KVS for which a hostel grant of Rs.385/- per student per month is being given by the KVS Headquarters.

Adventure activities

The KVS organises trekking programmes on a mass scale every year.

Scout/Guide activities

The Scout/Guide movement has taken deep roots in Kendriya Vidyalayas. The number of registered scouts and guides has shot up to about 60,000 and of trained teachers to about 5000. Every year several programmes for the training of teachers and students are undertaken. These include training courses at various levels from the preliminary to the leader-trainers course for teachers and training camps for the award of various proficiency badges, Prime Minister Shield competitions and training camps leading to the award of Rajya Puraskar and the President's medal for students. All these programmes are undertaken at the unit, district, divisional and KVS State levels. The KVS State Rally for 960 scouts and guides was held at Bhubaneswar on 6-9 January, 1991.

Science Exhibition

In order to pursue excellence in Science education several programmes are undertaken in Kendriya Vidyalayas which include field trips, science exhibitions, science quizzes and discussions on scientific topics. Such participation not only reveals to teachers the scientific talent possessed by students; it also motivates the students to design and devise something new in the field of science and develop among them a love for science, scientific temper and social and environmental awareness. Science exhibitions are held every year at various levels school, regional and national.

Youth Parliament

In order to equip students with the knowledge of parliamentary procedures and practices and also to inculcate in them a healthy habit of discipline, tolerance of the views of others, a habit of arriving at decisions after fee and frank debates and discussions and developing in them an awareness of social needs, parliamentary ethos and culture, youth parliament competitions are held in all kendriya Vidyalayas.

7

POA 1992

Till 1976, according to the Constitution of India, education was the exclusive responsibility of the State Governments, although the Union Government was concerned with certain areas such as "Coordination and determination of standards in institutions for higher education or research and scientific and technical institutions". By the Constitution Amendment Act, 1976, the Seventh Schedule was amended making education "including technical education, medical education and universities... vocational and technical training of labour", a joint responsibility of both the State and Union Governments.

Though decisions regarding the organisation and structure of education largerly continue to be the concern of the State Governments, the Union Government has also a clear responsibility regarding the quality and character of education in general and that of the higher and technical education in particular. In addition to policy formulation, the Department of Education in the Ministry of Human Resource Development (MHRD) shares with the states the responsibility for educational planning. The Central Advisory Board of Education (CABE) set up in 1935, continues to play a leading role in the evolution and monitoring of educational policies and programmes. The most notable outcome of its activities was the formulation of the National Policy of Education (NPE), 1986 and the Programme of Action (PoA), 1986 drawn up within the policy framework. The NPE and PoA have been revised in 1992.

The NPE,1986 and the PoA,1992 envisaged that free and compulsory education of satisfactory quality should be provided to all children up to the age of 14 years before the commencement of the 21st century (See also Update). The government committed itself to earmark about six per cent of the Gross Domestic Product (GDP) for education by the year 2000 AD and 50 per cent of the outlay would be allotted to Primary Education. Both the targets however seem to be unachievable even in the distant future. The expenditure on education as a percentage of GDP could not even cross the 3.5 mark.

The system of education in India consists of three streams: (i) the School Stream, (ii) the University (including the College) Stream, and (iii) the Non-university Stream. The school stream (along with ITIs and Polytechnics) and the university stream may be called the formal sector of Indian education. The non-university stream consists, on the other hand, of both formal and informal sectors.

THE SCHOOL STREAM

The school stream comprises three stages: (i) pre-primary, (ii) primary (or elementary), and (iii) secondary. The pre-primary or pre-learning stage consisting of nursery and kindergarten schools terminates when the children attain the age of five years. At the age of six , they enter the primary stage. There are two levels at the primary stage - the primary (Classes I to V) and the upper primary (Classes VI to VIII). Students are expected to complete the primary stage at the age of 13 years and enter the secondary stage. Article 45 of the Constitution of India stipulates free and compulsory education for all the children until they complete the age of 14. In 1993, the Supreme Court, in its order in the Unnikrishnan case, has also declared education of children up to the age of 14 years to be a Fundamental Right. However, the target of universalisation of primary (or elementary) education is yet to be achieved.

The secondary stage, in turn, has two levels - the secondary (Classes IX and X) and the higher (or senior) secondary (Classes XI and XII). There is a public examination at the end of Class X called the Secondary School Leaving Certificate (SSLC) examination or the Secondary School Certificate (SSC) examination. This examination corresponds to the Matriculation examination of yesteryears.

Another public examination is conducted at the end of Class XII called Higher Secondary Certificate (HSC) examination or "10+2 examination". In some states, higher secondary education (Classes XI and XII) is also called the Intermediate education and the corresponding examination Intermediate examination. Secondary and higher secondary education are regulated by State Boards of Secondary Education and State Boards of Higher Education (or Boards of Intermediate Education) respectively.

In several States there is only one Board for both the levels. Secondary and Higher Secondary schools are managed by state governments as well as by private societies and trusts. The State Boards accord recognition to schools, formulate syllabuses and conduct public examinations. Besides the State Boards, there are two Boards whose jurisdictions extend all over the country, viz., the Central Board of Secondary Education (CBSE), established in 1929 by the Government of India, and the Council for the Indian School Certification Examination (ICSE). Any school in the country can get affiliated to these Boards. Both the Boards conduct Secondary School Certificate (Class X) and Senior School Certificate (Class XII) examinations.

There is yet another Board named the National Open School (NOS). It provides secondary and higher secondary education through distance learning mode, and conducts public examinations and awards certificates like any other Board. A brief account of the NOS has been given in Chapter 6 (Learning from a Distance). The Annexure gives a list of Secondary and Higher Secondary Boards. By the time students complete the higher secondary education, they should have attained the age of 17 years. The minimum age prescribed for admission to many post-higher secondary courses is, therefore, 17 years.

In addition, there is a parallel system outside the School Stream - Industrial Training (ITIs) and the polytechnics. Polytechnic education is of three-year duration after Class 10. These institutions, sponsored both by the government and private organisations, are under the control of the State Boards of Technical Education, and as such belong to the formal sector.

THE UNIVERSITY STREAM

In the Indian system, education imparted beyond the 10+2 stage, is called higher education (or tertiary level education). Education at this level is provided by universities and a network of colleges, affiliated to them but not exclusively. There is also a parallel Non-university Stream, the third stream of the Indian educational system which is also a significant component of higher education. The universities are established by State and Central Acts. Several States have consolidated the individual University Acts into a single Act, e.g., Karnataka State Universities Act, 1975, Andhra Pradesh Universities Act, 1991. Besides such universities, there are also two other categories of institutions of higher learning which enjoy university status - institutions deemed to be universities (or simply "deemed universities" and institutions of national importance.

The University Grants Commission (UGC) constituted under the University Grants Commission Act, 1956, is the apex body which oversees the standards of teaching, examinations and research in universities. It also looks into the financial needs of universities and allocates and disburses grants to universities and colleges. All the universities are members of the Association of Indian Universities (AIU), an autonomous inter-university organization. It liaises between universities and other official and non-official agencies in the field of education, both at the national and international levels.

The University Stream offers degree courses at three levels - first degree (or graduate degree, i.e., Bachelor's degree); postgraduate degree (i.e., Master's degree); and Doctoral and post-Doctoral degrees (i.e., PhD, DLitt/DSc). There is also a pre-Doctoral degree (M Phil). Besides, universities also offer certificate and diploma level courses. A brief overview of the duration of courses at these three levels follows. Bachelor's degree is obtained after three years of study in one of the streams - Arts (BA), Science (BSc), and Commerce (BCom). Most of the first degree professional courses are of four-year duration although there are variations. For example, in the case of medicine (MBBS), the duration is four and half-years, while the dentistry course (BDS) is of four-year duration. For both the courses there is a compulsory period of internship. The duration of Master's degree programme also varies. MA, MSc, MCom, MBA programmes are of two-year duration. In the case of ME/MTech, the duration is only one and half years; but the computer application course (MCA) needs three years of study. There are also postgraduate courses of one-year duration leading to the award of Bachelor's degree, e.g., BEd (Education), BLISc (Library and Information Science), BCJ (Communication & Journalism).

A further study of one-year leads to Master's degree in the concerned subjects. The duration of law course is three years leading to the award of a postgraduate degree (BL/LLB), although integrated BL/LLB programmes of five-year duration after 10+2 are also available. This decision perhaps, has led to the introduction of integrated Master's degree programmes in several subjects after 10+2. By and large, the students attain the age of 20 years when they obtain the first degree, and 21-22 years in case of first degree in professional courses. They are about 23 years when they complete the Master's degree programmes in most of the disciplines.

The MPhil course which is the preparatory programme for doctoral level(PhD) studies, is of one and half year duration. PhD programme takes two years or more depending upon individual students. There are also two higher post PhD degrees leading to the awards of DSc and DLitt degrees. Many universities and institutions offer part-time courses in selected subjects (mostly in management), the duration of which is more than that of a full-time programme. For example, a part-time course in management (MBA) needs three years of study instead of normal two years for regular courses. In addition to the degree courses, all the universities offer a plethora of diploma and certificate courses. Their range is wide and covers subjects from "Religious Dialogue" to "Computer Aided Design". Some are undergraduate diploma courses while some others are postgraduate courses. The duration, depending upon the subjects, varies from one year to three years.

NON-UNIVERSITY STREAM

Like the ITIs and polytechnics which function outside the School Stream, there are a large number of educational institutions which function outside the university stream. Most of them offer professional programmes, the largest concentration being in the management and information technology areas. While many of them are recognised by the concerned regulatory authorities, some are not. This stream is an important component of the national system of education and supplements the educational and training programmes offered by the university stream.

Regulatory Authorities

An important aspect of the Indian educational system is the role of the statutorily established regulatory authorities for the regulation and maintenance of uniform standards of education and training in professional subjects. Prior approval of these authorities are essential for starting new institutions, introduction of new courses and fixing the intake capacity in each course.

Distance Education

A recent development in the Indian educational system is the introduction of the system of distance education. As the name suggests, unlike face-to-face teaching, it is the mode of education wherein instruction is provided to students located at distant places, even the remotest areas of the country. The distance learning, all over the world, is now considered an important mode of delivering education at the door steps.

National Policy On Education

Educational policy and progress have been reviewed in the light of the goal of national development and priorities set from time to time. In its Resolution on the National Policy on Education in 1968, an emphasis on quality improvement and a planned, more equitable expansion of educational facilities and the need to focus on the education of girls was stressed. About a decade ago and a half later, the National Policy on Education was formulated which was further updated in 1992. The NPE 1986 provides for a comprehensive policy framework for the development of education upto the end of the century and a Plan of Action (POA) 1992, assigning specific responsibilities for organising, implementing and financing its proposals.

India's commitment to the spread of knowledge and freedom of thought among its citizens is reflected in its Constitution. The Directive Principle contained in Article 45 enjoins that " the State shall endeavour to provide within a period of ten years from the commencement of this Constitution, for free and compulsory education for all children until they complete the age of fourteen years". Article 29 (i) provides that any citizen having a distinct language, script, special care of the economic and educational interests of the underprivileged sections, particularly, the Scheduled Castes and Scheduled Tribes is laid down as an obligation of the State under article 46.

Though education is in the concurrent list of the Constitution, the State Governments play a very major role in the development of education particularly in the primary and the secondary education sectors.

STRUCTURE AND PROGRESS OF EDUCATION IN INDIA

The focus in on the broad dimensions and magnitude of the structure, organisation and progress in education. Further it also highlights growth and priority areas in education in India that point to the challenges of the future. There are about 888 thousands educational institutions in the country with an enrolment of about 179 millions. Elementary Education System in India is the second largest in the World with 149.4 millions children of 6-14 years enrolled and 2.9 million teachers. This is about 82% of the children in the age group.

Structure of School Education

A uniform structure of school education, the 10+2 system has been adopted by all the States and Union Territories of India. However, within the States and the UTs, there remains variations in the number of classes constituting the Primary, Upper Primary, High and Higher Secondary school stages, age for admission to class I, medium of instruction, public examinations, teaching of Hindi and English, number of working days in a year, academic session, vacation periods, fee structure, compulsory education etc.

Age Restriction For Admission

The minimum age for admission to class I of the Primary School stage is generally 5+ or 6+ years. In 22 States/UTs the minimum age for admission to Class I is 5+ years and in 7 States/UTs the minimum age for admission is 6+ years. There is no age restriction in the case of Mizoram. In Gujarat, the minimum age for admission is 5+ years (voluntary) and 6+ years (compulsory). In Lakshadweep, the minimum age for admission is 5 ½ years.

Number Of Working Days

The number of working days of School Education in a year is generally more than 200 days in all the States/UTs.

Academic Session

The academic session begins from different months of the year in the different States and Union Territories. However, in most of the States, the long vacation periods are availed in the summer season while in some of the hilly States, these fall in the winter months.

Compulsory Education

Compulsory education has been enforced in four States and Union Territories at the primary stage of education while in eight States/UTs there is compulsory education covering the entire elementary stage of education. As many as 20 States/ UTs have not introduced any measure of compulsion upto the year 1997-98.

Free Education

A majority of States and Union Territories have introduced free education in Classes I-XII of their schools.

Tution Fees Per Annum Per Child In Govt Schools

In the States/UTs where education is not free for classes IX and above, the annual fee varies considerably from the highest level of Rs. 360/- for classes XI and XII in the case of Meghalaya to the lowest at Rs. 48/- in the case of Assam.

Financing of Education

From 1968 onwards, goal has been to set apart 6% of National Income on education. In spite of resource constraints as well as competing priorities, the Budgetary expenditure on education by Centre & States as percentage of Gross National Product has steadily increased from 0.8% in 1951-52 to 3.3% in 1994-95.

Para 11.4 of NPE, 1986 states "that the investment on education be gradually increased to reach a level of 6% of the National Income as early as possible. Since the actual level of investment has remained far short of that target, it is important that greater determination is shown now to find the funds for the programmes laid down in this policy. While actual requirements will be computed from time to time on the basis of monitoring and review, the outlay on education will be stepped up to ensure that during the 8th Five year Plan and onwards it will uniformly exceed 6% of the national income".

The total budgetary expenditure on Education by the Education Departments of the Centre and States has increased from Rs. 644.6 millions in 1951-52 to Rs. 300,000millions in 1995-96. In terms of its share in total budgetary expenditure, it has increased from 7.9% in 1951-52 to 11.1% in 1995-96.

There are, at present 130 plan schemes in the Department with a total Eighth Plan outlay of Rs. 74430 Millions. The total plan outlay of the Department for the year 1996-97 is Rs. 33827 millions. There are 18 Centrally Sponsored Schemes which account for 65.7% of the total plan outlay. Mid-Day-Meal Scheme is the major Centrally Sponsored Scheme with 1996-97 outlay of Rs.14,000 millions. Other major Centrally Sponsored Schemes are Operation Blackboard, Non-formal Education, Teacher Education, Post Literacy and Continuing Education and Vocational Education with 1996-97 Outlay of Rs. 2790 millions, Rs. 1582.5 millions, Rs. 1170 millions, Rs. 755 millions and Rs. 820 millions respectively

Since independence, the central and state governments have been expanding the provision of primary formal and non-formal education to realise the goal of Universilisation of Elementary Education (UEE). The challenge now is to sustain and deepen current reforms in education and encourage local planning and management of strategies for expanding and improving primary education.

With a view to cushioning the impact of rising costs of text books and exercise books, the government has exempted writing and printing paper supplied to all State Text Book Corporations from excise duty. It is expected that this would make school text books more affordable for students from weaker sections of society.

Removal of systemic deficiencies in the implementation of UEE and forging ahead necessitates the creation of informed public opinion and a facilitative environment akin to that of the Total Literacy Campaign. This has to be achieved through effective and sustained advocacy, massive community mobilisation and consciousness building. With this perspective, a national programme of media publicity and advocacy has been planned. The programme will target: i) teachers and all those involved in education of children; ii) students and parents of students, particularly non-literate parents; and iii) community opinion leaders.

The Kasturba Gandhi Shiksha Yojana, a programme to establish residential schools for girls in all the districts which have a particularly low female literacy rate has been announced. A sum of Rs. 2500 million has been provided in this year's budget. The central government has also decided to grant financial incentives and scholarships for the girl child born in families living below the poverty line.

Several central and state level initiatives have been in operation from the early 1980s. While the design of these projects vary substantially, all of them address the objectives and strategies of the National Policy on Education 1986. They pay special attention to increasing girls' enrolment, improving educational outcomes, strengthening community involvement, improving teaching and learning materials and providing in-service teacher training. The status of some of these initiatives are discussed below.

Operation Blackboard

This scheme launched in 1987, is aimed at improving the school environment and enhancing retention and learning achievement of children by providing minimum essential facilities in all primary schools. The scheme has brought about a remarkable quantitative and qualitative improvement in primary education. In all, 523,000 primary schools have been covered as originally envisaged. These schools have been provided with central assistance

Decentralisation

Decentralised planning and management of elementary education is a goal set by the National Policy on Education, 1986. The Policy visualises direct community involvement in the form of Village Education Committees (VECs) for management of elementary education. The POA, 1992, emphasised micro planning as a process of designing a family-wise and child-wise plan of action by which every child regularly attends school or NFE centre, continues his or her education at the place suitable to him/her and completes at least eight years of schooling or its equivalent at the NFE centre.

The 73rd and 74th constitutional amendments provide for decentralisation of the activities and facilitate transfer of power and participation of the local self-government institutions or the Panchayati Raj Institutions. It has created a congenial ambience for the PRIs to play a more dynamic and proactive role. States are expected to evolve institutional arrangements both in rural and urban areas for undertaking these activities. These structures have been providing voice to women, Scheduled Castes and Tribes, minorities, parents and educational functionaries. They have also, been delegated with responsibilities with regard to location and relocation of existing primary and upper schools on the basis of micro planning and school mapping. In this regard, decentralisation of school management to grassroots level bodies is an important policy initiative.

During the 8th plan period several innovative efforts hove been made under the ongoing projects to establish decentralisation. For instance, the District Primary Education Programme has shifted the planning mechanism from the state to the district level, and Lok Jumbish has gone one step further by assigning decision making processes to a block level committee. At the village level, a VEC has the main responsibility for community mobilisation, school mapping, micro planning, renovation and construction of school buildings and improvement of pedagogical curriculum. In fact, the VECs of Shiksha Karmi schools have been activated as a result of the Lok Jumbish programme.

Since 1993-94, the scheme has been expanded to cover upper primary schools. More then 47,000 upper primary schools have been granted central assistance of Rs. 40,000 each for purchase of teaching- learning materials. Also, primary schools with enrolment exceeding 100 have been augmented with a third teacher. A Special Orientation Programme for Primary Teachers (SOPT) to facilitate optimum utilisation of materials supplied has also been launched to cover all primary school teachers in the country.

The total expenditure under the scheme from 1992-93 to 1995-96 has been Rs. 8,163 million. The outlay for 1996-97 is Rs. 2,910 million.

National Programme of Nutritional Support to Primary Education (School Meal Programme)

This scheme was launched on 15 August, 1995 to give a boost to UEE in terms of increasing enrolment, retention and attendance in primary classes by supplementing nutritional requirements of children attending primary schools. It is an ambitious scheme that has been operationalised throughout the country in a very short period. The programme envisages provision of nutritious and wholesome cooked meal of 100 gms of food grains per school day, free of cost, to all children in classes I-V by 1997-98.

During 1995-96, 378 districts, 225,000 schools and 33.5 million children have been covered with an expenditure of Rs. 4,412 million. In 1996-97, the scheme was extended to cover 55.4 million children with an expenditure of Rs. 8,110 million. The scheme has become fully operational in 1997-98 covering nearly 110 million children in primary classes. A positive impact on school enrolment and retention has been reported.

District Primary Education Programme

The DPEP launched in November, 1994 is conceived as a beachhead for overhauling the primary education system in India. The programme aims at operationalising the strategies for achieving UEE through district specific planning and disaggregated target setting. It draws upon the accumulated national experience of several state level initiatives that were started earlier. It moves away from the schematic piecemeal approach of the earlier programmes and takes a holistic view of primary education with emphasis on decentralised management, community mobilisation and district specific planning based on contextually and research based inputs. The basic objectives of DPEP are:

— To provide all children with access to primary education either in the formal system or through the non-formal education (NFE) programme.

— To reduce differences in enrolment, dropout rates and learning achievement among gender and social groups to less than 5%.

— To reduce overall primary dropout rates for all students to less than 10%.

— To raise average achievement levels by at least 25% over measured base line levels and ensuring achievements of basic literacy and numeracy competencies and a minimum of 40% achievement levels in other competencies by all primary school children.

The Government of India finances 85 % of the project cost as a grant to the DPEP State Implementation Societies and the concerned state government provides the rest. The central government's share is resourced by external funding. As of now, IDA has approved credit amounting to $260 million and $425 million under Phase-I and Phase-II respectively. The European Union (EU) is providing a grant of 150 million ECU. The ODA (UK) is extending a grant of $80.21 million. The grant from the Netherlands amounts to $25.8 million.

The first phase of the programme was launched in 42 districts in the states of Assam, Haryana, Karnataka, Kerala, Maharashtra, Tamilnadu and Madhya Pradesh. In the second phase, the programme has been launched in 80 districts of Orissa, Himachal Pradesh, Andhra Pradesh, West Bengal, Uttar Pradesh and Gujarat and in Phase I States.

DPEP has been able to set up project management structures at district, state and national levels, create the environment and capacity for micro planning, take up the challenge of pedagogical innovation, create a responsive institutional base which includes both government and non-government institutions, enhance community participation and strengthen the process of catering to special focus groups such as tribals, scheduled castes, women and other marginalised sections.

The first phase of the programme is under evaluation. The initial trends of impact studies are very positive. DPEP has made a decisive impact on increasing enrolment, reducing repetition rates and improving class room processes.

While the DPEP has been targeting backward districts with female literacy below the national average and where TLCs have stirred up a demand for elementary education, several state level initiatives have shown tremendous potential. These are directed at improving literacy levels in the five low literacy states of Andhra Pradesh, Bihar, Uttar Pradesh, Madhya Pradesh and Rajasthan.

BIHAR EDUCATION PROJECT

Bihar Education Project (BEP) was launched in 1991 with the express purpose of bringing about quantitative and qualitative improvement in the elementary system in Bihar. The project lays emphasis on the education of deprived sections of society, such as SCs, STs and women. Participatory planning and implementation are crucial ingredients of the project. A midterm review highlighted certain major achievements such as: a) a strong Mahila Samakhya component; b) organisation of VECs and community involvement in programme implementation at grassroots level; and c) non-formal education through NGOs. The review suggested:

- consolidation of the programme in the existing seven districts,
- establishing strong linkages between BEP and the education system in Bihar,
- giving greater focus to the primary stage of classes I-V,
- building better linkages with the activities in other states under DPEP and other programmes,
- providing more emphasis to MLLs and teacher training, and conducting periodic base line studies.

It has now been decided to extend the project to the second phase of two years duration. The total outlay for the second phase is estimated to be Rs. 613 million to be shared between UNICEF, Government of India and Government of Bihar as per the existing funding formula of 3:2:1. The total project outlay for BEP is Rs. 3600 million. It is proposed to merge the project with DPEP during the next five years.

UTTAR PRADESH BASIC EDUCATION PROGRAMME

A project "Education for All" prepared by the Government of Uttar Pradesh was approved by The World Bank in June, 1993. The project is currently in operation in 12 districts. It is planned to expand the coverage to 15 districts under DPEP-II. It has an outlay of Rs. 7,288 million spread over seven years. International Development Agency (IDA), the soft loan window of The World Bank, would provide a credit of US$163.1 million and the state government's share would be approximately 13 per cent of the total project cost.

The progress of implementation of the project so far has been satisfactory. The construction work of schools and Block Resource Centres is being completed as per schedule. Training materials for teacher trainers on DIETs have been prepared. The first cycle of in- service teacher training was completed in October, 1995. About 40,000 teachers have been trained.

Community Mobilisation and Participation

Many educational innovations of recent years are based on the strong foundation of community support and participation. When progress is discussed and analysed of different levels within the project, "people's acceptance and participation" is used as an indicator.

Mobilising the village community to take responsibility to ensure quality education for every child, is the core strategy of both Lok Jumbish (LJ) and Shikhsa Karmi Project (SKP) in their efforts to universalise primary education and deliver quality education. It would not be far removed from truth if we say that community involvement has been the key factor for the success of the two projects. LJ has had a positive effect on the empowerment of locally elected people, especially on female representatives at village level, who are often active members of the LJ core teams or women's groups. The Village Education Committees(VECs), carefully formed and trained though environmental building activities in the LJ programme, are actively involved in school matters.

SKP has constituted VECs in 2000 villages to promote community involvement in primary education and encourage village level planning. The role of the VEC is to mobilise resources for maintenance, repair and construction of school infrastructure. The VEC also helps in determining the school calendar and school timings in consultation with the local community and Shiksha Karmis (educational workers).

The positive impact of the LJ and SKP, focusing on supporting the teachers and the students by involving, the village community in taking responsibility for all educational activities of the village school, is serving as a demonstration of how deeply rooted problems of education in India can be addressed. Wide dissemination of these innovative approaches could inspire other educational programmes all over India and the world.

Andhra Pradesh Primary Education Project

The Andhra Pradesh Primary Education Project (APPEP), practised in the south central state of Andhra Pradesh, with a female literacy of just 34 %, adopts a two-pronged strategy of improving classroom transaction by training teachers and giving a fillip to school construction activities. The project has trained an estimated 80,000 teachers in 23 districts and more than 3,000 teaching centres have become operational. The project is assisted by the ODA with an estimated outlay of Rs. 1,000 million in the 8th Plan.

Shiksha Karmi Project

The Shiksha Karmi Project (SKP) is being implemented since 1987, with assistance from the Swedish International Development Cooperation Agency (SIDA). The project aims at universalisation and qualitative improvement of primary education in the remote and socio-economically backward villages of Rajasthan, with primary focus on girls. Since teacher absenteeism has been found to be a major obstacle in achieving the objective of UEE, the project uses the novel approach of substituting teachers in dysfunctional schools with local youth known as Shiksha Karmis who are provided with rigorous training and supervisory support. An important feature of this innovative project is the mobilisation and participation of the community in improving the functioning of primary schools.

The project is being implemented as an externally aided scheme with reimbursement of 90 % in Phase I and 50 % in Phase II, from SIDA. The project, with an outlay of around Rs.212 million in Phase I and Rs.490 million in Phase II, places strong emphasis on vigorous and continuous in-service training.

The SKP also runs non-formal classes called Prehar Pathshalas-schools of convenient timings. For girls' education, Angan Pathshalas are being run in three blocks. The programme at present covers over 150,000 students in 1,785 schools and 3,520 Prehar Pathshalas, involving over 4,271 Shiksha Karmis.

The project is known for its open participative style and continuous experimentation to achieve its objectives. The approach, strategies and achievements of the SKP have attracted national and international recognition. The project is slated for a major expansion with SIDA assistance in the 9th Plan. The total projections for the 9th Plan are estimated to be Rs. 4260 million.

Lok Jumbish Project

Barely five years old, Lok Jumbish (LJ) has made an indelible impression in the primary education landscape of Rajasthan. The coverage of the project has extended to 75 blocks, covering a population of approximately 12 million. Significantly, it has also achieved a major breakthrough in welding together government agencies, teachers, NGOs, elected representatives and the people into an interactive group effort to promote universalisation of primary education. The seven guiding principles of Lok Jumbish are:

— a process rather than a product approach;

— partnerships;

— decentralised functioning;

— participatory learning;

— integration with the mainstream education system;

— flexibility of management; and

— creating multiple levels of leadership committed to quality and mission mode.

Special focus has been given to environment building in all training programmes under LJ. This helps in the development of an understanding about issues involved in people's mobilisation, use of different media forms and clarity about the messages to be given to the people.

The first phase of the project was for a period of two years from 1992-94, with the expenditure shared between SIDA, Government of India and Government of Rajasthan in the ratio 3:2:1. The second phase stretches up to 1998, with the sharing modality remaining the same. The allocation for LJP is Rs.1100 million for Phases I and II and Rs.4000 million for Phase III. A Norwegian grant of Rs. 200 million is also available.

THE STATUS OF THE TEACHING STAFF

The role of the teacher has been well recognised in the traditional Indian thought through the centuries. The 'Guru' (teacher) was to be revered as an imparter of knowledge and a guide. In the present context, the role of the teacher remains as critical as ever. The teacher plays a major role in implementing the policies and schemes formulated to achieve a breakthrough in the quantitative expansion and qualitative improvement of education. Reflecting the crucial role of teachers in national development, the NPE 1986 called for a substantial improvement in the conditions of work and quality of teacher education The important determinants of the status of teachers could be identified as follows:

— The academic and professional requirements for entry into the profession
— The financial and other economic benefits
— The freedom of teachers to take part in public affairs
— The professional responsibility assumed
— The degree of public recognition.
— Growth of the teaching profession

The teaching profession has the largest number of members as compared to other professions in India. During 1994-95, about 4.3 million teachers were working in different levels of schools. Of these, 2.7 million [66 per cent] were engaged in primary and upper primary schools [grades I to VIII] of which 2,018,050 teachers were in government schools. Of the 1.5 million [34 per cent] in high/higher secondary schools [grades IX to XII] 609,121 were in government schools. During the period 1990-95, the total strength of teachers at different levels of school education increased from 4.0 million to nearly 4.3 million, marking an increase of 6.5 per cent. If this trend continues, the number of teachers, particularly primary and upper primary teachers, will grow significantly over the next decade.

A sex-wise analysis of the teacher force indicates that there are 3 times more male teachers than female teachers at all levels of school education. Although the number of female teachers has increased, yet, their share in the total teaching force is very small, particularly, in rural, remote and educationally backward areas. The number of women teachers in schools increased from 1,141,015 in 198788 129.4 per cent) to 1,343,667 in 1993-94 132.08 per cent).

System of teacher education

The NPE 1986, called for an over-haul of the Teacher Education System in the country. It emphasised the need for continuing education for teachers to meet the thrust envisaged in the policy. A new Centrally Sponsored Scheme of Restructuring and Reorganisation of Teacher Education was launched in 1987-88 which primarily envisages establishment of DIETs to provide pre-service and in-service training to elementary school teachers and to AE and NFE personnel. In addition, upgradation of Secondary Teacher Education Institutions into Colleges of Teacher Education (CTEs), establishment of Institutes of Advanced Studies in Education (IASE), strengthening of SCERTs and University Departments of Education through the University Grants Commission are components of this restructuring which has the basic objective of providing training and resource support to elementary and secondary education at the grassroots level. Central assistance is meant for the construction of buildings, procurement of books and equipments, additional expenditure on staff salaries and training programmes. In view of the high priority accorded to the achievement of the target of UEE, emphasis under the Teacher Education Scheme has so far been on setting up of DIETs. It was proposed to establish DIETs in 425 districts in the country (as per 1987-88 configuration when there were 451 districts in total) by the end of the VIII Five Year Plan. Against this target, 424 DIETs have been sanctioned as on 31 st March, 9h. Seventy three CTEs and 34 IASEs have also been sanctioned. Eighteen SCERTs have been assisted under strengthening of SCERT component of the scheme.

A Special Orientation Programme for Primary Teachers (SOPT) has also been taken up during the VIII Plan period 11992-971. Started in late 1993, this programme is aimed at orienting an estimated 1.8 million primary teachers in the country in the use of Operation Blackboard material and MLLs strategy. The NCERT is the apex body implementing this programme through state nodal agencies which are mostly SCERTs. Ministry of Human Resource Development releases grants to the NCERT based on the needs. Within the provision of the Centrally Sponsored Scheme of Restructuring and Reorganisation of Teacher Education, so far about Rs. 450 million has been released to the NCERT for the purpose.

According to the NCERT, State Governments have reported training of about 0.3 million primary teachers under the SOPT. Details on the implementation of Teacher Education Scheme have been presented earlier.

Qualifications and training

The minimum general qualification prescribed by some states for the recruitment of primary school teachers (teaching grades I-V} is 10 years of formal education (matriculation/secondary, whereas, it is senior secondary or 12 years of education prescribed in certain states (e.g., Haryana, Maharashtra, Tamil Nadu, Uttar Pradesh and Delhi). The minimum qualification prescribed by most states for the appointment of upper primary school teachers (teaching grades VI-VIII) is graduation (second level diploma) whereas in some states it is matriculation/senior secondary (first level diploma!. The educational qualifications of teachers have been gradually increasing.

According to the Fifth All India Educational Survey in 1986, as many as 2.1 million 177 per cent) primary and upper primary school teachers had been trained through first level diploma (under-graduation), 0.5 million (18 per cent) through second level diploma (graduation) and 0.1 million (5 percent) through third level diploma. All states in India require at least a graduation degree (second level diploma) for secondary school teachers (grades VI-X) and post-graduation degree (third level diploma) for higher/senior secondary school teachers (grades XI-XIII. As many as 58 per cent teachers teaching at the secondary and higher secondary levels had second level diploma, 33 per cent had third level diploma and only about 9 per cent had first level diploma (under-graduation).

Pre-service teacher training

The Fifth All India Educational Survey indicates that about 87 per cent primary and upper primary teachers are trained, that is they have acquired a primary or elementary teacher training certificate of one or two years' duration or bachelor's degree in education. There are, however, significant regional variations. The percentage of trained teachers at primary and upper primary level is more than 99 per cent in the states of Haryana, Tamil Nadu, Chandigarh and Delhi. It is less than 50 per cent in Arunachal Pradesh, Meghalaya, Sikkim, Nagaland and Tripura.

The Centrally Sponsored Scheme of Restructuring and Reorganisation of Teacher Education taken up in 1987-88 in pursuance of NPE 1986 envisages, on the one hand, strengthening of institutional base of teacher training and, on the other, takes up special programmes for training of teachers in specified areas and other non-institutional programmes of orientation for teachers. The Scheme provides for the setting up of DIETs to provide training and resource support to elementary education (both formal and non-formal) and AE systems at the grassroots level. The scheme for establishing the DIETs envisaged raising the general education of primary teachers to 12 years of schooling. With the establishment of DIETs, almost all states are now moving towards a two-year diploma in education for those teaching at the elementary level following 12 years of schooling.

Of the total number of teachers working in high or higher secondary schools, approximately, 90 per cent are trained, i.e., they have acquired a bachelor's degree in education (B.Ed.). The percentage of trained teachers at both the levels is the highest in Chandigarh and lowest in Assam. A comparison between male and female teachers indicates that the number of male untrained teachers is more than that of female teachers at all school levels in the country.

The National Council for Teacher Education

The NCTE was established in May, 1973 by a Government resolution to advise Central and State Governments on all matters pertaining to teacher education, with its Secretariat located in the NCERT. The NCTE's status and role till 1993 have been purely advisory and it did not have statutory powers to enforce its guidelines. As per the provisions laid down in the NPE 1986 and the Programme of Action for its implementation, the NCTE has been conferred statutory status as per the NCTE Act No. 73 of 1993 passed by the Parliament and assented to by the President. It has come into existence with effect from 17th May, 95. The Act provides for establishment of the NCTE with a view to achieving planned and coordinated development of teacher education system throughout the country, regulation and proper maintenance of norms and standards in the teacher education system and for matters connected therewith.

Programmes and activities taken up by the NCTE so for include:

— Preparation of a framework for competency-based curriculum for elementary teacher training institutions.

— Restructuring of pre-service teacher education curriculum for all stages.

— Human Rights and National Values- preparation of materials and orientation of teacher educators.

— Preparation of a video film on teacher training in physical education.

— Preparation of a project proposal on Teacher Education in States/UTs-current status, issues and future projections.

— Development of material for teacher educators on specific subjects.

Instructors in NFE

In the NFE system, the instructor is the key person. The instructor is a nominally paid volunteer who is usually employed on a part time basis. He/she could be an educated housewife, a girl from the village, an educated unemployed youth, a retired teacher, a qualified social worker, an anganwadi worker or even a professional semi-skilled person. Among the qualities expected of an instructor are dedication to work, and volunteerism. Girls' NFE centres have only lady instructors. The minimum qualification of the instructor is class 10 pass. But studies show that the qualifications of instructors vary from class 8 to Master's degree with a professional degree in education. In fact, there are many remote areas-rural and tribals-where individuals who have studied beyond class 8 are not available. In such cases, the VEC is empowered to relax the minimum qualification of the instructor. In the case of lady instructors, this problem is even more acute.

The basic skill which an NFE instructor is expected to have or develop is multi-class teaching as the group of learners he/she has to deal with is a heterogeneous one. The methodology of teaching at the NFE centre has to be different from the one used in formal schools. Therefore, to orient the instructor in the teaching methodology and also to acquaint him with the content of the learning materials, a four-tier system of training has been developed.

During the first year, the minimum training period for the instructor is 30 days and in the subsequent year it is 20 days. The first phase is usually divided into three phases and focused on training in pedagogy! content, evaluation and monitoring. The second phase of training is devoted to discussion focused at finding solutions to the problems faced by the instructors while teaching at the centre. Various packages of training materials have been developed to cope with the needs of training. The training of instructors at the district level is done through DIETs. The overall responsibility of training NFE functionaries at the state level rests with the SCERTs.

In the NFE centres, the instructor is the link between the centre and the community and is expected to perform a more dynamic role. He is also expected to take care of the individual needs of the learner and help him/her in solving day-to-day problems. The responsibilities of instructors include the organisation of the daily activities of the centre, identification of out-of-school and non-school going children, the selection of the site for the centre in consultation with the VEC, organising teaching-learning activities by drawing on supervisors, primary school teachers, TLC volunteers, ECCE Centres, the community, nearby voluntary agencies, mobile village library, Block Development Office, Primary Health Centres, etc. The monitoring of the NFE programme is done on a continuous basis at all levels viz. village, district and state through the VEC, DIETs, SCERTs and Directorate of Education.

The teachers working under TLCs are volunteers and are not paid any salary for their services. Since the qualification of these volunteers is not fixed, any educated person capable of working as a volunteer is appointed and trained. The responsibility of training volunteers of TLCs is that of the State Resource Centres (SRCs).

Conditions of work

Salary

Good conditions of work play a significant role in attracting and retaining the right type of persons in the teaching profession and enabling them to function efficiently. The working conditions include teacher's salary and benefits, availability of o suitable school building and essential facilities in the school, teacher's workload, method of recruitment, availability of teaching and non-teaching materials and opportunities for promotion.

Today, teacher's pay is probably the most important element affecting the quality of education. The calories of different levels of teachers ore established separately by each state and are determined on the basis of academic qualifications, training and experience. In addition to salary, price-index linked 'dearness allowance' is given to all teachers Various other allowances are also granted to all categories of teachers to compensate them for the special stress under which they work.

These allowances are: city compensatory allowance, house rent allowance, hill allowance and other special allowances such as winter allowance, backward, remote and tribal area allowance, island allowance, etc. These allowances differ from state to state and within the state from stage to stage of education. Entry level salaries for trained primary teachers are only slightly higher than those for untrained teachers. The maximum salary for a trained teacher is 3 to 4 times his/ her entry salary, and is achieved only after 1 & 20 years of service in most states.

In the majority of states, the salary scores of trained and untrained graduate teachers in upper primary/middle schools are at par with those in secondary and higher/senior secondary schools. Teachers with a Master's degree working in higher/ senior secondary schools hove separate salary scales and ore designated as post-graduate teachers (PGTs) or "Lecturers". There is a provision of selection grades for all categories of teachers. Twenty per cent of senior teachers of different categories get selection grades after 10 to 15 years of service.

In addition, most states provide fixed medical allowance or reimbursement of medical expenses, advances for house building and purchase of conveyance, and free education for the children of teachers, as well as retirement benefits of pension, gratuity and group insurance. In the majority of states, there is also a provision of incentives for some special categories of teachers. For instance, in Assam, Bihar, Gujarat, Maharashtra and Tamil Nadu, a certain percentage of elementary (primary and upper primary) women teachers working in rural and remote areas are given residential accommodation. In some states, physically handicapped teachers are offered conveyance allowance.

Working environment and facilities

Working conditions for primary school teachers are different from secondary and higher secondary school teachers, particularly, for those in primary schools in rural areas.

According to the fifth all India educational survey 56.25 per cent primary schools, 69.36 per cent upper primary, 72.97 per cent secondary and 89.39 per cent higher secondary schools are housed in buildings. There is a tremendous demand in provision of more facilities such as classrooms and instructional materials. Library facilities are available in only one-fourth primary schools as against 90 per cent in secondary and higher secondary schools.

A plan provision of Rs.500 million has been made in the budget for the year 1996-97 for financing a new Teacher's Housing Scheme under the Central Plan which will be implemented through the State Governments. It has been observed that teachers serving in remote and inaccessible areas do not have suitable residential accommodation. As a result, they have to commute to their schools from a distance and this affects their punctuality and attendance, adversely. The provision made in this year's budget could be utilised for construction of residential accommodation for teachers in such areas

Teaching material

Recent studies at primary level in selected educationally backward districts have revealed that charts, maps and globes were available in the blocks covered by the Operation Blackboard (JOB) Scheme introduced by the Central Government to provide some minimum infrastructure to primary schools e.g., two classrooms, a kit consisting of some teaching-learning materials and provision of an additional teacher. Teachers in remote areas now handle 2-3 classes, whereas, earlier they used to handle 4-5 classes Thus, it is evident that the minimum essential facilities needed for a smooth school functioning and a teaching-learning process need to be upscaled at all school levels, particularly, at primary level.

Other conditions of work

Some of the problem areas identified in the teaching field arc teacher absenteeism, non-availability of adequate housing facility, frequent transfers, etc.

The workload of teachers is often judged in terms of amount and type of work done by them. More than 60 per cent of teachers teach about 50 students on an average, 34 per cent teach between 51-100 and about 5 per cent more than 100 students. This means that on an average about 39 per cent teachers teach more than 50 students in the primary school. At high/higher secondary levels, however, the teacher-pupil ratio was 1:16 in 1994-95. It is evident that there is too much stress on primary school teachers, specially those handling multi-grades. Education codes in different states specify the number of class or periods teachers at different levels have to teach. In middle schools, nearly half of the teachers teach 31-40 class periods a week, whereas, 12 per cent teach more than 40 class periods.

Besides teaching, elementary and secondary school teachers have to spend a fair amount of time on co-curricular activities, specially in private schools. In addition, teachers have to do clerical work and other miscellaneous work like organising relief work, collecting census data, participating in family planning campaigns, and population control drives, helping in the smooth conduct of elections, etc.

Promotional prospects for teachers

In most states, the promotion of teachers in government primary and secondary schools is either on the basis of seniority or seniority-cummerit. Acquiring higher qualifications also helps in promotion provided a departmental vacancy exists which suits the qualification of the candidate. In the case of teachers working in private and aided schools, the chances of promotion are rare because in privately managed schools there is a shortage of senior positions and so only one or two persons have the opportunity to reach the level of headmaster/head teacher In secondary and higher secondary schools, a Trained Graduate Teacher (TGT) may become a PostGraduate Teacher {POT) provided he gets some higher qualifications i.e. a Master's degree in any school subject and depending upon the availability of a vacancy in the school. It may well be that teachers in private aided schools or privately managed recognised schools or public schools remain in the same post from the beginning to the end of their service of 30 to 35 years.

Teachers in government schools can aspire for higher administrative posts in the Education Department of the Government of India. Though a certain percentage of posts in the. higher categories of education are reserved for teachers, yet, avenues of promotion in the teaching profession are comparatively more limited than in other sectors such as industry, commerce and business.

Teacher support material

A number of agencies such as the NCERT, NIEPA, SCERTs and Departments of Education in universities have developed documentation services for teachers. A number of educational journals addressed to school teachers are published by national and state institutions such as NCERT, SCERTs, Boards of School Education, Teachers' Associations, NGOs and private publishers to disseminate research findings and information regarding innovations attempted by teachers, teachers' educators or researchers in different settings. Materials (multi-media packages, self-learning materials, etc.) for training and upgrading the knowledge and skills of teachers/functionaries of minority institutions through Distance Education are prepared by the NCERT, IGNOU, NIEPA and NOS, etc.

Some leading newspapers also sometimes bring out supplements or special editions on education. In addition, several institutions and NGOs bring out educational material in audio and video format. Professional associations have also made their contribution in this field. The UGC supports these efforts at the higher education level through a chain of EMRCs (Educational Media Research Centres) and AVRCs (Audio Visual Resource Centres). These efforts are coordinated through a Consortium of Educational Communications (CEC) The IGNOU also has a media programme service. These programmes are telecast throughout the country under the programme 'Country-wide Classroom'. Even though the programmes are targeted at students, teachers are also able to upgrade content and methodology-related delivery and evaluation techniques. Computer software has also been developed to upgrade the knowledge content in various school subjects. At the school level, the CIET in the NCERT and the SIETs which have been set up in six states are responsible for producing these programmes. Besides these, broadcasts and telecasts cater to regular and out-of-school children and teachers at the primary and secondary level. Several other technological aids and other audio-visual aids have been developed to help teachers in their instructional tasks. A large number of films have also been produced on teacher training, including the teaching of difficult concepts and content areas to children. The films produced include films on the methodology of teaching science, and the needs of children with special problems. Science kits, too, have been developed to enable children to perform experiments related to the prescribed syllabi.

Influenced by the advent of new technologies of communication, the teacher's role has been changing rapidly and teacher education curricula have been revised periodically reflecting this. Interpersonal skills for making instruction interactive and the two-way communication effective have become an integral part of the changes. These curricular reforms have provided teachers an opportunity to participate in the designing of instructional material using locally available resources. A number of newspapers and magazines extend support to teachers in their work. Many teachers, through their writings in newspapers and magazines, provide additional material to students. School broadcast and school telecast programmes addressed to students of different levels are organised with the help and cooperation of practicing teachers. Teachers participate in the planning, organisation and evaluation of these programmes. Since, these programmes are meant to provide syllabus-based enrichment material to children, they supplement the work of teachers. The government provides a satellite channel to educational and development programmes, the telecast of which is available to students in all parts of the country. This would also give a boost to the development of educational software

Motivational efforts for teacher development

Private educational establishments-government-aided and government recognised but unaided-make special efforts to maintain their teachers' motivation. Both incentives and disincentives are used. Good work in these institutions is rewarded by giving additional responsibility which is often linked with monetary incentives. In government schools, this is not possible as the head of the institution is not empowered to extend monetary incentives to teachers. Teachers in private education establishments have relatively less security of service. It is relatively easier to dispense with their services if their performance is not found satisfactory. In government schools, though teachers are accountable, teachers' unions make it difficult to enforce accountability, and it is extremely difficult to dispense with their services.

Teachers are involved in the formulation of education policies, development of curricula, syllabi and instructional material. They are also represented on decision-making bodies of universities, boards of school education, SCERTs and DIETs.

Moreover, teachers are autonomous in the management of their own classes. They are encouraged to undertake experimentation and action research and are provided incentives both at the state and national level. Every year, the NCERT conducts an All India Competition of Innovations and Experiments undertaken by school teachers and Teacher Educators. Teachers are invited to submit papers on the basis of the work done by them in their schools and as many as 50 primary school teachers and 20 secondary teachers are given national level awards. Similar awards are also available for elementary and secondary teacher educators. In the management of educational institutions, teachers at some places enjoy partnership in decision-making. The School Education Acts in vogue in some states have a provision for the membership of teacher representatives on the managing committee of the institution. For example, in the Delhi School Education Act and Rules, 1973, teacher representatives have to be on the managing committee of every recognised school. In the last few years there has been a move that even government schools should have an advisory or managing committee with representatives of the teachers working in the school as members.

To ensure parental support, many schools have either Parent Teacher Associations or Mother Teacher Associations. Parents are invited periodically to the school to discuss the performance of their children with the teachers. In some schools, particularly private schools, parents support the teachers in the organisation of co-curricular activities, art education activities and work experience activities by providing the materials required for these activities. In the DPEP, large scale efforts are underway to facilitate a constructive involvement of parents and the community with the school through the formation of grassroot structures such as VECs, Mother Teacher Associations and Parent Teacher Associations. Another aspect of enhancing motivation is through the institution of on annual Teachers' Day, on September 5. This day is observed in all the schools throughout the country, according a special place to the teacher. Under the aegis of the Ministry of Human Resource Development, a National Foundation for Teachers' Welfare has been set up. This Foundation provides facilities for teachers' welfare.

Similarly, with the objective of raising the prestige of teachers and giving public recognition to teachers, the Scheme of National Award for Teachers was launched in the year 1958-59. Primary, middle and higher secondary school teachers are eligible under the scheme. Each award carries a certificate-of merit, cash payment of Rs. 10,000 and a silver medal. In 1993, the number of awards given was raised from 296 to 302.

HIGHER EDUCATION

The enrolment in universities has been on the rise over the past years, with approximately a teaching staff of 0.301 million, catering to a student population of 6.1 1 million students. The pay scales of university teachers have been revised periodically and are considered to be on par with the highest pay scales of civil servants. Benefits include provident fund, residential accommodation (depending on seniority), retirement benefits. etc. Various incentives exists for teachers to improve their qualifications during their service by way of training and research. They are sent abroad under bilateral programmes of research, area studies, conferences, etc. There are fellowships and scholarships offered by various countries besides travel grants to go abroad. Approximately, 250 scholars visit various countries under these programmes.

Involvement of teachers in decision making is also a vital component of teachers' service conditions. University and college teachers, are involved in the formulation of curricula and the management of university/college affairs They are autonomous in planning their research. In Autonomous Colleges, teachers have been given the freedom to formulate and teach their courses of general curricula and evaluate their students. A scheme of Academic Staff Colleges provides training programmes in various subjects as a support for professional development of University and College teachers.

Teachers in technical education

With a large network of technical institutions established and developed since independence, and the programmes and initiatives launched in India during the successive plan periods, the technical education system has made significant contributions in producing one of the largest reservoirs of technically trained manpower which has been a source of strength for scientific and industrial development. The role of teachers in technical education is quite central and crucial. To be effective in their task, the technical teachers have to maintain fine balance between their professional competence and teaching potential. The job of technical teachers is multifarious, "to guide and inspire the students, to enrich self-discipline, to foster the area of specialisation by keeping abreast of the latest technologies and changing trends and, ultimately, to provide services and expertise to the industry and community for finding solutions to real life problems".

The Government of India, over years has taken a series of steps for developing the overall performance of the technical teachers. Significant among them are mentioned below:

Quality Improvement Programme (QIP)

The programme was launched in 1970 with an objective of upgrading the expertise and capabilities of the teachers of engineering colleges and polytechnics in the country. The aspect of upgradation of academic qualifications is achieved with the help of seven major centres located in the IITs, University of Roorkee, IISc., Bangalore and 18 other centres through which the engineering college teachers can acquire their masters and doctoral degrees with full salary and allowance. They are also paid a monthly stipend. Over the years, about 2,000 engineering college teachers have acquired and about 1,700 teachers have acquired masters degrees in engineering/technology.

The ISTE, a national professional body in technical education conducts summer/winter schools for improving the knowledge, skills and capabilities of engineering college teachers as well as polytechnic teachers. The ISTE conducts a large number of short term courses and programmes at various institutions and industries in the country. The teachers are provided travelling and other allowances as per the rules. So far over 25,000 college level teachers have participated in such programmes and over 4,500 polytechnic teachers have been benefited under such programmes. In addition, QIP centres in the IITs, IISc., Bangalore and University of Roorkee also have established curriculum development centres for upgrading curricula of engineering colleges with the help of teachers and experts.

The statutory AICTE has also launched some innovative schemes for teachers of technical institutions which include:

— Travel Grants Scheme

— Seminar/Conference grant

— Career award for young teachers

— Emeritus fellowship

— Professor of Eminence.

Under the scheme of continuing education programmes, presently handled by AICTE, the working professionals in the industry are provided knowledge-based skills and training with the help of teachers of various technical institutions, both at the degree and diploma level. Continuing education has been a very significant aspect of the World Bank assisted project for polytechnics as also the CIDA funded Canada India Institutional Cooperation Project for 12 polytechnics in Southern India. Despite several measures taken so far, the overall position of filling up the sanctioned posts and attracting competent engineers/ technologists to the teaching profession has been a matter of concern and debate. Efforts are, therefore, afoot to launch some new schemes and programmes for attracting brilliant young ,teachers by taking them up at a young age and sponsoring them for acquiring higher qualifications. At the same time, designing some new scientific methods of selection and providing adequate research facilities and challenges so as to keep the teachers motivated, professionally satisfied and result-oriented. Several new measures are also required in order to fill up the existing vacancies and the vacancies likely to be created because of mass scale retirement in the near future, especially, in the old reputed technical institutions. The aspects of providing need-based training and also to engage eminent experts as visiting faculty and contract faculty are also being encouraged.

UNESCO-ILO recommendations on the status of teachers in the Indian context:

The recommendations concerning the Status of Teachers adopted on 5th October, 1966 by the Special Inter-governmental Conference on the Status of Teachers convened by UNESCO, Paris in cooperation with ILO in 1966 recognised that the document was a unique instrument which recognised that education is fundamental to development and that teachers are the key to educational process. In the Indian context, the major aspects of the recommendations viz. the guiding principles recognises the importance of education and the fact that the status of teachers should be given its due regard in society. This is already incorporated in the NPE. As far as the educational objectives and policies are concerned the items concerning the interface between the world of learning and the world of work in the field of education is well recognised and has been implemented in India. In fact, the EFA commitment speaks of a financial commitment to the extent of 6 per cent of the GDP by the turn of the century for the education sector.

In the recommendations concerning Preparation for programmes, Educational objectives and policies and Preparation for the profession, there is evidence that there is widespread availability of teacher training facilities as well as comprehensive selection and recruitment facilities for each in the country. The various incentives that are given to employment and career opportunities to teachers have also been well documented. The security of tenure is particularly well established in government run schools. In the domain of the Rights and Responsibilities of teachers, the Indian context enjoins a fair degree of freedom and flexibility based on a framework outlined by the respective state governments on the issue of freedom of association. In every state, teaching and non-teaching personnel have their unions/associations. These organisations have powers of collective bargaining to secure teeter service conditions for their members.

State level organisations have joined together to form federations of educational organisations for primary, secondary and college stage of education. These federations negotiate with the central government to secure teeter pay scales and other service conditions. The central question under Indian laws is whether a "teacher" can be equated to a "workman", the latter being defined in the Industrial Disputes Act 1947. Various suggestions in this respect are being considered by the Ministry of Labour to amend the Industrial Disputes Act and initiate reforms to grant teachers the same protection as other workers. On the question of the rights of teachers, (in particular, salaries), these are structured as per government norms as laid down by the government from time to time.

On the Conditions for Effective Teaching and Learning, due consideration has been given in the context of the Indian teachers incorporating the recommendations of ILO. According to NPE 1986, development of Teachers' Code of Professional Ethics has been the responsibility of National level Teachers' organisations and they have themselves evoled such a code. On the issue of Teacher Shortage and Social Security, there are provisions for various benefits and salary revisions commensurate with inflationary trends that protect the pay of teachers.

It is also a fact that with the expansion of enrolment brought about by active interaction of the government, the requirement of teachers is constantly assessed, monitored and shortages are filled up through regular recruitment procedures. In short, it may be seen that the spirit and letter of the ILO recommendations have been incorporated in the Indian context and that the status of teachers in India is under constant review to keep pace with the growing and expanding reach of educational opportunities.

8

ROLE OF CBSE, SCERT, NCERT, DIET

The National Council of Educational Research and Training (NCERT) was established on 1st September, 1961, Us an autonomous organization. Qualitative improvement and excellence in school education and teacher education are some of its major concerns. For realization of its objectives the NCERT undertakes programmes related to research, development., training, extension and dissemination of educational information through its constituent Departments, — CIET, the Regional Colleges of Education at Ajmer, Bhopal, Bhubaneswar and Mysore and seventeen Field Offices located all over the country, mostly in the State Capitals.

During 1991-92 sustained and concerted efforts were made to implement programmes related to school education and teacher education, including the implementation of Centrally Sponsored Schemes for school improvement in the States.

The NCERT also continued to coordinate and monitor activities related to the Unicef-assisted projects in the education sector, the NPEP. Close liaison was maintained with State and Union Territory Governments through the network of Field Offices and the Regional Colleges of Education and by actively collaborating in different programmes organized by the

Departments/Directorates of Education, SIEs/SCERTs and similar other agencies in the States and Union Territories.

The National Council of Educational Research and Training (NCERT) is an apex resource organisation set up by the Government of India, with headquarters at New Delhi, to assist and advise the Central and State Governments on academic matters related to school education.

The NCERT provides academic and technical support for improvement of school education through its constituents which are as follows:

— National Institute of Education (NIE), New Delhi
— Central Institute of Educational Technology (CIET), New Delhi
— Pandit Sunderlal Sharma Central Institute of Vocational Education (PSSCIVE), Bhopal
— Regional Institute of Education (RIE), Ajmer
— Regional Institute of Education (RIE), Bhopal
— Regional Institute of Education (RIE), Bhubaneswar
— Regional Institute of Education (RIE), Mysore
· North-East Regional Institute of Education (NE-RIE), Shillong
— Field Advisers' Offices in the States

National Institute of Education

The National Institute of Education (NIE) in New Delhi through its various Departments carries out research and development functions related to pedagogical aspects of curriculum; prepares prototype curricular and other supplementary instructional' material; develops school education-related database and undertakes experiments in preschool, elementary and secondary stages to nurture all-round development of the learner. The NIE also organises in-service training of key resource persons and teacher educators associated with implementation of centrally sponsored school improvement schemes.

Department of Pre-School and Elementary Education (DPSEE)

Issues and problems related to pre-school and elementary education including research and development of prototype teaching-learning materials and functions of the National Resource Group in teacher training, pedagogy and curriculum, as a part of the District Primary Education Programme- (DPEP) jointly with the Department of Teacher Education and Extension. Department of Education in Non-Formal and Alternative Schooling (DENFAS) Issues and problems of non-enrolled and drop-out children including research and development of prototype models of non-formal education, alternative schooling, studies related to open schooling for NFE, instructional materials and training strategies for NFE personnel.

Department of Education of Groups with Special Needs (DEGSN): Issues and problems related to education of scheduled castes/ scheduled tribes, minorities, disabled and other groups with special needs.

Department of Women's Studies (DWS): Issues and problems related to education of girls and related, research and development activities.

Department of Education in Science and Mathematics (DESM): Issues and problems in the education of science and mathematics and research and development of prototype curriculum and instructional materials, and designing and developing of science equipment's.

Department of Teacher Education and Extension (DTEE): Programmes for capacity-building of teacher education institutions at state/sub-state levels and academic support to the centrally sponsored scheme of teacher education; functions of the National Resource Group on training, pedagogy and curriculum jointly with the Department of Pre-School and

Elementary Education; coordination with the National Council for Teacher Education (NCTE), and issues related to extension education.

Department of Education in Social Sciences and Humanities (DESSH): Issues and problems of education in social sciences and humanities, research and development of prototype curriculum and instructional materials; population education activities as a part of the National Population Education Project (NPEP).

Department of Educational Psychology and Foundations of Education (DEPFE): Studies related to psychological, sociological and philosophical foundations of education; comparative education; and their implications for school education.

Department of Educational Measurement and Evaluation (DEME): Measurement and evaluation related concerns in school education; examination reform including continuous and comprehensive evaluation, and related research and development activities.

Department of Educational Surveys and Data Processing (DESDP): Periodic thematic educational studies including All India Educational Surveys.

Department of Educational Research and Policy Perspectives (DERPP): Promoting policy research in education; organising activities for operationalising 'think tank' function; undertaking, coordinating, sponsoring, and commission in research and innovations in school education and functions of the ERIC Secretariat.

Department of Computer Education and Technological Aids (DCETA): Issues and problems in computer education and related research and development in modern technological aids/ multi-media educational support and the functions of Computer Resource Centre.

Planning, Programming, Monitoring and Evaluation Division (PPMED): Coordination of educational programme formulation, monitoring of programme implementation, evaluation of programme utilization by the target groups, and impact assessment of programmes of the constituents of the NCERT.

International Relations Division (IRD): Coordination of international relations with educational institutions' in other countries, and serving as an academic secretariat for the National Development Group (NDG).

Publication Division (PD): Publishing school level textbooks, instructional and supplementary material, journals and research monographs.

Division of Library, Documentation and Information (DLDI): Documentation of educational information, and providing library services.

Central Institute of Educational Technology (CIET): The Central Institute of Educational Technology (CIET), also located in New Delhi, performs educational media-related research, development, training, production and extension functions, and provides academic and technical guidance and support to the State Institutes of Educational Technology (SIETs).

Pandit Sunderlal Sharma Central Institute of Vocational Education (PSSCIVE): Pandit Sunderlal Sharma Central Institute of Vocational Education (PSSCIVE), located in Bhopal, organises research and development functions related to vocational education in the school sector.

Regional Institutes of Education: The Regional Institutes of Education (RIEs) located in Ajmer, Bhopal, Bhubaneswar and Mysore provide in-service training support to state and district level teacher training institutions in the school sector. To a limited extent, pre-service professional training to prepare school teachers for teaching Science and Mathematics and teacher educators of Elementary Teacher Training Institutiohs is also offered by the RIES. A new North-East Regional Institute of Education (NE-RIE) was set up at Shillong in December 1995 to cater to the educational needs of the North-Eastern States (Assam, Arunachal Pradesh, Meghalaya, Mizoram, Manipur, Nagaland, Tripura and Sikkim).

Field offices

The Field Offices of the NCERT, mostly located in the state capitals, carry out educational liaisoning with Departments of Education and other related institutions on problems and issues of school education in the states and apprise them of activities and programmes of the NCERT.

Programmes and Activities

The NCERT undertakes the following programmes and activities.

Research

Being an apex national body for research in school education, the NCERT performs the important functions of conducting and supporting research and offering training in educational research methodology. The different Departments of the National Institute of Education (NIE), Regional Institutes of Education (RIEs), Central Institute of Educational Technology (CIET) and Pandit Sunderlal Sharma Central Institute of Vocational Education (PSSCIVE) undertake programmes of research related to different aspects of school education, including teacher education.

Besides conducting in-house research, the NCERT supports research programmes of other institutions/organisations by providing financial assistance and academic guidance. Assistance is given to scholars for publication of their Ph.D. theses. Research fellowships are offered to encourage studies in school education to create a research base for developmental, training and extension programmes and to create a pool of competent research workers. It also organises courses for educational research workers. The NCERT also organises educational research in the country. It has computer facilities for storing, processing and retrieval of data. It collaborates with international agencies in inter-country research, projects.

Development

Developmental activities in school education constitute an important function of the NCERT. The major developmental activities include development and renewal of curricula and instructional materials for various levels of school education and making them relevant to changing needs of children and society. The innovative developmental activities include development of curricula and instructional materials in school education in the area of pre-school education, formal and non-formal education, vocationalisation of education and teacher education. Developmental activities are also undertaken in the domains of educational technology, population education, and education of the disabled and other special groups.

Training

Another important dimension of NCERT's activities is the pre-service and in-service training of teachers at various levels; pre-primary, elementary, secondary and higher secondary, and also in such areas as vocational education, educational technology, guidance and counselling, and special education. The pre-service teacher education programmes at the Regional Institutes of Education (RIEs) incorporate innovative features such as integration of content and methodology of teaching, long-term internship of teacher trainees in the actual classroom setting, and participation of students in community work. The RIEs also undertake the training of key personnel of the states and of state level institutions and training of teacher educators and in-service teachers.

Extension

The NCERT has comprehensive extension programmes in which various Departments of the NIE, RIEs, CIET, PSSCIVE and the offices of the Field Advisers in the states are engaged in various ways. It works in close collaboration with various agencies and institutions in the states and also works extensively with Extension Service Departments and Centres in teacher training colleges and schools with the purpose of providing assistance to various categories of personnel, including teachers, teacher educators, educational administrators, question-paper setters, textbook writers, etc.

Conferences, seminars, workshops and competitions are organised as regular on-going programmes as a part of the extension activities. Several programmes are organised in rural and backward areas in order to reach out to the functionaries in these areas where special problems exist and where special efforts are needed. Special programmes are organised for the education of the disadvantaged sections of the society. The extension programmes cover all States and Union Territories of the country.

Publication and Dissemination

The NCERT publishes textbooks for different school subjects for Classes I to XII. It also brings out workbooJks, teachers guides, supplementary readers, research reports, etc. In addition, it publishes instructional materials for the use of teacher educators, teacher trainees and in-service teachers. These instructional materials, produced through research and developmental work, serve as models to various agencies in States and Union Territories. These are made available to state level agencies for adoption and/or adaptation. The textbooks are published in English, Hindi and Urdu.

For dissemination of educational information, oı the NCERT publishes six journals: *The Primary Teacher* is published both in English and Hindi and aims at giving meaningful and relevant educational inputs to primary school teachers for direct use in the classroom; *School Science* serves as an open forum for discussion on various aspects of science education; *Journal of Indian Education* provides a forum for encouraging original and critical thinking in education through discussion on current educational issues; *Indian Educational Review*contains research articles and provides a forum for researchers in education; and *BharatiyaAdhunik Shiksha,* published in Hindi, provides a forum for encouraging critical thinking in education on contemporary issues and for dissemination of educational problems and practices. Besides these, a house journal called *NCERT Newsletter* is also published in English and Hindi. The title of the Hindi version of the newsletter is *Shaikshik Darpan.*

Exchange Programmes

The NCERT interacts with international organisations such as UNESCO, UNICEF, UNDP, NFPA and the World Bank to study specific educational problems and to arrange training programmes for personnel from developing countries. It is one of the Associated Centres ofAPEID. It also acts as the Secretariat of the National Development Group (NDG) for Educational Innovations.

The NCERT has been offering training facilities, usually through attachment programmes and participation in workshops, to educational workers of other countries. The NCERT also acts as a major agency for implementing the Bilateral Cultural Exchange Programmes entered into by the Government of India with the governments of other countries in the fields of school education and teacher education by sending delegations to study specific educational problems relevant to Indian requirements and by arranging training and study visits for scholars from other countries. Educational materials are exchanged with other countries.

Textbooks are once again in the news, especially those

dealing with history. The Government recently constituted a panel of Historians to look into the current NCERT textbooks. The panel submitted its report and stated that "we are convinced that the current NCERT textbooks brought out after 2000 are so full of errors and substandard that we find it impossible to recommend their continuation. However, we have made an effort to point out some salient errors and also the common strand of bias that runs through the entire series." (Report of the panel of Historians, MHRD, June 2004). A brief summary of the report is given in the following section.

The Executive Committee (EC) of NCERT accepted the report of the panel, but in the light of its utmost concern for the problems and dislocation faced by students and teachers, *decided not to withdraw the flawed books in the middle of the ongoing session*. However, for the current session 2004-05, to help teachers cope with the substandard and flawed history books, NCERT is immediately reprinting its pre-2000 history books (for Classes VI-VIII and XI-XII) to provide a few copies free of cost to each school, to serve as a ready reference. This is not being done for Classes IX and X, because the present integrated social studies syllabus is different from that of the pre-2000 books.

The EC also decided to initiate a participatory process of textbook writing, in line with a comprehensive curriculum review, which is meant to be undertaken every five years. In his letter to the Director NCERT, the Education Secretary, who is also a member of the EC, had stated that:

> "The textbooks of the NCERT have drawn serious academic criticism during the last few years. You are already in the process of handling the controversy regarding the History books. While undertaking the review, you may like to address the question of how books emanating from a new curriculum framework could be insulated from such distortions. While undertaking the review, we are sure you would take into account the Yashpal Committee Report

on 'Learning Without Burden' and Chapter 8 of the Programme of Action, prepared under the National Policy on Education 1986. The National Curriculum Framework should always be in harmony with the idea of India, as enshrined in its Constitution".

This short advisory note is meant to directly communicate with school teachers the academic and pedagogic bases of these decisions and to help them cope with the problematic situation for this year.

In view of the issues of inadequacies and bias of the textbooks the MHRD appointed three eminent historians to review these books. This panel was asked to recommend the removal of 'distorted and communally biased portions and inclusion of short passages to fill certain gaps'. The panel came to the conclusion that the textbooks prepared since 2000 are full of errors and a common strand of bias runs through the entire series.

"A running bias of more weight to Hindu religious practices and revival movements distinguished from other religious or modernising traditions that have been in the last 1000 years as much a part of India's composite culture as the one's of earlier origin was seen."

The panel acknowledged that debate is the substance of all historical interpretation and that there can be many ways of corroborating, verifying and contesting facts. However, for the school level, the interpretation should be generally acceptable, not from one or even from a dominant and majoritarian point of view, but from as harmonious a consensus as is possible. According to them the textbooks show printing errors, inaccuracies and a strong bias in favour of one interpretation of the Hindu religion that challenges the coexistence over time of varied currents in India's historical unity in diversity.

The panel also felt that it may not be possible to surmount all the shortcomings and drawbacks in the books by altering a word, a few words, a sentence or a series of sentences, as some thoughts and ideologies run through the chapters or hide between the lines.

The panel concluded that: "The present slant on political and administrative history of the ruling class should be forsaken in order to accommodate the large masses of people and distinct social groups as well as neglected sections of society, in a reframing of the syllabus. It is necessary to highlight interrelations and diffusion of ideas and customs among different ethnic, religious and social groups in every period of history. The past has a value of its own and distinctive fact of its own, not to be twisted for present purposes, either of the state or regional predilections of that element of the past *as it was*, distinct from the past *as we would like it to be today*. If this can be reasserted, then the professional practice of Indian history can genuinely redeem itself and in the process become more interesting for children of the future."

EXECUTIVE COMMITTEE OF THE NCERT

The Minister of Human Resource Development made the following statement in Parliament on July 20, 2004, regarding the decision of the Executive Committee (EC) of the NCERT: "I had ...hoped that the EC will no doubt keep the interest of students as their foremost concern. The report of the panel was accordingly considered by the EC for two days and they have taken the following decisions: The Executive Committee accepted the report of the Committee of Historians in so far as their finding that the history books were biased, badly written and full of inaccuracies rendering them unsuitable for continuation.

In view of the above it was decided that for the academic session 2005-06, the earlier books of history will be restored with appropriate modifications in line with the existing curriculum and minor corrections wherever required.

Because of the already advanced stage of the current

academic session, it was, unfortunately, not practical to change the books at this stage. It was, however, decided that the NCERT textbooks which were replaced by the present textbooks will be printed in sufficient numbers to enable at least 5 copies to be sent free to each school taking the CBSE syllabus. These textbooks would also be available in the market for purchase. These could be used by teachers and students for reference.

A short advisory should be expeditiously issued by the NCERT in close consultation with school teachers and historians to help them develop an appropriate perspective in teaching. In accordance with these decisions the HRD Ministry will issue appropriate direction to the CBSE to suitably guide the question paper setters and evaluators. The NCERT and CBSE could constitute joint teams for this purpose.

The Committee was also deeply concerned about the quality and content of textbooks other than in history. While it expected that the proposed curriculum framework review will take care of the concerns in the medium term, it was important that all the text books are subjected through a quick review to take corrective steps wherever required before the next academic session."

Clarifications Sought by Teachers and Students

Different aspects of the announcement may need clarification in the minds of different sections of the school community. The suggestion about making available the pre-2000 textbooks for reference only for this year (2004-5) has caused some confusion in the minds of teachers and students. A number of questions are being raised:

- Should the students also buy the 'old' book? If they are available in the school library should they consult them regularly? If so, how?
- Can a student use only the current book? Will this matter in the Class XII Board examination?

— Can a student use only the 'old' one for certain portions?

— If the 'old' books are meant only for teachers' reference, how should a teacher use the two books, which in some sections have contradictory facts and opposing views?

— How should the teacher help correct the biases and help the child to learn correctly?

— How will evaluation be done - will a student, especially of Class XII, be penalised for writing answers from the existing books?

Some General Suggestions on How to Tackle these Issues

For Classes VI-VIII

Schools that prescribe the NCERT books in Class VI, VII and VIII may ask students to continue with the current books and there should be no pressure on them to buy the 'old' book in addition.

Most teachers are familiar with the 'old' books so they should not find it difficult to refer to these in order to correct factual errors and obvious bias. It may need some convincing to make children accept a view not given in 'their' textbook. The teacher could talk and let children discuss about alternative views. This could be a good opportunity for a discussion about interpretations. The teacher could do an activity to show how a simple event that happened in class or school could be viewed differently by different children. Or they can read out reports of the same event from different newspapers to see how it is reported differently. The teacher may also do a few activities with artifacts, and textual materials like an inscription, and get children to form opinions from these.

In a chapter like that on Vedic culture where the panel has reported many distortions, the teacher may need to tell children how a historian is supposed to examine sources and arrive at conclusions.

Children often ask 'what is the truth?' One could talk about how it may be difficult to know this, particularly about an event that happened so long ago. Archaeologists and historians study different sources to arrive at valid conclusions supported by the evidence.

For Classes XI and XII

Students will continue to use the current books and should not be forced to buy the 'old' book. Teachers will be sent some copies of the pre-2000 'old' books (free of cost) to be used for reference to avoid blatant inaccuracies or bias. Examples of how the 'old' book may be used for reference.

Class XII: Modern India

— *Example 1*: The concept of Rule of Law is discussed on p. 75 of the current book. Reference could be made to p. 84 of the 'old' book for more clarification.

— *Example 2*: Achievements of the Moderates are given on p. 165 of the current book.

Reference could be made to p.168 of the 'old' book for a more organised presentation.

Class XII: Contemporary World

— *Example 1:* For Chapter 1 (p. 1 to 11) of the current book, reference could be made to the old book (p. 1 to 10) for a clearer presentation.

— *Example 2:* Developments leading to the First World War are discussed on p. 49 to 63 of the current book. For a better understanding reference could be made to p. 11 to 16 and p. 39 of the 'old' book.

In Classes XI and XII, the teacher needs to correct the inaccuracies and biases using his or her judgement. This will give the teacher an opportunity to talk about sources and historiography. The teacher may be able to get the students to interpret any source she or he could lay hands on. An interesting example of two historians who looked at the same set of events from completely different points of view is the following: Badauni and Abul Fazl were both employed at Akbar's court. Badauni wrote a strong critique of Akbar's religious policy, while Abul Fazl praised it as the strategy of a good statesman.

TOWARDS CHILD-FRIENDLY TEXTBOOKS

The discipline of History has a critical role to play in the school curriculum. It can equip children to understand diversities in terms of environments, cultures, languages, religions, gender and social practices. It can develop skills in understanding social relations, institutions and processes of social change. Moreover, it can stimulate children to understand how people have grappled with different ideas at different times, and how even the scientific theories that are accepted as valid knowledge today have been questioned and examined over time.

But unfortunately a subject that could help children analyse people, events and ideas, to discriminate and judge for themselves, does not attract the interest of most students. Being part of Social Studies which is a compulsory subject till Class X, children have to go through the motions of 'doing' history. There are many factors responsible for this. These include the overburdened and linear nature of the course, textbooks which are usually not child-friendly, and the little scope these leave for the subject to be taught in an interesting and engrossing manner in the classroom. Unfortunately, public debates on textbooks tend to overlook these factors while taking notice only of the ideological slants and tilts and factual inaccuracies.

It is true that history is politically contentious and there have been debates in several countries about how to represent historical events and individuals in school textbooks, whether it is about racism and the policy of Apartheid in South Africa, war crimes committed by the Japanese army or the role of Hitler and Nazism in Germany. However, in most countries history teaching is not assumed to be doling out mere 'facts' to children, taken as passive recipients, but is meant to actively engage them in critical analysis and knowledge construction.

They are trained to understand the methodology of how historians construct history, and also to reflect on different perspectives offered by various sources. In our own context there is an urgent need for a pedagogy that helps raise questions and prevents indoctrination, and textbooks that stimulate and excite children.

A large majority of our children are denied the luxury of formal studies after Class 8; it is *our* responsibility to make history a pleasant memory for them, not an inexplicable jumble of facts and dates painfully memorised. Children love stories of 'real' people and places, and narratives of emotion, action and change; they relish the suspense of investigation, the joy of exploration, and the drama of dilemmas.

History offers us a rich canvas of possibilities, to creatively engage their inquisitive and imaginative minds. Why not present it in a way they can truly enjoy? Children love visuals and cartoons (and so do we!), but our textbooks are devoid of illustrations and humour that can tease or tickle their imagination. Why are our children not trained to 'see' monuments, appreciate architecture, analyse paintings, feel the textures of terracotta, wonder at how textiles are designed or how musical instruments are crafted?

One crucial aspect that has often been ignored in the ongoing debates on history textbooks is that of how children construct their understanding of historical ideas and facts. People often say that school history should offer 'nothing but facts', without realising that 'facts' acquire a meaning for children only when they can place them in a perspective. Isolated 'facts' cannot be 'understood' when the child cannot link them to her own mental map of concepts. Whether we say 'the earth is rotating on its axis' or 'cave paintings about hunting were made by pre-historic humans' the child has to make sense of these 'facts' by relating these to what she understands. Each of these 'statements of fact' involves a canvas of several concepts, some of them even too abstract for the mind to grasp before she may be, say, 14-15 years old.

For instance, it is now well researched across the world that most children younger than 15 years find it difficult to think of 'this earth', referring to the ground beneath their feet, as something like a sphere, rotating at an unimaginable speed on some imaginary axis! Even when they are old enough to imagine that we are standing on a huge rotating sphere, they continue to wonder why we do not *feel* anything - 'no dizziness, no gushing winds'!

The human mind needs to develop a whole perspective to deal with such mind-boggling abstraction before it can understand that 'fact'. Early astronomers too struggled similarly to understand this. And yet, this fact is usually 'told' in school, to children as young as 8-9 years old, sometimes with models of balls and rotating tops, without realising the conceptual problem they face in comprehending it.

For a sense of history a child must develop a concept about time and things in the past. For this she must know how we know what we know about the past. To convey this, several 'real' examples of sources such as archaeological artifacts, maps, original documents, newspapers, photographs, biographies, diaries and books can be used to very good effect.

Teachers need guidance from textbooks, to be able to consciously address how children think about certain concepts that are routinely used in the discipline. For instance, recently in a government aided school, a teacher asked the children (from relatively poor and disadvantaged families) what they understood by the term "*anusoochit jaati*" (scheduled caste) that often appeared in their social studies textbook. A few vocal ones spoke, and said it referred to persons 'with small teeth' or 'dirty clothes' whom their mothers did not allow in the kitchen because they would steal their utensils! These alarmingly incorrect ideas reflected how children internalised strong upper caste biases. There were children in the class who were from Scheduled Caste families, but who did not speak. Textbooks normally deal with issues such as caste discrimination, 'untouchability' or dowry very briefly and mechanically, calling them 'social evils'. The challenge both for textbook writers and teachers is how to sensitively and effectively address such issues.

How do children interpret historical processes mentioned in textbooks and relate them to their own experiences? How does formal school knowledge relate to the 'common sense' children imbibe from their peer group and family, or from popular narratives of the past and present? These are issues that must be addressed seriously and imaginatively.

Textbooks must help children to build concrete and living images of the concepts being discussed. This can be done through imaginative accounts with human characters, through case studies, role play and by drawing analogies from the lived experience of the child. The textbook and the teacher cannot hurriedly offer conclusions, but must allow children to think, to relate with their experiences and debate with each other to arrive at a reasoned opinion. This had been strongly emphasised by the Yashpal Committee Report.

This advisory is not exhaustive. It attempts to indicate some of the problems with the present textbooks with suggestions for dealing with them. The teacher may use his or her innovative skills, experience and available resources to tackle the immediate problems at the classroom level.

Ultimately the teacher is the best judge. It is the teacher who can kindle interest and also create curiosity in children's minds to critically seek new knowledge and examine what they already know. The teacher needs to be supported in this process, by the best educators and academics, and the NCERT will endeavour to provide such a participatory platform. The challenge of reviewing curricula and moving towards more child friendly textbooks will also be taken up this year and conducted in an academically sound and participatory manner.

Since 1981, the Ministry of Human Resource Development, with academic support from the NCERT, has been engaged in making concerted efforts to review school textbooks from the standpoint of national integration to ensure that the school curricula designed in this country, while matching the cultural, geographical and ecological diversity of the land, do not contain any material or approach which can directly or indirectly perpetuate untouchability, racism, regionalism, casteism and communalism in the impressionable minds of our school students.

Two distinct phases of this programme of review of school textbooks from the standpoint of national integration have been completed by covering the school textbooks in use in States/ Union Territories in situations where NCERT textbooks have not been adopted without any change or where textbooks printed by non-NCERT organisations are in use. The built-in system, which the States/Union Territories were advised by NCERT to establish, for continuous evaluation of textbooks as part of textbook preparation and development, has stood the test of time.

With the publication of new textbooks on the basis of revised curricula, the need for undertaking another programme of their evaluation from the point of view of promoting communal harmony, secularism and national integration was felt and a fresh programme initiated during 1989-90. To oversee this fresh programme, to be coordinated and monitored by the NCERT, a Steering Committee at the national level was set up. Under this fresh programme, the textbooks brought out by the State level agencies and private publishers are being used in schools under all types of management, will be evaluated.

The Committee has met twice since it was constituted and has considered the reports of evaluation of school textbooks, used in some States prepared by the NCERT. The main focus of the NCERT in its textbook evaluation programme was on textbooks in history and languages which were prepared after the adoption of NPE.

ACHIEVEMENTS OF NCERT

Major achievements in various areas of work of the NCERT during 1991-92 are presented below:

Early Childhood Care and Education (ECCE)

The NCERT carried out various activities aimed at strengthening the Early Childhood Care and Education (ECCE) programmes in the country. The activities in ECCE focused primarily on development of material for teacher educators; training programmes for teacher educators of Pre-primary Teachers Training Institutions and functionaries of voluntary organizations running ECCE Centres; research studies related to impact of pre-school education programme in the Municipal Corporation of Delhi Schools; process based programme for development of number concept; try-out of audio programme with visually handicapped children and impact of toy making competitions.

Under the UNICEF-assisted ECCE project, which has entered a new Master Plan of Operation, State plans for the 12 participating States had been finalised and an intensive one month training programme for key functionaries for these states was conducted. A training film on the Training of Anganwadi Workers in ECCE has been developed. Three publications titled (i) Early Childhood care and Education Programme, (ii) Stimulation Activities for the Young Child, and (iii) Child to Child have been broughtout.

Curriculum for Teacher Education

The primary teacher, specially, in the first three grades is expected to teach mainly literacy, numeracy and life skills. Besides these, the teacher is required to have knowledge of the process of a child's growth, development and learning. At the secondary stage, a teacher is expected to be familiar with adolescent psychology and social processes, in addition to knowledge of school subjects

The curriculum for primary teacher education is developed by state governments/State Boards of Teacher Education and is reviewed from time to time. The curriculum for secondary teacher education developed by universities is also reviewed and updated periodically in the light of changes in the school curriculum, advances in pedagogical science, societal demands, technological advancements and changes in the socio-economic structures in the country. The NCERT has developed model curricula for elementary and secondary teacher education. State governments and universities may adopt/ adapt this in their teacher education programmes. The NCERT revises these curricula from time to time.

Teacher training for special needs

To look after children with special needs, the NPE 1 986, recommended integrating children with locomotor and mild disabilities in general schools. The implementation of the UNICEF assisted 'Project Integrated Education of the Disabled (PIED) in ten demonstration sites in different contexts further encouraged policy makers to integrate children with moderate disabilities in general schools.

The Multi Site Action Research Project also promoted the need to develop 'effective' schools for all. All these experiences focus on the preparation of the general school system to meet the special needs of not only those with physical impairment but also of those with mental impairments and learning disabilities. A provision has thus been made by the NCERT to orient all teachers and education officers by incorporating a component on special needs in all major in-service training programmes. The emphasis is on preparing general teachers and also moving towards the organisation of primary schools as inclusive schools focusing on meeting individual needs in the classroom. Teachers receiving this training are supported by multi-category trained teachers who were provided training by 4 RIEs of the NCERT. Teachers absorbed into special schools, mostly single disability schools or those with multiple disabilities such as spastics, cerebral palsy, etc., are trained under the guidance of the National Institutes for the Handicapped as well as some non-governmental organisations with courses accredited by the Rehabilitation Council of India. A number of universities have also started offering B.Ed., and M.Ed., courses in special education.

RECRUITMENT OF TEACHERS

Different states follow different recruitment procedures. In some states, the recruitment is made on the basis of the candidate's performance in a competitive examination, whereas, in some other states, recruitment is made on the basis of the academic and professional background of the candidate. The merit of each candidate is determined on the basis of his/her score in the examinations he/she has passed in addition to previous teaching experience, if any. In some other states, a combination of the two procedures, i.e., performance in a competitive examination and merit determined on the basis of academic credentials is adopted. Some weightage is given to the performance of candidates in an oral examination held through interviewing the candidates.

The qualifications required for the recruitment of a Lecturer in a university/college are:

- Qualifying in the National Test conducted by the UGC or any agency approved by it.
- A Master's degree with at least 55 per cent marks or its equivalent grade and a good academic record.

At the higher education level, 45 Academic Staff Colleges are involved in teacher training and university departments also organise orientation programmes and refresher courses.

Institutional Infrastructure for Training

The infrastructure for in-service training of teachers exists at the central, state, regional, district and sub-district levels. At the national level, there are the NCERT, the NIEPA, the Central Institute of English and Foreign Languages (CIEFL), Hyderabad, and the Central Institute of Indian Languages (CIIL), Mysore.

At the regional level, there are Regional Institutes of Education located in the four regions of the country—Northern, Western, Eastern and Southern. One Regional Institute has been set up recently at Shillong for the states in the north-eastern part of India.

At the state level, there are the SCERTs, State Institute of Education (SIE), State Institute of Science Education. IASE. CTEs. SIETs.

Districts have DIETs and In-service Training Institutes. DIETs cater to the in-service education of teachers working at primary and upper primary level. In-service education of secondary teachers is being looked after by CTEs. It is proposed to strengthen 200 CTEs, of which 73 have already been established. The IASEs are looking after the in-service education of senior secondary school teachers, including principals of these schools and the faculty of DIETs. Recently, in-service training centres have been set up at sub-district level, i.e., block and cluster level. To begin with, these centres are being established in the districts covered under the DPEP.

National Policy on Education and In-service Training of Teachers

In the context of the NPE 1986, the Government of India formulated a national scheme of in-service training of teachers to reach out to primary and secondary school teachers. The objectives of the scheme known as the Programme of Mass Orientation of School Teachers (PMOST) was to sensitise teachers to the emerging concerns in education, UEE, use of learner-centred approach, action research, the emerging role and responsibilities of teachers, enrichment of their knowledge in curricular areas, and other thrust areas enlisted in the NPE.

The duration of training was 10 days The programme was in operation from 1986-90 and about 1.8 million teachers were covered by it. The training programme was strengthened by media support. Films relating to various modules constituting the training print package were telecast on the national network for the benefit of teachers in different parts of the country. Each viewing session was preceded and followed by discussion. A participatory, interactive approach was followed in the training. The programme was implemented by the NCERT in collaboration with the SCERTs in different states.

After the PMOST, another programme/scheme known as the Special Orientation Programme for Primary School Teachers (SOPT) was launched from the year 1993-94 to improve the quality of primary/elementary education as part of the strategy to achieve UEE. The main focus of this programme is implementing the MLLs identified for the primary stage, training in the use of Operation Blackboard materials provided to primary school teachers, and encouraging teachers to adopt a child-centred approach to teaching. It envisages covering 0.45 million teachers every year. During the past few years, these two schemes of mass orientation have covered more than 2 million teachers. Like PMOST, this programme too, is strengthened by media support. Films on various themes covering the course design are shown to teachers during training programmes.

In most of the states, pre-service teacher education is essential for appointment as a teacher. Therefore, most states do not organise induction programmes for new entrants. However, some organisations like Kendriya Vidyalaya Sangathan and Navodaya Vidyalaya Samiti do organise a short induction programme for newly appointed teachers.

Training for Addressing the Needs of Disadvantaged and Minorities

In-service programmes are organised to realise three objectives- awareness, content upgradation and fine-tuning of teaching skills. The duration of a course differs from the others depending upon their nature, objectives and content

At present, the in-service education of teachers through distance mode is organised on a very limited scale. In-service education is mostly provided through face to face modality. However, recently a programme has been developed to provide in-service education to primary school teachers through distance education mode in the districts covered under the DPEP in which a multi-media approach would be used The programme will be implemented by the IGNOU in collaboration with the NCERT. Recently, NCERT has successfully experimented with using interactive teleconferencing for training of Primary teachers of Karnataka and Madhya Pradesh. This intervention will be upscaled as an important strategy for in-service education.

Besides sensitisation to general problems and priorities of education, the in-service training of teachers is also focused on specific areas requiring different kinds of competencies. These specific competencies include educating groups with special needs like SC and ST children, disabled children and those belonging to minority communities. Since, these groups have different social, linguistic and physical problems, training and orientation programmes for key persons and teachers working with them have been formulated keeping these in view.

From time to time, the NCERT provides orientation at the national level to key persons working for the education of SCs. This orientation is used by them during the training and also during the orientation programmes they organise for teachers of their states associated with the education of the SCs.

The Welfare Department/Tribal Development Departments in the states, and the UGC through the state colleges also organise remedial programmes to enrich and facilitate teachers working in the areas predominantly inhabited by the SCs and STs.

Training programmes addressed to teachers working in educational institutions of minority groups are in the formulation stage and will be implemented in the coming years. However, as a start, NCERT has designed some orientation and training programmes to help educationally backward minorities. Steps have also been initiated to update the list of minority concentration districts and these shall be made available to voluntary agencies and SCERTs requesting them to include teachers/functionaries of minority schools from these areas in their training programmes.

From the standpoint of promoting integration based on the appreciation of the national goals and ideas in conformity with the objectives of the core curriculum, a study on the analysis of curriculum in terms of specified MILs at the primary stage is being undertaken by the NCERT. The analysis of curriculum and new instructional material would help in the training of teachers to fill the gaps.

Other Areas of Training

Inspectors of schools are provided training to equip them with competencies essential for providing academic support to teachers in improving their performance. Principals of schools are also provided training to equip them with competencies required for planning and management of resources, human as well as material, by NIEPA.

The NCERT prepares a resource base of key persons and master trainers at the national level, who in turn provide training to teachers in their respective states.

The following training programmes are currently being organised: training of teacher leaders/teacher educators working in tribal areas. These key functionaries, trained and oriented by the NCERT, organise training programmes in their states to orient teachers in the life, culture and educational problems of the tribal people. The base line studies conducted in the tribal areas of seven states led to the identification of a number of educational problems. Based on these, orientation programmes for master trainers/key persons are organised from time to time. These master trainers in turn, train teachers working in tribal areas.

A programme of Regional Resource Centres to extend training facilities to principals and managers of educationally backward minorities through selected universities has been implemented by the NCERT. The NCERT's Regional Institutes of Education also offer training facilities under this programme. Till now, 467 principals and 947 school teachers have attended these orientation/training programmes.

Training of teachers is a vital and key area of work which has lead to the setting up of infrastructure to prepare hundreds of thousands of teachers for their profession as well as the tailoring of training for specific needs such as those for special education and the education of disadvantaged sections of society.

Training and Recruitment of Teachers

The professional skills of teachers in all categories of institutions except the unrecognised ones are determined by the regulations of the state education departments and examining bodies. The level of professional skill required is fixed in terms of academic and professional qualifications which are taken into consideration for granting recognition and affiliation. Therefore, institutions of various types set up in the public and private sectors adhere to the norms prescribed by the state.

Initial training of teachers (pre-service teacher training) is organised at the following three levels, i.e, pre-school teacher education, elementary teacher education, and secondary teacher education

Pre-school teacher education

Pre-school teacher education is organised to prepare teachers for teaching pre-school classes, i.e., nursery and kindergarten. The minimum qualification for admission into the pre-school teacher education programme is secondary or senior secondary examination, i.e., 10 years or 12 years schooling. The duration of the course is one to two years. Pre-school teacher training institutions are mostly unaided private institutions

In the case of nursery teacher education and primary teacher education courses, State Education Departments prescribe a minimum percentage of marks in the qualifying examination as a requirement for admission. Some universities have also fixed a minimum percentage of marks in the B.A./B.Sc. examinations for admission to the Bachelor of Education (B.Ed.) course

Elementary Teacher Education

Elementary teacher education is organised to train teachers mainly to teach primary classes from 1 to 5. The minimum qualification for admission into the elementary teacher education programme is either 10 or 12 years of schooling. Recently, most states have prescribed 12 years schooling as the minimum requirement though some states still have the entry qualification as secondary school examination pass. The programme duration in the majority of states is two years, while in others it is one year. Elementary teacher training institutions are of three types-government, private aided and private unaided. Recently, DIETs have been set up in all the states. An important feature of these is that besides providing pre-service teacher education, they also provide in-service education to teachers. Thus, both pre-service and in-service education are provided under one root. The number of such institutes is 424. These institutes ore government institutions and are fully financed by the Central Government. The total number of elementary teacher training institutions is 1,179.

Secondary teacher education

Secondary teacher education institutes prepare teachers to teach classes 6 to 12. The minimum education required for admission to a secondary teacher education programme is graduation in science, social sciences, humanities, commerce, agriculture, etc. A large number of postgraduates also seek admission to these training institutions.

Secondary teacher education is offered by secondary colleges of education which are affiliated to different universities. Some university departments also offer a secondary teacher education programme. The minimum qualification for admission to this programme is graduation. These institutes are of three types: government, private aided and private unaided. At present, there are around 586 secondary colleges of education.

Four Regional Institutes of Education (RIEs), constituent units of the NCERT offer a 4-year integrated course in secondary teacher education. The minimum qualification for admission into this programme is senior secondary, i.e., 12 years of schooling. Recently, the University of Delhi has also started a four year programme in elementary education leading to the degree 'Bachelor of Elementary Education'.

Teacher education institutions follow the reservation policy of the Government of India with regard to the disadvantaged sections of society like SCs and STs and Other Backward Classes (OBCs). At present, 15 per cent posts in the Education Departments and seats in teacher education institutions are reserved for candidates belonging to the SCs. Likewise, 7.5 per cent posts are reserved for candidates belonging to STs. Recently, 27 per cent posts in all services including teaching have been reserved for candidates belonging to OBCs.

9

IT Education in Schools

COMPUTER LITERACY PROGRAMME

Computer Society of India, the association of IT professionals in India, as part of its 'IT for masses programme ' in association with SSI Education and Aptech Computer Education has announced a computer literacy programme, India Akshar Mission, which aims at empowering 2.5 lakh citizens across the country.

Under the drive, SSI Education and Aptech Computes will offer computer literacy programme at a nominal fee of Rs 490 throughout the country. As a special gesture, the two institutions will offer 10,000 courses free of cost to the underprivileged across the country.

To implement the scheme, CSI will associate NGOs, Government and Municipal schools throughout the nation. Courses catering to different segments of the population including women, children and others have been created as part of the scheme. For this drive, Aptech will offer its 'Vidya' and SSI Education 'Connect for Beginners'.

Computer Literacy and Studies in Schools (CLASS) 2002

To create awareness among school students about the computer and its usage in teaching-learning process and in modern world so that they make full benefit of information and communication technology in their daily life and in education at every level.

Long Term Objectives

Recognising that some of the State Governments and private schools have taken initiatives to introduce computer education in schools, the project is intended to accelerate the pace of introduction of IT in schools and create models of school computer education – so as to achieve the goals of universalisation of computer literacy among school passed outs within five years.

CLASS Project was initially introduced as a Pilot Project during the year 1984-85 in the wake of the British Aid of BBC Microcomputers. A total of 12,000 such Computers were received and distributed to Secondary and Senior Secondary Schools through State Governments. The Project was subsequently adopted as a Centrally Sponsored Plan Scheme during VII Plan (1993-98). During the Eight Five Year Plan the Scheme was widened to provide financial grants to institutions which were provided BBC Micros and also coverage of new Govt. Aided Sec./Sr. Sec. Schools. Assistance included annual maintenance grant for BBC micros, and purchase as well as maintenance of equipment for new Schools.

2598 schools having BBC Micros were covered under the CLASS during the 8th Plan for providing Instructors, maintenance of hardwares, consumables and textbooks for students and training of teachers in schools. In addition, 2371 schools were covered with new hardwares and services which included Rs.1.0 lakh for hardware configuration and Rs.1.30 lakh per annum for recurring cost. Rs.0.80 lakh per annum was kept as the recurring cost for schools which had already been covered under the BBC-Micros scheme.

The Scheme began with the identification of the NIC as the notal agency for finalising the contract for the supply of hardware. The use and supply of software were restricted, coverage was confined to Sr. Secondary Schools and the students of class XI & XII had to undergo a rigid Computer Course Module.

Based on the feedbacks and suggestions from the states, guidelines for the implementation were modified from time-to-time. In may 1996 the states were given flexibility to procure hardware directly, develop and introduce the software operating system and extend computer education to classes other than class XI & XII.

In a subsequent exercise to review various Centrally Sponsored Scheme, and in the wake of Prime Minister, IT Initiatives, it was decided to revise the CLASS so as to address the new vision and and long term objectives as stated above. Funding under the old scheme was stopped in 1996-97 and the revised scheme has been operatianlise and funding started from 20001- 02.

Features Computer Literacy & Studies in Schools (CLASS) Scheme 2002

Each State/UT would be requested to formulate a Computer Education Plan (CEP). The CEP would indicate the steps already taken by the State Government/UTs and the assistance which they now require.

The Department of Secondary & Higher Education would set up a Project Monitoring and Evaluation Group at the national level which would consider the CEPs. Funds would be allocated on the recommendations of the Project Monitoring and Evaluation Group.

The State Governments would have to contribute a minimum of 25% of the funds required for the scheme. The Scheme also provides for contribution of 25% of funds from the MPLAD Scheme for Members of Parliament in addition or as an alternative to the State Govt. contribution.

The assistance of the Government of India would be for the following items and upto the limits indicated against each item:

— PC / Printer / CRT not exceeding Rs. 60,000/- per set

— Software / curriculum / CDs not exceeding Rs. 25,000/- schools per annum

— Furniture (one time) not exceeding Rs. 10,000/- per school

— Computer stationery not exceeding Rs. 20,000/- per school per annum

— Maintenance – 50% of the cost of the annual maintenance contract (after the period of warranty is over)

— Internet connectivity, not exceeding Rs. 5,000/- per annum

— Teacher's Training – not exceeding Rs. 10,000/- per school per year (for teachers teaching in such schools for which the grants are agreed to be given)

— An amount of Rs. 1 crore would be kept aside for the Department of S & HE for development of software, teaching tools, designing training models, evaluation, monitoring and other contingent expenditure

— Only such schools which have computer education as an elective subject at the secondary state would be eligible for the grants under the scheme. However, the scheme could be implemented in English/Hindi or the regional language

— The CEPs received from the State / UTs will be examined by a Project Monitoring and Evaluation Group Consisting of the following:

  — Secretary, Department of Secondary Education and Higher Education : Chairman

  — Joint Secretary (Secondary Education), DSEHE : Member

— A representative of the Department of Information Technology : Member

— A representative of the National Informatics Centre : Member

— Financial Adviser, MHRD : Member

— Two Technical Experts nominated by the Chairperson of the PMEG : Members

— Kendriya Vidyalayas / Navodaya Vidyalayas would be converting one of their schools into SMART school with a grant of Rs. 25 lakhs per school

— Kendriya Vidyalayas and Navodaya Vidyalayas would be given funds @ Rs.15,000/- per neighbourhood school to impart computer literacy to not more than 10 neighbourhood schools to cover 10,000/ - such schools over three years

COMPUTER USE IN CLASSROOMS

School computers are being used in many different ways and to very different extents. Educational leapfrogging, however, is only possible if the potential of hardware and software is fully exploited. Computers can used as:

— *Gaming tool* - Computers are used for games, especially in primary education where a playful approach to computers helps students prepare for future computer use and stimulates their creativity and imagination

— *Teacher tool*- Teachers themselves may use computers for administration tasks, production of documents, and the creation of lessons. This includes keeping of records, manipulating information, producing individual letters to parents or a class newsletter, creating customized follow-up work for lessons, making personalized certificates of achievement, creating student lists or name tags, etc

— *Research tool* - Computers are used to provide students with access to information on the Internet. The Internet facilitates gathering data for class projects, taking online excursions to travel reports and photos from various countries, reading work written by other students, following up on current news and issues, reading fiction, taking virtual field trips to institutions such as museums on the Internet, etc

— *Communication tool* - The use of computers in the classroom helps students get used to email and it facilitates communication among students, teachers, etc both within class and outside of class

They learn to communicate via Internet be it by emailing with another class working on similar subjects/projects, especially if a school network exists, or be it by consulting an expert or another "significant person" on issues that arise during coursework

Training tool for repetitive tasks - This includes the use of drill and practice programmes in the fields of reading, grammar, or simple arithmetic. This also includes solving equations, studying irregular verbs, learning vocabulary in a foreign language, spelling, recalling historical dates, etc

Teaching tool for the development of intellectual and thinking skills - Computers may be used for interactive games and real world simulations ie. Interdisciplinary comprehensive explorations that cannot be provided by any medium other than the computer

Teaching tool for computer use in itself - Students have to be prepared for computer used in their future lives, ie develop easiness in dealing with both software and hardware tools. The former includes word processing, and dealing with spreadsheets, databases as well as graphics applications that they are likely to encounter at their future work place.

Hawkridge et al. identified four principal rationales for introducing computers in schools:

— *The social rationale* is concerned with the overwhelming importance of the computer in modern society that seems to make it imperative for all students to become familiar with it and accept it in everyday use.

— *The vocational relates* the need for computer education to the possibility of better access to the job market. This sees the teaching of computer applications or programming as providing skills vital for employment.

— *The pedagogic rationale* asserts that computers assist the teaching-learning process and enhance the instruction of traditional subjects in the curriculum.

— *The catalytic rationale* sees the introduction of computers as improving the overall performance of schools thus having a positive impact on the education system in general.

The use of computers per se cannot make up for poor pedagogy and content. According to some schools of thought, there are two types of pedagogy, namely *instruction and construction.* It is essential to acknowledge the difference between instruction and construction. The former is the approach usually followed by traditional classroom teaching, the latter refers to a way of teaching that facilitated full exploitation of the potential of ICT but demands rethinking and a redefinition of the traditional approach in education as well as of the teacher-student relationship.

A School ICT policy

A whole-school ICT policy is a statement of the beliefs, values and goals of a school's staff working co-operatively in the context of using ICTs. Like any formulated strategy it is a management tool. A whole-school ICT policy, recommends including elements such as:

— The aims of ICT and how it relates to or contributes to the school's aims

— The distinctive contribution of ICT to the curriculum
— The contribution ICT makes to other subjects
— How the subject will be monitored and evaluated
— A strategy for implementation
— Teaching and learning styles
— Recording, assessment and reporting
— Monitoring and review
— Classroom and resource management
— Continuity and progression
— Staff development and training issues
— Leadership and management roles
— Links to the Management Information System
— After-hours and community use
— Things to consider in configuring technology in schools

Since infrastructural questions are dominated by a complex mix of technical factors, requirements, and options, decisions about infrastructure often are divorced from educational concerns and driven by technical matters and technology experts. In reality, infrastructure questions and decisions are coupled with educational needs, opportunities, and outcomes.

Therefore, to achieve optimum educational results, each school or school system should base infrastructure decisions on an assessment of a mix of technical factors and educational needs and objectives. The results of such an assessment then must be compared to the costs and benefits of a variety of computer system configurations and infrastructure options. When carrying out an educational/infrastructure assessment, the following questions may need to be considered:

Educational goals

What educational goals will be accomplished by integrating technologies into the classroom? Different computer configurations will directly affect or decide how computers and the Internet can and will be used by teachers and students to enhance education.

Professional development

Will the technologies be used to train teachers, for management, and to supplement classroom teaching? If so, teachers may need to be given special access to the technologies, with a mix of initial and ongoing training and support. If online professional development is planned, suitable Internet connectivity will need to be established, and time given for the teachers to learn the new facilities.

Student-to-computer ratio

What target ratio of students per computer is your school/ educational institution aiming for? How much computer and Internet access is to be offered, as well as frequency and duration of use for students in different disciplines will need to be considered.

Students per classroom

What is the average number of students per classroom, and what is the expected growth of the school population over time? Classrooms already overburdened with large numbers of students will clearly be limited in terms of space for computers. For younger students in may be possible to have groups of students for each computer, but for older students more than two per computer is quite restrictive. Space between computers, as well as aisle space for which teachers to patrol must also be considered.

Community use

Will the computer system be used by the local community during after school hours? Often the high costs of investing in technology are balanced with offering the facilities to the public at a small fee. If this is part of the school plan, then staff, security and configuration issues will need to be considered.

Electrical system

What is the availability and quality of electrical output in the school and how is the wiring distributed throughout the building? Inconsistent, discontinuous voltage can be highly disruptive and even damaging to computers, yet many schools lack sufficient electricity supplies. Cables may not be the correct gauge to withstand the additional load of connecting computers to the school system, or made be made of aluminum, which oxidizes with time and can even become a fire hazard. To avoid having to install an entirely new supply system, many schools chose to install computers in labs to limit the amount of refurbishment necessary.

Also, computers, especially those connected to a LAN, require a grounded electrical system, which is also less costly if applied only to one or two labs. Problems of inconsistent or interrupted voltage may be met by installing line stabilizers that make the voltage constant, and provide a 10-20 minute window, in case of power cuts, of electricity, so work can be saved, and computers safely closed down. All this can add to costs considerably. Some schools may choose solar power as an alternative power source, but equipment can be very expensive.

Other physical conditions

What are the sizes and shapes of classrooms? What is the quality of natural/electrical lighting? What types of furniture is available? Are telephone lines present throughout the school?

Physical security

How secure are the schools/rooms in which the technologies are to be installed? Security can be costly. Security plans must also consider a balance between protecting against theft, and allowing flexible and easy access. Fear of being blamed for damaging the computers, or for loss of equipment has been shown to restrict actual use of ICTs during class time.

Technical support and management

What strategies will be developed to deal with support, maintenance, and management of computer systems? This concern has serious financial implications, and its importance can not be stressed enough, especially in terms of technical support.

Movement of students throughout the school

What is the school routine? Do students tend to move around from class to class or stay in one room? This factor should be considered when deciding whether to set up labs, or to install computers within classrooms.

Climate – temperature and air quality – Will rooms need to be air-conditioned or sealed against excessive dust? Technologies can generate a lot of heat. Lack of ventilation can make the study areas uncomfortable, and in extreme cases, even lead to computer malfunctioning. Open windows, however, can let in potentially damaging dust and be a security risk.

Special needs or disabled students – Will special needs/ disabled students need access to the computer systems? If so, ramp access should be provided for those in wheelchairs and special desks will be needed. For students with special needs, specialized software may need to be installed, such as new graphic/audio presentations to help the visually impaired read. Large lettered keyboard may be needed, or printers that can produce Braille. Recent advances show immense potential in educating these students, a potential that will not be realized unless these factors are considered from the beginning of the planning process.

Funding resources – How much money is available to purchase and install the equipment, train teachers and staff, buy software, support, maintain and use the equipment? Is there a budget for ongoing maintenance, upgrading aging systems and technical support? Clearly, financial considerations are central when deciding which configuration is best. While funds to purchase/install equipment and initial training may come out of national/state budgets, funds for maintenance and running costs are usually expected to be provided by schools or local governments. It may be necessary then to devise special fund-raising schemes, such as offering the computers for commercial use after school hours, or soliciting the help of local businesses.

· Educators' technology skills – Do the teachers know how to use computers, and even more importantly, do they know how to teach with them; how to integrate them into classroom learning? Teachers clearly play a pivotal role in maximizing the educational benefit of computer systems. In providing learning opportunities for teachers, configuration of computer facilities will need to be considered.

Connecting computers together- Will the computers be installed as stand alone systems or linked together to form local area network (LAN)? While creating a LAN can have great educational benefits, its creation has financial and infrastructural effects that need to be taken into account.

Internet connectivity – Will the computers be connected to the Internet? If so, what kind of connection is possible and affordable.

One of the most difficult challenges is balancing educational objectives with technical limitations and hard financial realities. Ultimately, the goal of assessing objectives, needs, conditions, and options is to determine the optimum configuration for integrating computers into education at a specific school.

There are three basic ways that computers can be distributed in schools to meet educational goals. They can be provided to individual classrooms, installed in central computer labs and placed in libraries and teachers' planning rooms. Each of these options, and their combinations, has associated benefits and costs that need to be carefully considered. Below presents an analysis of these options.

One of the greatest potential benefits of distributing computers to individual classrooms is to provide teachers and students with easier access to these educational tools. This can make it potentially easier for teachers to integrate computer and Internet use into routine educational programs. But it cannot be guaranteed. Also, not all schools and classrooms can accommodate computers in sufficient numbers. Providing only one or a few computers in all classrooms of a school will likely have little or no impact on learning since it will be difficult for teachers to make computer use an integral part of their teaching.

ALTERNATIVE COMPUTERS IN CLASSROOM STRATEGY-COWS

COWs or Computers On Wheels are carts that hold a set of computers (10 to 20), usually laptops, often a printer, with the possibility to connect to a school network via one network connection. COWs can be wheeled into a classroom when the teacher wants to use computers for a specific activity. COWs can be beneficial because it makes it possible to provide teachers access to computers in their classroom without having to significantly remodel the room, provide special furniture, or reserve space for dedicated computers. Using battery-powered laptops makes it possible to avoid the need to provide special electrical power.

COWs allow schools to optimize the use of expensive equipment by enabling any teacher to request a cart of computers. Since software only needs to be purchased for the computers on the carts and not for dozens of computers in each classroom, the cost for software can also be much less with COWs than with conventional classroom computer installations.

However, the initial cost of COWs with laptops and wireless networking capabilities has a higher cost per computer than conventional stationary computers. COWs can be seen as "communal" property and therefore it can be more costly to maintain them, especially when using laptops, than with stationary systems. There is also a greater risk of equipment damage from accidents, hard use or dropping with COW using laptops than with stationary equipment.

Computer Rooms or Labs

Establishing one or more computer rooms or labs is a popular way to provide equitable access to computers for the greatest number of users at the lowest possible cost. Computer labs enable schools to concentrate expensive resources in a common space that can be used for student educational activities, teacher professional development events and community groups.

When using computer labs, it is important to arrange computers along the walls of the room rather than in rows so that teachers can view all the students' work from a common point and move quickly and easily from student to student, providing feedback and support. It can also make it easier and less costly to provide electricity and network access to the computers. Some of the benefits and challenges of using computer labs are discussed below.

Among its benefits are: (i) establishing a computer in a lab or dedicated room only requires schools to install quality electricity, network cabling and servers, effective security, climate control systems, good lighting, and specialized furniture in one or two rooms in a school rather then in many different rooms; (ii) equipment and software costs can be less for computer labs used by all classes than by classroom-based systems; (iii) it can be easier and less costly to provide access to the Internet via computer labs than with classroom systems; and (iv) computer labs can make it easier to encourage collaborative projects among groups of teachers and students.

However, computer labs can quickly become oversubscribed and competition for use may make it difficult for teachers to engage their students in longer-term on-going projects and activities. Furthermore, scheduling conflicts can frustrate teachers and inhibit their use of computer labs. Also, users, as with COWs, can see computer labs as a communal resource and thus reduce the feeling of responsibility and make it more difficult to maintain.

Computers in Libraries and Teachers' Rooms

When funding and staff resources are scarce, schools can optimize investments in computers and Internet access by installing a few computers in public spaces such as the library and the teachers' planning room. Giving teachers private access to computers and the Internet can encourage teachers to learn to use these technologies and enable them to carry out planning activities involving the use of computers.

Hybrid Options

Where possible, the greatest educational returns on technology investments can result by strategically using combinations of the above configuration options. For schools with sufficient room, suitable infrastructure, funds and technical resources, the strategy of distributing computers to classrooms either as stationary systems or via COWs can be an effective means of enabling easy access to computers and the Internet. Library computers can be used to focus on research activities, while special classrooms can be outfitted with computers, especially for special needs students, to enable and enhance benefits that are difficult to achieve from computer labs. The combination of these two options with one or more computer labs can create an ideal solution to providing students and teachers with rich and powerful educational tools.

ICTS IN SECONDARY EDUCATION

"Headstart": Computer-Assisted Education in Madhya Pradesh

'Headstart', one of the largest computer-enabled education programmes India, is aimed at making the learning process interactive and interesting through computers. Initiated by the Rajiv Gandhi Shiksha Mission (RGSM) of Madhya Pradesh government, this is a project essentially aimed at improving the quality of learning through the use of computers in the classroom in primary and middle schools. Launched in the year 2000 as a pilot project in about 648 schools, the programme was later expanded to over 2,718 rural schools across the state at the elementary level. In future months, project organisers hope to make Headstart lessons available for use by other state governments and private schools.

In order to prepare children from rural areas for life and work in the modern age, Pradeep Lokhande, under the aegis of "Rural Relations", a rural consumer relations organisation that he runs in Pune, is working towards taking second-hand computers to 28,000 village schools in India. Having personally visited over 4,000 villages in India since February 2000, he has installed 102 used computers. Used computers are collected from donors and given to schools free of cost, after a through analyisis of ICT readiness. After the schools see the value of using the computers in their classroom, it is hoped that the school will seek funds on its own to either upgrade the existing computer or then buy a new one and initiate computer education in the school. The current figures show that 37 of the 102 schools have been pushed into buying new computers or upgrading the systems by the students.

Goa Computers in Schools Project (GCSP)

This is a community-based project attempting to improve the levels of computer literacy and computer access to students in Goa, while training teachers to use them to teach effectively. In addition, the Project seeks to promote after-hours use of the computer facilities by adults in the community for email access, information and income generating schemes. With a high drop-out rate at the secondary school level in Goa, imparting computer skills to secondary school students and IT entrepreneurship development are particularly relevant.

The vision of the project is to help all secondary schools obtain a lab of at least eight internet ready computers with the help of the government, industry, and the community, relying on teamwork and networking among volunteers. Being based on Linux, the software used in the project is freely distributable, moderately priced and legally copyable. Since 2002 the Goa Government has been providing a few new PC's to each of Goa's 350 secondary schools, thus enabling every school in Goa to have at least 1 PC - the first state in India to achieve this goal. Simultaneously GSCP has provided over 450 mainly recycled PC's to over 100 schools.

Project Shiksha - Computer Literacy

Shiksha, which means "education" in Hindi, is about empowering students to learn in ways that can vastly elevate quality of life. The project aims to accelerate computer literacy by providing an end to end solution which includes software solutions, comprehensive training for teachers and students, IT curriculum development, and scholarships for teachers and students across India. Over 80,000 school teachers and 3.5 million students across government schools will have an opportunity to strengthen their IT proficiency via the initiative over the next five years.

Committed as of November 2002, Microsoft plans to set up 10 Microsoft IT Academy Centres under the project in partnership with state education departments in addition to collaborating with over 2000 partner-driven school labs. The software giant will also be sponsoring teacher and student scholarships to recognise teachers committed to delivering effective IT education, and students for driving innovation through technology.

Karnataka CLC in Schools Initiative

The Karnataka government launched 55 more community-learning centres across the state during the end of 2002, after the success of the pilot project, where 34 CLCs were set-up in Bangalore and surrounding rural areas. The project, a joint initiative between the government of Karnataka and the Azim Premji Foundation, aims to demonstrate, that technology initiatives, such as the use of software to reinforce certain aspects of mathematics, geography, environmental sciences and Kannada, have a positive impact on the interest levels of children and increase their learning achievement levels. So far, this aim has been realised, as student motivation levels have been stimulated by the introduction of computers, and attendance and enrolment rates have been shown to increase. A chronic shortage of teachers in government schools has prompted the Foundation to train volunteers, rather than taking Government school teachers away from their current classrooms. After a two-week training and orientation programme, they were equipped to supervise work at the CLC.

Mobile Classrooms: IT Buses in Rural India

Using buses converted into mobile computing classrooms to spread IT literacy among rural school students, this World Bank project is being piloted in Maharashtra's Pune district, India. An initial investment of $1 million will be used for buying computers, the salaries of the instructors and for buying new buses and reconditioning old ones. Under the plan, 20 buses will be converted into mobile computing units by removing the seats and replacing them with battery-powered computers. The buses will travel from one school to another in rural Pune, teaching basic computer skills along with typing knowledge through local language curriculum. If successful, the project will be replicated in other parts of the country.

Indira Soochna Shakti - "Empowering a Quarter Million Schoolgirls through ICT"

Indira Soochna Shakti, or "Empowering a quarter million schoolgirls through ICT" is a project in Chhattisgarh, India whose goal is the "seamless access to IT education for all girls in high schools". The project mission is to work in all 1605 of the state's government high schools by delivering four years of IT instruction to girls through an innovative public-private sector partnership, where a private entrepreneur has been provided space in schools and permitted commercial IT use outside school timings. Volunteers then share networked handheld community computers in villages and help route information and information-enabled services of local relevance to the communities.

Pratishrishti Computer Assisted Learning (CAL) Centres in Western India

Encouraging children in primary municipal schools to use computers by playing games and learning basic computer functions, Pratishrishti has set up 13 Computer Assisted Learning (CAL) centres in municipal primary schools of Mumbai. The Pratishrishti Computer Assisted Learning Model uses a LAN of 10 computers per school, thereby covering up to 8000 children per week in total. The project also generates maths and language educational games in local languages. After school and during holidays, the centres are used for adult computer training, revenues from which are used to sustain and upgrade the centres.

The NIIT mission

Obliteration of the Digital Divide and taking Indian citizens towards computer literacy is the mission that is driving NIIT's World Computer Literacy Day 2003 campaign. The successes WCLD has achieved over the past two years, have further encouraged us to broaden the scope and footprint of the movement. Today, WCLD 2003 is touching virtually every geography where NIIT has a presence and where there are computer illiterates who need to be made aware of the wonder tool.

Swift Jyoti program, which has touched the lives of over 2.5 lakh global citizens in the past two years, will enable over two lakh citizens to cross the digital divide this year. The program is being used to familiarize one lakh school children with computers-one of the most ambitious goals of the movement in its third year. As in the past, massive support for the WCLD 2003 cause is expected from the country's elected leaders, chief ministers, academicians, industry captains and ordinary citizens

DRAFT SCHEME OF INFORMATION & COMMUNICATION TECHNOLOGY IN SCHOOLS

Information & Communication Technology (ICT) is universally acknowledged as an important catalyst for social transformation and national progress. However, disparities in the levels of ICT readiness and use could translate into disparities in level of productivities and hence could influence a country's rate of economic growth. Understanding and leveraging ICT is therefore critical for countries striving for continued social and economic progress.

India shows enormous geographic and demographic disparity in ICT use. India has one of the largest ICT workforces in the world. One can find intense ICT use in technology clusters such as Bangalore and Gurgaon or amongst the upper middle brackets of incomes. The other side of the story is that large parts of the country lack even telephone connectivity.

Background

India recognized the importance of ICT in education as early as 1984-85 when the Computer Literacy And Studies in Schools (CLASS) Project was initially introduced as a pilot with the introduction of BBC micro-computers. A total of 12,000 such computers were received and distributed to secondary and senior secondary schools through State Governments. The project was subsequently adopted as a Centrally Sponsored Scheme during the 8th Plan (1993-98). During the 8th Five Year Plan the Scheme was widened to provide financial grants to institutions which were given BBC Micros and also to cover new Government Aided Sec./Sr. Sec. Schools. Assistance included annual maintenance grant for BBC micros and purchase as well as maintenance of equipment for new Schools.

2598 schools including 325 Kendriya Vidyalayas having BBC Micros were covered under the CLASS scheme during the 8th Plan for providing Instructors, maintenance of hardware, consumables and text books for students and training of teachers in schools. In addition, 2371 schools including 376 Kendriya Vidyalayas were covered with new hardware and services which included Rs.1.00 lakh for hardware configuration and Rs.1.30 lakhs per annum for recurring costs. Rs.0.80 lakh per annum was kept as the recurring costs for schools which had already been covered under the BBC-Micros scheme. For this purpose, financial assistance of Rs.100.00 crores was provided to the States/UTs/KVS/CTSA etc.

NIC was identified as the nodal agency for finalising the contract for the supply of hardware. The use and supply of software was limited, coverage was confined to Sr. Secondary Schools and the students of class XI & XII had to undergo a Computer Course Module.

During the 9th Plan period, Computer Literacy and Studies in Schools (CLASS) scheme was discontinued and only maintenance grant were given to the States/Uts for 1850 schools. A revised Computer Literacy and Studies in Schools (CLASS) scheme was launched during 2001-02, i.e., the last year of the 9th plan for a period of one year. Under the revised CLASS scheme, Rs.70.00 crores were released to 19 States/UTs covering 3112 schools. Besides, Rs.3.63 crores were released to KVS and NVS for establishment of 68 SMART schools (35 KVS and 33 NVS) and for covering 600 KVs and 400 NVs under the Universalisation of Computer Literacy component of the revised CLASS scheme.

Evaluation of the Revised Class and ET Scheme

Evaluation of the revised CLASS scheme has been done by Shiksha India which is a non-profit initiative of the Confederation of Indian Industry (CII) and World Economic Forum (WEF). The review of the scheme has shown that in spite of challenges in implementing the CLASS scheme, the overall response that it has generated in the various states has been extremely encouraging. Some states like West Bengal, Andhra Pradesh, Tamil Nadu, Chattisgarh and Manipur have achieved remarkable success. Broadly the findings of the evaluation are :

(i) Financial parameters need more flexibility as there is not enough provision for connectivity, teacher training, monitoring & digital content.

(ii) Regular power supply needs to be ensured and thus additional inputs like generators need to be included in the provisions of the scheme.

(iii) Guidelines for procurement and deployment of equipment and services need to be framed. A work shop could be conducted which show cases best practices in implementation.

(iv) The need for Digital content and its dissemination is vital.

(v) In a large and diverse country, standardized content may not meet local aspirations. States should be encouraged to set in place initiatives to create regional language versions of curriculum and reference content which will increase the reach of the CLASS programme.

(vi) A separate provision should be made for educational and vernacular software in the budget.

(vii) There should be a nodal agency for monitoring the implementation of the scheme and to consult the states in terms of vendor selection, exchanging. successful models, liasoning with Government and corporates on regular basis.

State Governments should submit progress reports every quarter or at least 6 months mandatorily.

There is a need for a robust Management Information System (MIS) to monitor the implementation right from Central Government to the school level.

(viii) Greater financial assistance should be provided to special category states.

(ix) The scheme should be harnessed to create an effective learning environment for children with special needs.

(x) Unaided, private and aided schools systems should be included in the scheme provided they admit disadvantaged and disabled students (without or with nominal fees). Besides, they should also share their resources with nearby Government school.

(xi) There is a need for the states to develop a comprehensive technology education plan for schools over 1-5 year period.

(xii) There is a need to mention explicitly in the scheme that the State/UT Governments are free to integrate the scheme with other similar programmes to make maximum use of the scheme.

A Committee under the Chairmanship of Dr. Kiran Karnik had already reviewed the functioning of SIETs and also suggested restructuring of SIETs. It recommended that SIET's should be restructured to ensure greater accountability to the Union Government, there should be greater functional autonomy and operational flexibility. Greater coordination with related schemes like DPEP, DIET is desirable as are uniform service conditions.

National Task Force on Information Technology and Software Development (IT Task Force) – constituted by the Prime Minister – in July, 1998 has made specific recommendations on introduction of I.T. in the education sector including schools. The relevant paragraphs are reproduced below:

Vidyarthi Computer Scheme, Shikshak Computer Scheme and School Computer Scheme to enable students, teachers or schools respectively, desirous of buying computers to do so under attractive financial packages. These schemes will be supported by a suite of initiatives such as lowering the cost of PCs, easy installment bank loans, computer donations by IT companies and other business houses, bulk donations of computers by NRI organizations, large-volume bargain price imports, multi-lateral funding, etc.

Computers and Internet shall be made accessible to schools, polytechnics, colleges, and public hospitals in the country by the year 2003.

The concept of SMART Schools where the emphasis is not only on Information Technology in Schools, but also on the use of skills and values that will be important in the next millennium, shall be started on a pilot demonstrative basis in each State.

The Report recommended provision of computer systems to all educational Institutions upto Higher Secondary/Secondary Schools by suitable investments (about 1-3%) of the total budget during the next five years.

The recommendations of the Task Force have been approved by the Council of Ministers.

The 'ICT in Schools' scheme is a window of opportunity to the learners in the schools of India to bridge this digital divide. The scheme is not a simple merger of the earlier CLASS and ET Schemes but is a comprehensive and well thought-out initiative to open new vistas of learning and to provide a level playing field to school students, whether in rural areas or in the metropolitan cities. The 'ICT in Schools' Scheme is not a stand-alone scheme but actively solicits the partnership of States, Union Territories & other organizations in a mutual endeavour to bridge the heterogeneous proliferation of ICT across different socio-economic and geographic segments in the country. This partnership is manifest in the structure of financing the initiative, in encouraging the development of long-term Computer Education Plans, the setting-up of Smart Schools by KVS/NVS in States as technology demonstrators and in providing for supplementing the States efforts in these areas with no attempt being made to supplant the State Schemes.

The centrally sponsored scheme of 'Educational Technology' and 'Computer Literacy and Studies in Schools' have been suitably modified keeping in view the past experience, the feedback which has been received and changing needs to form the new scheme of 'Information and Communication Technology in Schools'. The component regarding financial assistance to States/UT's for purchase of RCCPs and CTVs under the erstwhile Educational Technology Scheme has been weeded out.

Objectives

1) To establish an enabling environment to promote the usage of ICT especially in Higher Secondary and Secondary Government Schools in rural areas. Critical factors of such an enabling environment include widespread availability of access devices, connectivity to the Internet and promotion of ICT literacy.

2) To ensure the availability of quality content on-line and through access devices both in the private sector and by SIETs.
3) Enrichment of existing curriculum and pedagogy by employing ICT tools for teaching and learning.
4) To enable students to acquire skills needed for the Digital world for higher studies and gainful employment.
5) To provide an effective learning environment for children with special needs through ICT tools.
6) Promote critical thinking and analytical skills by developing self-learning. This shall transform the classroom environment from teacher-centric to student-centric learning.
7) To promote the use of ICT tools in distance education including the employment of audio-visual medium and satellite-based devices.

Scheme Components

The present scheme has essentially four components. The first one is the partnership with State Governments and Union Territories Administrations' for providing computer-aided education to Secondary & Higher Secondary Government Schools. The second is the establishment of SMART schools which shall be technology demonstrators. Universalisation of Computer Literacy through the network of KVS and NVS to neighbouring schools is the third component. The fourth components relates to the activities of SIETs.

Implementation Partners

States/UT Governments, State Institutes of Education Technology, Kendriya Vidyalaya Sangathan, Navodaya Vidyalaya Samiti, Government and Government aided schools systems. Moreover, financial assistance would also be provided to short-listed NGOs/Trusts/Societies and Companies for software development, teaching tools, designing training models, evaluation, monitoring and other contingent expenditure. The State/UT Governments shall be free to partner with private organizations or integrate it with other similar schemes for implementation of the 'ICT in schools' scheme including providing for maintenance. The National Council for Teachers Education shall be associated with the scheme in the context of training of teachers in computer-aided learning. The Rehabilitation Council of India would play an important role in projects involving introduction of use of technology for the education of children with special needs.

Financial Parameters

(a) Under the CLASS component of the ICT scheme, the Union Government would provide 75% of financial assistance to State/UTs. The balance 25% of funds would be contributed by the State Governments/UTs. The scheme also provides for contribution of 25% of funds from the MPLAD scheme in addition or as an alternative to State Government contribution. Assistance shall be provided to special category states in the ratio 90:10. The assistance of the Government of India would be for the following items and upto the limits indicated against each item.

1	10 PCs/Printer/CRT per school inclusive of facilities like scanner, web camera, modem etc. or one server with 10 workstation with accessories	4,05,000
2	Operating System & Application Software	20,000
3	Educational Software	45,000
4	Furniture	16,000
5	Computer Stationery	50,000
6	Teachers' Training	60,000

7	Internet	30,000
8	Maintenance - 50% of the cost of annual maintenance contract	20,000
9	Monitoring Cost	24,000
	Total	***6,70,000***
10	Recurring Costs, which includes consumables, hardware and network maintenance, monitoring costs, telephone for Internet usage	1,34,000

It may be noted that even in the revised norms, it is proposed to have greater in-built flexibility. The States would have the option to incur expenditure on the above items or any other item like generators, preparation of labs for computers including civil repairs and cabling and provision of electricity depending upon their needs and resources, subject to a overall maximum limit of Rs.6.70 lakhs per school. The Central Government's share would be restricted to Rs.5.00 lakhs per school.

At least two schools in each of the identified Educationally Backward Blocks would be taken up for assistance under the ICT @ Schools scheme.

The provision for software shall include Learning Management Systems & curriculum based courseware apart from operating systems & other application software.

An amount of Rs.1 crore would be kept aside annually for the Department of Secondary and Higher Education for development of software, teaching tools, designing training models, evaluation, monitoring and other contingent expenditure.

KVS and NVS would convert one school per State/UT into a SMART school subject to availability of funds. A grant of not more than Rs.25 lakhs would be given per SMART school. This limit may be reviewed in the future if needed. A sum of Rs.2.5 lakhs shall be provided as recurring costs which includes maintenance, consumable, Internet usage & monitoring costs.

In SMART Schools the emphasis would not only be on the use of Information Technology but also on the use of skills and values that will be important in the next millennium. It is hoped that at least one section (of 40 students) in each of the class IX – XII will be fully computerized. Thus a school having 160 computers @ 40 computer for each IX to XII classes may be called a SMART school under the scheme. However, keeping in view the fact that this target cannot be achieved in one go, it is proposed to provide 40 computers to such identified schools. A grant of not more than 25 lakhs per school would be given to KVS/NVS for the purpose. Both KVS and NVS have identified the schools which will be converted into a SMART School.

Kendriya Vidyalayas and Navodaya Vidyalayas would be given funds at the rate of Rs.15,000/- per neighbourhood school to impart computer literacy to not more than ten neighbourhood schools within a radius of 3 to 4 kilometers to cover 8,000 such schools over 3 years. The course shall be imparted in the local language if such a demand is received from the beneficiary school.

The financial assistance to SIETs shall be in the project mode. The financial assistance would be provided to SIETs on the basis of the project proposals submitted by SIETs. These project proposals shall be submitted to the Project Monitoring and Evaluation Group which shall assess the proposals submitted as to their utility and quality. Progressively, the administrative expenses of SIETs shall be reduced to zero within five years.

Illustrative list of activities

— Production of Audio, Video and Multi Media programmes

in the project mode by the State Institutes of Educational Technology established at Pune, Bhubaneswar, Patna, Lucknow, Hyderabad, Ahmedabad and Thiruvananthapuram.

— Assessment of need for multi-media programmes, preparation of profiles of target groups, design and development of audio-video programmes and other teaching aids, training of State level personnel in the process of educational technology viz. scripting, production of programmes and technical operations of equipment and studios for their production by Central Institute of Education Technology (CIET)/State Institutes of Education Technology (SIET).

— Training to teachers and teacher trainers in the production of low-cost audio-visual aids, help in script development, media production, editing, communication research, setting up and operation of audio and video studios and computerization of its various processes by Central Institute of Education Technology (CIET)/State Institutes of Education Technology (SIET).

— Feeding telecast and broadcast service titled Tarang and Umang respectively on DD-I and AIR and dedicated educational channel Gyan Darshan and Gyan Vani by CIET and SIETs

— Coordination of academic production and technical activities of the 6 State Institutes of Educational Technologies by CIET.

— Organising Educational Film Festivals/Multimedia contests.

— Financial support to States/UTs on the basis of their Computer Education Plans (CEPs).

— Support to KVS/NVS for opening of SMART schools and for imparting computer literacy to students in neighbourhood schools.

— Development of multimedia content for use in schools.

— Digitisation of video and audio cassettes produced by SIETs on the basis of fresh assessment and in partnership with non-governmental agencies so as to make them viable and self-sufficient.

— Establishing and Conferring National Awards for development and use of ICT tools.

— Development of teaching tools, designing training modules for teachers.

— Financial support for conversion of content into regional languages.

— Projects for introduction of use of technology for the education of children with special needs.

— Sale of audio and video programmes made by SIETs on a commercial basis.

— Leasing/hiring of studios and equipment by SIETs to other agencies both Government and non-Government on a commercial basis.

— Training of teachers and master trainers/resource persons in the use of ICT tools for enrichment of curriculum and pedagogy.

Process of Execution

Each State/UT would formulate a Computer Education Plan (CEP). The CEP would indicate the steps already taken by the State Government/UTs and the assistance, which they now require. The project proposals should inter-alia indicate number of schools in the state (government, government aided), the number already having computers, the number of schools now proposed to be covered and within what period, number of students likely to be benefited, whether State Government/UT's have made provision for the States share in their budget, vendors which have been short listed for procurement of equipment, provision of training, availability of infrastructure etc.

The proposals for the existing components must indicate the funds received earlier for them, the status of their utilisation and benefits accrued in qualitative and quantitative sense. Efforts would be made for convergence and dovetailing with schemes of other Departments like Ministry of Information Technology whose representative will be invited to the meeting of the Project Monitoring and Evaluation Group. The States/UTs shall be free to dovetail this scheme with existing or proposed schemes of the State Governments.

Funds will be allotted to KVS/NVS for SMART schools and Universalisation of Computer Literacy on the basis of the proposals submitted by KVS/NVS. The GIAC shall be empowered to affect modifications in the scheme based on the feedback received and depending upon changes in the technological environment. As the shift in technological parameters is rapid, this would ensure that the scheme is able to adapt itself to changing conditions and requirements. Financial norms and budgetary outlays shall, however, be strictly adhered to.

Detailed guidelines to facilitate implementation of the scheme shall be formulated and issued by the Ministry of Human Resource Development

Grant–in–Aid Committee

A Project Monitoring and Evaluation Group headed by the Secretary (Secondary and Higher Education) would consider the Computer Education Plans (CEPs) received from the States/ UTs. The committee would also include a representative of Ministry of Information Technology, NIC and representatives of organizations engaged in the field of computer education. This Group shall also consider the project proposals submitted by SIETs.

Release of Grant

On approval of the project / CEP the grant shall be released to the State/UT/SIET on an annual basis in two or more installments – the first installment of 50% will be released immediately after the issue of sanction. After the State/SIET has utilized 75% of the 1st installment it may make a request for release of the subsequent installment along with progress report and statement of expenditure with full details. The release of grants in the second and subsequent years will be made on a similar basis, provided that before release of the second installment in a particular financial year (beginning with the second year) the utilization certificate and audited statement of accounts in respect of grants released till the end of the proceeding year shall be furnished.

Disbursement

The grants of SIETs/KVS/NVS would be remitted either by Demand Draft drawn in its favour by the Ministry of Human Resource Development or by telegraphic transfer to the savings bank account opened in its name. The grants to States/UTs would be given through Inter Government adjustment advice.

MONITORING AND EVALUATION

The Project Monitoring and Evaluation Group would also function as the Monitoring Committee. In addition, the SIETs and the State/UT Government submitting the proposal would be required to submit progress reports every quarter. The Department would also explore the possibility of getting the 'ICT in Schools' scheme evaluated through an independent agency.

Anticipated Outcomes

The Scheme shall enable the widespread use of ICT in schools during the 10th Plan period leading to enrichment of existing curriculum and pedagogy.

The scheme shall enable the students to acquire necessary skills needed for both higher education and for gainful employment.

During the 10th Plan period a total number of 9380 schools shall be covered for employment of ICT tools.

Efforts shall be made to ensure coverage of the scheme in all States and Union Territories of the country during the 10th Plan.

A system of hosting and accessing quality educational content on a nation-wise basis shall be established. This shall be available online as well as through other access devices.

Two SMART schools shall be established in each State and Union Territory by KVS/NVS, which shall serve as technology demonstrators.

KVS and NVS shall operationalise the component relating to Universalisation of Computer Literacy and shall cover a minimum of 8,000 schools.

Projects to introduce the use of technology for the education of children with special needs shall be established.

State Institutes of Educational Technology shall become substantially self-financing.

Each SIET shall produce and transmit at least 200 programmes each year.

10

QUALITY IMPROVEMENT IN SCHOOLS

DRAFT SCHEME OF QUALITY IMPROVEMENT IN SCHOOLS

There is no exact definition of what constitutes quality in school education. However, there is a general perception that students' performance in terminal public examinations conducted by the Autonomous Boards make a school "good" or "very good". In contrast to such perception, conventional researchers in quality and school effectiveness have stressed on the identifiable inputs that would go into improving the quality in schools. Such inputs would include infrastructure linked with the curriculum transactions, teaching and learning processes, teachers' qualifications and experiences and their training.

Against this, a new model, also known as the *'contextual modes'*, is developing at the international level which takes into account the context, 'which means a *school's linkage* with the community, its *intake,* that is students seeking admissions in it, and *autonomy* given to its teachers to chalk up their plan and strategy in organizational as also in respect of curriculum and pedagogy'. The spirit of this model has been well captured in the National Policy on Education as modified in 1992, which says, *'To promote equality, it will be necessary to provide for equal opportunity to all not only in access, but also in success'.* Assuming a direct co-relationship between 'success' and quality, one can argue that the national policy sees no conflict between quality and equity, and it conforms to the international trend, which advocates, 'The successful schools in the post industrial era will be ones that *achieve excellence and equity simultaneously indeed one that recognizes equity as the way to excellence.'*

Any quality improvement programme in schools has to keep these perspectives in the background. Private schools, which largely accommodate the upper middle class students in urban areas, are becoming models of 'effective schools' and government schools are increasingly being perceived as a failing system. This trend has to be arrested by a carefully designed strategic policy and programmatic interventions that could include a marriage between quality and equity, bringing diversity in student population, extending common school system policy to private schools and better cooperation and networking with different systems of schooling for sharing resources and expertise so that there is a systemic quality improvement in schools.

The proposed scheme takes it cue from the National Policy on Education and the Programme of Action, 1992 as under:

The POA in its section on 'quality improvement and facilities' stresses on the *key issues* in secondary education, which apart from *access,* are *quality, modernization and diversification.* It calls for evolving standards regarding minimum facilities such as classrooms, sanitary facilities, science laboratories/equipments, libraries etc. by the NCERT in consultation with the school boards. It also suggests that in view of past experience of equipment once given not getting replaced or maintained, there should be a mechanism of community participation by way of student contribution at the rate of Rs. 10 to Rs.15 per month, except from girls and others exempted from the tuition fee. It further says that the collection should remain in schools for replacement and maintenance purposes.

The POA has also called for the professional development programmes for Heads of Secondary/Higher Secondary Schools.

For reorienting the content and process of education, the NPE recommended development of many areas for *curriculum enrichment such as cultural perspective, education technology, environment education, population education, science education, work experience, sports and physical education and yoga.* Centrally Sponsored Schemes relating to some of these areas were launched, which continued in the Ninth Plan and is proposed to continue during the Tenth Plan as the components of the Quality Improvements in Schools.

Objectives

— To identify and encourage the development of such infrastructures that would have a bearing upon the improvement in quality in school education.

— To encourage and undertake the curriculum enrichment projects in the areas such as Science, Environment, Population Education, Human Rights, Languages, Fine Arts, Music, Folklore, Yoga, Sports activities, etc. Special emphasis will be laid towards making environmental education and yoga education an integral part of the curriculum in school education.

— To encourage networking and sharing of resources and expertise between different systems of schools - Government aided or unaided, so that there is an overall improvement in quality education in schools.

— Curriculum reforms involving continuous re-organization and up-gradation of content and process of education.

— Identification of learning outcomes in the form of competencies or levels of learning for secondary and higher secondary stage.

— Strengthening and reforming the Secondary School Boards towards national uniformity in standards in learning and in the examinations.

— To reform the curriculum in the Teacher Training Institutes for incorporating the process for development of competency based teaching and learning.

— To encourage the States to recruit teachers through objective methods of testing and to provide regular in-service training to the teachers for upgradation of their skills.

Components

The following Centrally Sponsored Schemes will constitute new components of the scheme under the title "Quality Improvements in Schools". The details and the guidelines of the existing scheme will continue to be valid unless they are contrary to the new provisions in the new QIS Scheme. The annexures given in the existing scheme will also be valid unless revised.

1. Improvement of Science Education in Schools

The emphasis on Science Education in schools will continue in the coming years. Need for developing scientific temper, a pool of scientifically and technologically trained manpower and importance of basic science call for continued impetus on science education. The existing scheme of Improvement of Science Education in Schools through the State Governments and the voluntary agencies will continue to be implemented with the objective of achieving the goal set in the scheme. The financial parameters of the scheme are being revised to take into account the inflation factor. However, the scope of the scheme of science education is open ended with the intention to allow the scheme to meet the emerging needs.

2. International Science Olympiads

At present, five Olympiads in the subjects of Mathematics, Biology, Chemistry, Physics and Informatics are being held every year in the different cities of the world. Students upto senior secondary schools in the country have been participating in these Olympiads with very good results. Selection and preparation of the team for the Olympiads are made by concerned bodies. Under the scheme the cost towards international airfare of the participants is met.

3. Introduction of Yoga and Environmental Orientation in school education

The Expenditure Reforms Commission under para 2.13 of its report has recommended that the two schemes relating to Environment Education and Yoga Education can be terminated as the outlays of the scheme is such that these schemes cannot be implemented effectively in more than a handful of centers and there is no reason to continue such schemes in the central sector. These recommendations were placed before the Committee of Secretaries on 19th September, 2003. The following views/observations were made during the meeting :

(1) National policy on education 1986 underlines the importance of environmental consciousness and yoga and it is proposed that environment consciousness be taught in schools and colleges. The integrated development of body and mind through yoga also needs special attention. The scheme of Environmental Orientation to School Education and promotion of yoga would become part of quality improvement programme in schools.

(2) The Department of Secondary and Higher Education partially accepts the recommendation of the ERC, and shall recast the scheme for environmental teaching and promotion of yoga into a comprehensive scheme.

In order to expand the scope, activities and the outreach of the scheme of Introduction of Yoga in Schools the following steps are to be taken:

(i) Reputed yoga institutes/organizations will be identified to work as Resource Centers at national and State levels. While smaller States may have one Resource Centre each the bigger States may have two to four such centers. These centers would act as nodal points for imparting yoga education to school yoga teachers and NGO Instructors/ Teacher trainers.

(ii) The Resource Centers will create a network of yoga institutions/organizations for consultation, sharing of ideas, conducting periodic workshops for improving, constantly, the yoga education and practice as an instrument of self improvement.

(iii) The Resource Centres will also appraise the proposals of other yoga institutes/NGOs which are desirous of taking up programmes under the scheme. The financial assistance to all NGOs for a State will be routed through the resource center for implementation of the scheme in association with the concerned NGOs in the State.

(iv) The methodology and strategy in imparting the training course will be designed by the concerned Resource Centres.

(v) In order to achieve higher coverage the programmes on yoga training for teachers and teachers instructors shall be for a minimum of one months duration. There will be complete flexibility in the duration of the training course as decided and reviewed by a group of experts to be constituted by Central Government till the recommendation of expert group, the existing structure of training courses will continue to be in force.

(vi) The training module and syllabus for each course of training of yoga teachers will be reviewed by the experts groups mentioned at para 3.(v) above.

(vii) Yoga is one of the stand alone elective subjects for the students for the 10th class board examination of Council for the Indian School Certificate Examinations. It is also included as one of the activities in the physical education subject for 12th class board examinations of Central Board of Secondary Education (CBSE) and Council for the Indian School Certificate Examinations. In the case of schools affiliated to CBSE , yoga is one of the physical activities upto 10th standard, which is evaluated internally by the schools. When the coverage of yoga is increased in all the schools including those affiliated to the State Boards by including yoga in the school curriculum, the activities in terms of training the instructors and providing the facility for such training will increase several folds.

(viii) In order to support the above mentioned activities, the outlay for yoga in schools during the Tenth Plan will have to be proportionately raised to achieve higher coverage.

Similarly, while implementing the existing scheme of Environmental Orientation to School Education the following new steps will also be taken to expand the scheme:

(i) Identification and designation of well known NGOs in the field of Environment Education as Resource Center and Nodal agency at national and the State level. At least, one Resource Centre and nodal agency may be identified for each State to coordinate with the State Government, Central Government and sister NGOs in the States. The Resource Centre will have well defined functions like development and distribution of resource materials, training of trainers including teachers and NGOs instructors, and appraisal of NGOs in the State. It will also have the function of monitoring the implementation of the programme and evaluation at the end of the programme to see if the set goals are achieved or not.

(ii) Each Resource center at the beginning of the year, preferably in January/February shall prepare State programme in consultation with sister NGOs for the whole State and submit the same both to Central and State Governments. The State Governments shall furnish their comments on the proposals to the Central Government within two months. In case of delay in receipt of comments from the State Governments, the Central Government may proceed further on the proposal.

(iii) New proposals of the NGOs not included in the State Programme shall be appraised by the Resource Centres. Financial assistance for such NGOs shall be routed through the Resource Centre for implementation of the programme in association with the former.

(iv) The implementation strategy for the programme shall be worked out by the Resource Centres and shall be shared with all the stakeholders.

(v) Development of materials, programmes and activities shall be in keeping with the requirement of the area.

(vi) The outlay for environmental education has been raised. However, there is need to raise it further to have wider coverage.

4. Population Education

National Population Education Project (NPEP) launched in 1980 completed a very significant phase in December 2002. The goal of NPEP has been to institutionalize population education in school education and teacher education. The objectives are as given below:

— To develop awareness and positive attitude towards population and development issues leading to responsible behaviour amongst students and teachers. And, indirectly, among parents and community at large;

— To contribute to the realization of India's demographic goals which affect the overall national development of the country.

Major Project Activities

To achieve the above mentioned objectives, both curricular and co-curricular activities as detailed below are to be implemented : -

A. *Curricular Activities* (i) Various activities will be conducted to ensure effective integration of new population education elements, such as gender equality and equity, sustainable development, changing structures of the family and roles of its members, and under-served population groups (adolescents and elderly people).

(ii) Special efforts will be made to incorporate elements of adolescence education (process of growing up, HIV/AIDS and drug abuse) and create space in the school and teacher education curriculum for facilitating the organization of activities focused on skill development. This demands urgent attention in view of the initiation of the process of curriculum revision as a follow up of the *National Curriculum Framework for School Education prepared by NCERT in 2000.*

(iii) If the integration of these elements in school syllabi and textbooks and teacher education courses is expected to take time, alternative curricular strategy may be adopted to ensure that the concerned contents are integrated in the teaching-learning process.

B. Co-curricular Activities (i) In order to maximize the impact of project activities, organization of *co-curricular activities* will occupy the center-stage of NPEP during the X Five year Plan period. The momentum for doing so has already been created.

(ii) Co-curricular activities such as Long Distance Run at the district/sub-divisional/block headquarters, Poster/Painting/Debate/Elocution/Essay Competitions, Quiz contest, Special Interactive Lectures will be organized. These may be organized while observing World Population/AIDS/Environment/Women Day and other International/National Days/Events.

(iii) Some innovative activities such as Population and Development Seminar, Focused Group Discussion and other interactive activities may be planned.

(iv) Based on the experiences of some States, population education activities may be made an integral part of

Annual Science Exhibition. It is necessary that activities focused on population education/adolescence education themes may be initiated at the school level and those should culminate at the state level.

(v) Activities in adolescence Education, such as, Question Box, Role Play, Group Discussion, Value Clarification, Case study, etc. will be organized.

(vi) These activities will be organized with district centered approach, and DIETs under the supervision of State Population Education Cells in SCERTs will be made specifically responsible for this task.

(vii) These activities will be planned and organized in selected schools the number which will multiply every year.

(viii) Special efforts will be made to ensure media coverage of these activities to elongate their impact.

(ix) The organization strategy of these activities will ensure that they are *specific result oriented* and that the community in the neighborhood of concerned schools and local opinion leaders are actively involved.

(x) Over and above the monitoring process, continuous evaluation will be an integral part of the implementation strategy.

C. *Research Activities* (i) A National Survey will be conducted to create an authentic and comprehensive national data based on the needs of adolescents, the lack of which has been a major bottleneck in planning and implementing interventions.

(ii) Evaluation studies will aim at taking mid-way corrective steps.

(iii) Impact studies will be linked with every major project activity.

(iv) Efforts will be made to promote research and its utilization.

D. *Activities for Multiplier Effect* (i) The canvas of school education and teacher education in the country and even in a State is very vast, whereas the ability of the given infrastructure to cover the entire canvas within a definite time frame is limited. It will, therefore, require special efforts as an integral part of each significant activity to ensure that the activity results in creating multiplier impact. The following points may merit consideration in this regard :

(a) Effective co-curricular, advocacy, training or action research activities may be showcased and telecast/ broadcast.

(b) Print/electronic media may be involved in all major activities. Advocacy activities may be organized for media to create its interest in the project and to motivate it for providing effective coverage to project activities.

(c) Educational channel of electronic media and cable network may be utilized to the maximum.

Institutional Arrangement

(i) The existing infrastructure in all the implementing agencies of NPEP will implement the project in their respective areas. The infrastructures are being supported by respective governments.

(ii) The NPEP will be implemented and coordinated by NCERT on behalf of MHRD. Every state implementing agency (Population Education Cell located in SCERT/SIE/State Board) will prepare its Plan of Action and implement it as per the process mentioned below.

(iii) National Agencies like CBSE, COBSE, NIOS, KVS, NVS and NCTE will be implementing project activities planned by them under the overall supervision of MHRD.

The national population education programme continues to be relevant in the face of emerging challenges faced by the adolescents. United Nations Fund for Population (UNFPA) will also be collaborating with the Ministry of HRD to share resources and experiences in the implementation of the programme of Population Education during the 10th Plan.

NEW COMPONENTS OF QIS

Research and Development

Projects for undertaking research and development in the field of improvement of quality in schools, the issue of access and equity, networking and sharing of resources for improvement in quality of education, curriculum reforms, process of education, identification of learning outcomes in for form of competencies , strengthening and the reforming of secondary school course, reforms in the curriculum of teacher training institutes and process of recruitment of teachers.

Innovative Initiative and Projects, Workshops, Monitoring and Evaluation

State Governments, UT Administrations, Autonomous Bodies and NGOs may implement innovative projects with the objective of improving quality in education in schools. Workshops and seminars to share experiences in the areas of excellence in education with the overall objective of recommendations towards improvement in quality in school may also be financed by the Scheme. Monitoring and evaluation of the scheme will be in integral part of the scheme with funding under the scheme.

Examples of innovative programme funded by Ministry of HRD are given below:-

INNOVATIVE PROGRAMME FOR PROMOTION OF SCIENCE EDUCATION BY HYDERABAD SCIENCE SOCIETY

Title of the project : development of teaching aids for science education in schools :

(a) Demonstration system for satellite based communication consisting of table model real-time satellite, TV receiving equipment and table model transmitter- receiver for voice communication incorporating a miniature satellite model suspended in air.

(b) Dynamic full scale model of human blood circulation system depicting the heart's pumping action and purification of blood through lungs/kidneys.

INNOVATIVE PROGRAMME FOR PROMOTION OF ENVIRONMENT EDUCATION SUBMITTED BY CPR ENVIRONMENT EDUCATION CENTRE, CHENNAI

Title of the project : Environmental Education for Water Resource Management System in Kanchipuram district

Project outline: Kancippuram district has a major problem of water shortage. The project aims to create awareness among the teachers and school students about eco-technologies and its necessity in day to day life. Involving the school children in these action oriented activities will lead to the improvement of school campus.

Miscellaneous activities for improvement of quality in school education

In order to make the scheme flexible and responsive to the needs for improvement in quality of school education, which has multiple dimensions, it is proposed to provide a small lump sum amount each year to implement new programmes and initiatives which are not covered by the preceding paras. It could be for any activity which has great bearing on the improvement of quality in school education.

Some illustrative items of activities :-

1. Setting up of science laboratories, new as also up-gradation of existing laboratories.

2. Setting up of school libraries including initial acquisition of books.
3. Setting up of activity centers and acquisition of equipments relating to games and sports, art and craft etc.
4. Additional infrastructure facilities such as sanitation and drinking water facilities, common room etc.
5. Development of locale specific teaching learning materials, e.g. books, brochures, posters, maps, charts, audio and video Cassettes, CDs, multi media etc relating to science, environment, population and other curriculum related themes.
6. Action research/experimental/innovative activities with the objectives of curriculum enrichment in anyone or more areas of curriculum, such as science, environment, population, social sciences, mathematics etc.
7. Development of training modules, peer reviews and field trials for teachers, teacher educators, principals and head masters for their professional development.
8. Organization of workshops, conferences, seminars etc. by reputed organizations with very specific aim and objectives and outputs.
9. Development of institutional mechanism for sharing of resources and expertise between different school systems.
10. Development of minimum levels of competencies in each of the curricular areas keeping in view the learners' needs and sovereignty, which may lead to the national standards.
11. Action research, comparative evaluation, studies of different school systems- strengths, weaknesses and need for reforms.
12. Development of system of accreditation and grading of different schools taking into account variety of factors such as its response to equity, inclusiveness and social responsibility.

13. Inclusion of Population Education/ Adolescents life skills in the curriculum through Boards of Education.
14. Encouraging the building of models/ proto-types of innovative ideas/ concepts relevant to school curricula with a view to finally patenting them.
15. Development of competency based teaching learning for secondary and higher secondary stage.
16. Curriculum enrichment projects in Science, Humanities, Arts, Environment, Yoga, Human Rights, etc.
17. Development of system of accreditation and grading of schools.
18. Implementation of competency based teaching learning methods in Teacher Training curriculum and in-service training of teachers.

Implementation partners:

State Governments, UT Administrations, Ministries, Departments & Autonomous bodies of Central Government, local bodies and Panchayatiraj institutions, educational institutions, registered societies; public trusts and not-for-profit companies would be partners in implementation of the programmes. Their resources and expertise will be pooled together to make the programme successful.

As far as the voluntary agencies, public trusts and non-profit making companies are concerned, in order to be eligible for financial assistances under this scheme they should

i. have a proper Constitution/Articles of Association;

ii. have a properly constituted managing body with its powers and duties clearly defined in the constitution;

iii. be in a position to secure the involvement, on voluntary basis, of knowledgeable persons for furtherance of their programmes;

iv. not be run for the profit of any individual or a body of individuals;

v. not discriminate against any person or group of persons on the ground of sex, religion, caste or creed;

vi. not directly function for the furtherance of the interest of any political party;

vii. not in any manner incite communal disharmony;

viii. not proselytize; and

ix. eschew violence.

In some cases a registered society or a public trust fulfilling requirements spelt out above and designated as 'nodal agencies' would be given assistance for mobilization, involvement and provision of financial support to other voluntary agencies, social activities groups and individuals.

The grant-in-aid committee constituted under the scheme should carefully examine the credentials of the lead organizations or the nodal agencies and satisfy itself as to its reliability and capacity. The criteria for assistance through the Resource Centres/Nodal Agencies for sister NGOs as spelt out in preceding paras will be followed. The Resource Centres shall be accountable for proper utilization of funds by the implementing agencies, and the nature of its accountability should be clearly laid down in the sanction. Only those activist agencies, which have been in existence for 3 years, would be considered for assistance under this scheme. This requirement may be waived in respect of agencies with specially qualified workers or which can otherwise justify a special consideration.

Financial parameters:

The activities which would lead to the improvement in quality of school education are multifarious, it is proposed to keep flexibility in financing the activities which are considered to be of high priority and for which the implementing partners have evinced greater importance. Therefore, earmarking of funds for certain components will deprive the scheme of the desirable flexibility of financing the components as per demand. Even though the funds are earmarked and phasing indicated in the EFC memo, the Ministry of HRD is of the view that there should be complete flexibility in not only financing the components indicated in the scheme but also programmes/activities which will have great bearing on the improvement in quality of school education.

Since the gamut of activities for improvement of quality in schools is large, it would be necessary to pool in resources from all Ministries, Departments and organizations of Central and State Governments to achieve the desired goal. In so far as improvement in infrastructure in schools is concerned, funds under PMGY, SSA, schemes of Rural development etc have a substantially large component for civil works including construction of toilets. Hence no outlay for infrastructure is provided under QIS. Similarly, Ministries namely Youth Affairs & Sports, Health & Family Welfare, Culture & Tourism are expected to implement schemes and programmes for promotion of sports & physical education, health education and cultural values respectively. The proposed outlay in 10th Plan will focus on the existing five components of QIS specially on expansion of yoga and environmental education, Research & Development, Monitoring & Evaluation and miscellaneous activity for improvement in quality of education. Norms of financing will be as under:-

Quantum of Financial Assistance:

Improvement of Science Education in Schools:

Item	Amounts (in Rs.)
Laboratory Equipment to Schools for new laboratoriess	1,35,000

Laboratory equipment to school	
for inadequate laboratories	45,000
Library assistance to schools	27,000

Summer Institute programmes for Higher Education, Secondary teacher training programme, upper primary teacher training programme, orientation programmes for resources persons and workshops for development of instructional materials.

Unit cost for teachers (including the funds required for training of key persons, resource persons, development of training materials)

— Rs.1500/- per senior secondary teacher

— Rs.1125/- per secondary teacher

— Rs.750/- per upper primary teacher.

Assistance to NGOs for taking up project activities on fill projects, developments of teaching learning material and their dissemination, training or orientation of research, organization of seminars, co-curricular activities in schools in collaboration with education departments authorities etc.

Lumpsum amount based on the scope of the activities indicated in the proposed project by the NGOs without ceiling.

Environmental Orientation to School Education:

The quantum of assistance to the NGOs depends upon the activities proposed to be covered in the project report.

Promotion of Yoga in Schools:

Item	Amount (in Rs.)
Boarding & Lodging Charges	2200 per trainee per month
Lump-sum grant for conducting training courses in yoga	Upto 3 month course – Rs.20,000/- For 12 month course –

	Rs.40,000/-
TA/DA	As per State rates
Library Grant	Maximum of Rs.1,00,000
Construction of Hostel building for training	Maximum of Rs.15,00,000
Furnishing Grant for Hostel building	Maximum of Rs.4,50,000

National Population Education Project:

The activities under the scheme covers areas like material development, advocacy, training, co-curricular activities, research/evaluation, publication/ documentation and monitoring. The quantum of assistance will be as per various activities covered by Project proposal received from the State Govts/UTs and national level organizations under the Ministry of Human Resource Development.

International Science Olympiad:

The quantum of assistance is towards the cost of air travel in economy excursion class for the participants in the Science Olympiads, registration fees, contingencies, whenever applicable.

Research & Development:

Quantum of assistance will depend on the scope of works.

Monitoring, Evaluation, Innovative Initiative, Workshops:

Quantum of assistance will depend on the scope of works.

Though the QIS will be a hundred percent centrally sponsored scheme, but the implementation partners would be expected to contribute and also organize community participation for sustainability of the project.

As recommended by the POA, 1992 schools would be required to raise student contribution at the rate of Rs 20 to 30 per month, except from girls and others exempted from payment of tuition fees. The collection so made would remain in the school for replacement and maintenance of equipments etc.

Miscellaneous activities for improvement of quality in school education

Since the scope and the nature of activities is open ended it is not possible to indicate the quantum and rate of financial assistance for the programme. However, each proposal will be evaluated on the basis of the prevailing rate and the cost in the State. Tentatively a sum of Rs. Three crores is proposed to be allocated for the last three years of 10th Plan.

Process for implementation:

Project mode:

Implementation partners would be required to submit projects indicating the components intended for funding. The project proposals should clearly highlight the objectives, schools details, number of students likely to be benefited, commitment of schools, teachers and community involvement in the project and its ownership, provisions for maintenance and replacements of equipments, financial outlays, anticipated outputs and outcomes, phasing, monitoring, evaluation etc.

Proposals for the existing components must indicate the funds received earlier for them, the status of their utilization, and benefits accrued in qualitative and quantitative sense.

Proposals for new components as also for the existing ones must also indicate if the agencies are accessing funds also from other sources, government or otherwise for similar purposes. An account of such funding and sources may be given in the project proposal.

Efforts will be made for convergence and dovetailing with schemes of other Departments like sports and youth affairs, environment and forest, science and technology etc. The representatives of these departments will be invited to the GIAC meeting as and when required.

The proposals received from NGOs for the first time will be examined by GIAC after examination of the same by the SCERT of the State/ UT / Nodal agency concerned/ any other agency decided by the Department. Subsequent proposals shall be considered on the basis of an evaluation report from the concerned SCERT/ Nodal agency/ the agency decided by the Department.

In view of the proposed expansion of the programmes under QIS, Ministry of HRD will seek assistance from organisations like Edcil/NCERT for handling and scrutiny of the NGO's proposals before consideration by GIAC.

The project would target mainly the secondary and senior secondary schools. However, if upper primary and primary schools are part of the secondary schools the benefits of the project may also go to upper and primary children.

Time frame:

The project proposal received before September will be considered for assistance during the same year. The proposals received thereafter would ordinarily be processed for the releases next year. The project may be prepared for a period not exceeding the balance of a Five Year Plan period. The recurring liabilities, if any, arising out of the project, will have to be taken over by the management of the school or the state governments as the case may be.

Grant-in-Aid Committee:

The Grant-in-Aid Committee consisting of Secretary, Department of Secondary and Higher Education in the Ministry of Human Resource Developments as Chairman with Joint Secretary (Secondary Education), Joint Secretary & Financial Adviser, and representatives from NCERT, NIEPA, and three nominated experts as members would consider the project proposal for approval. Representatives from such other ministries as may be required in view of the nature and scope of the project would also be invited to the GIAC meetings. As and when required, the representatives from the state governments and the agencies submitting the proposals would also be invited to discuss with the committee the proposal concerning them.

Release of Grant:

On approval of the project the grant shall be released to the agency on an annual basis in two instalments -the first instalment of 50% will be released immediately after the issue of the sanction. After the agency concerned has utilized 75% of 1st instalment, it may make a request for release of the subsequent instalment along with a progress report and statement of expenditure with full details. Release of grants in the second and subsequent years will be made on a similar basis, provided that before release of the second instalment in a particular financial year (beginning with the second year) the utilization certificate and audited statement of accounts in respect of grants released till the end of the preceding year shall be furnished.

Disbursement:

Grants payable to a voluntary agency, public trust, non-profit making company, etc., would be remitted to it directly by a demand draft/cheque drawn in its favour by the Ministry of Human Resource Development. However, the preferred mode of release of grant will be by electronic transfer of fund. The implementing partners shall give the bank account No. along with the name and address of the bank where their accounts are maintained to facilitate electronic transfer of the grant.

Publicity and transparency:

Every year highlights of the project would be put up by way of advertisements in national and regional newspapers. The project would also be up linked on the ministry's website with the provision for submitting on-line proposals, queries etc. The expenditure on these activities would be met out of the component, 11.7 of the QIS programme.

Conditions for grant:

I. The grant-receiving agency will be required to execute a bond on a prescribed form (appended). The signed bond and pre-receipt will be submitted along with application.

II. An agency in receipt of financial assistance shall be open to inspection by an officer of the Union Ministry of Human Resource Development/ or National Council of Educational Research and Training or the State Education Department.

III. The accounts of the project shall be maintained properly and separately and submitted as and when required. They should be open to check by an officer deputed by the Government of India or the State Government. They shall also be open to a test check by the Comptroller and Auditor General of India as his discretion.

IV. The audited accounts together with utilization certificate in the prescribed form duly countersigned by the Chartered Accounts are required to be furnished within six months in respect of a preceding year or after expiry of the duration for which grant is approved.

V. The agency shall maintain a record of all assets acquired wholly or substantially out of Government grant and maintain a register of such assets in the prescribed Performa. Such assets shall not be disposed of or encumbered or utilized for purpose other than those for which the grant was given, without prior sanction of the Government of India. Should the agency cease to exist at any time, such properties shall revert to the Government of India.

VI. When the State Government /Government of India have reasons to believe that the sanctioned money is not being utilized for approved purpose, the payment of grant may be stopped and the earlier grants recovered.

VII. The institution must exercise reasonable economy in the working of the approved project.

VIII. The grantee agency shall furnish tile Ministry of Human Resource Development with such reports as may be prescribed.

IX. The decisions of the Secretary to the Government of India in the Ministry of Human Resource Development (Department of Secondary & Higher Education) on the question whether there has been breach or violation of any of the terms and conditions mentioned in the sanction letter shall be final and binding on the grantee.

MONITORING AND EVALUATION:

The GIAC would also function as the monitoring committee. In addition the state governments and the agencies submitting the proposals would be required to submit progress report every quarter. The state as also agencies' project particularly of high value may be evaluated by independent agencies. The entire programme of the QIS would be evaluated by independent agencies mid way and before the beginning of the 11th plan.

Anticipated outcomes:

As of now there are 115, 000 secondary and higher secondary schools in the country. The QIS would give priority to girls schools and schools in educationally backward districts. It is expected that over 25,000 schools be able to access the fund under the QIS during the current plan period. Besides, the programme would raise awareness and encourage a discourse on the quality and excellence in school education, its linkages with the equity and with the inclusive characteristics of our social fabric. It will encourage networking and collaboration among schools for sharing resources and expertise and improve total quality in the school education system. The overall quality of education in the country is anticipated to be on the upswing by the end of 10th Plan.

INDEX